POLITICAL ROLES
AND
MILITARY RULERS

POLITICAL ROLES AND MILITARY RULERS

AMOS PERLMUTTER

FRANK CASS

First published in 1981 in Great Britain by
FRANK CASS AND COMPANY LIMITED
Gainsborough House, Gainsborough Road,
London E11 1RS, England

and in the United States of America by
FRANK CASS AND COMPANY LIMITED
c/o Biblio Distribution Centre
81 Adams Drive, P.O. Box 327, Totowa, N.J. 07511

Copyright © 1981 Amos Perlmutter

British Library Cataloguing in Publication Data

Perlmutter, Amos
    Political Roles and military rulers
    1. Military government — Addresses, essays, lectures
    2. Near East — Politics and government — Addresses,
    essays, lectures
    I. Title
    322'.5'0956   JQ1758.A56M/

ISBN 0 7146 3122 1

Photoset in Baskerville by Saildean Limited.
Printed and Bound in Great Britain by
T. J. Press (Padstow) Ltd., Padstow, Cornwall

Contents

Acknowledgments   vi

Preface: Egypt Face-to-Face   1

1. The Praetorian Army and the Praetorian State   8

2. Prefatory Note by A.P.
The Birth of a New Class by Manfred Halpern   41

3. Egypt and the Myth of the New Middle Class
(A.P.'s critique)   71

4. Reaffirmations and New Explorations (M.H.'s reply)   97

5. The Myth of the Myth (A.P.'s rejoinder)   113

6. The Syrian Military and the Ba'th Party   130

7. The Arab Military Elite   160

8. Experiments in Praetorianism   196

9. Political Power and Social Cohesion
in Nasser's Egypt   230

10. Perspectives on Praetorianism   252

11. Military Incompetence and Failure   283

Index   307

Acknowledgments

The chapters in this book appeared in their original form in the following books and journals. Several have been revised and updated for publication in this collection. Chapters 2-5 constitute an exchange of views between the author and Prof. Manfred Halpern.

Chapter 1:   From *The Military and Politics in Modern Times* (Yale University Press, 1968).

Chapter 2:   From Manfred Halpern, *The Politics of Social Change in the Middle East and North Africa* (Princeton University Press, 1963).

Chapter 3:   From *Comparative Studies in Society and History,* Vol. X, No. 1, October 1967.

Chapter 4:   From *Comparative Studies in Society and History,* Vol. 11, No. 3, January 1969.

Chapter 5:   From *Comparative Studies in Society and History,* Vol. 12, No. 1, January 1970.

Chapter 6:   From *The Western Political Quarterly,* Vol. XXII, No. 4, December 1969.

Chapter 7:   From *World Politics,* Vol. XXII, No. 2, January 1970.

Chapter 8:   From *Egypt: The Praetorian State* (New Brunswick, N.J., Transaction, 1974).

Chapter 9:   Ibid.

Chapter 10:   A paper presented at the ASA/LASA Convention, Houston, Texas, November 1977.

Chapter 11:   From *The Journal of Strategic Studies,* vol. 1, no. 2, Oct. 1978.

Preface

This book is a collection of essays which represents my labours in the field of the military and politics in the last two decades. From the beginning I have tried to identify the political rather than the sociological and organizational explanation for military interventionism, demonstrated by the nature of military coups and praetorian corporatism among the emerging new states of the Middle East and Sub-Saharan Africa, the continuing role the military has played for over a century in Latin America and the emergence of its new corporative types in the major Latin American states. The politics of the military in the less developed countries as well as in the economically more highly developed Latin American states have become routine, a matter of fact and of life in over ninety per cent of the new states. In fact it is easier to identify the few nonpraetorian and non-interventionist states and regimes than otherwise. Only in India, Israel, Mexico, Kenya, Tanzania and Zambia (so far) and in the South Arabian and in Arab Gulf oil sheikhdoms and states has the military not been interventionist, yet in most of the above it has played and continues to play a most significant role in security-defence and strategic policy making and is an influential if not a major partner in the making of national security and foreign policy without seriously intervening in domestic politics.

1

When I began my studies and writing on the political role of the military in new states the field was still an undiscovered territory. Since then the number of political military interventions and military regimes has increased exponentially but not to the same degree as the literature on the subject. When I began my researches this comprised altogether less than five major books and under fifty articles. Today if the Kurt Lang bibliography (which badly needs updating) is taken as a guide the literature extends to well over a hundred books and over a thousand articles and published papers. This does not include the numerous unpublished dissertations, monographs and convention and seminar papers. Because the growth of literature has been so rapid and uneven, some generalizations and an overall view are needed. Most of the studies (with the exception of an outstanding few), both the empirical and conceptual endeavours, do not yet demonstrate sufficient confidence in differentiating the *political* explanations for military interventions from other respectable and valuable sociological and organizational explanations of civil-military relations. My publisher therefore thought it might be useful to collect my writings on the subject.

I have added new material to earlier essays but I have also included three new essays never before published, dealing with the political stimulus and cause for military interventions, regimes, coups and praetorianism. This book represents an integration of research papers and empirical country and area studies with overarching theoretical essays. The collection emphasizes my analysis of (1) types of direct and indirect military rule (ruler and arbitrator) (2) types of military intervention (coups, civilian-military alliances) and (3) corporate-professional types of interventionism.

I have attempted above all to demonstrate that corporatism, not professionalism, is a prima facie case for interventionism and that military professionalism is only one guarantee for non-interventionism. The major arguments I advance to persuade the student of modern military and politics are as follows:

(a)   There is no correlation between military interventionism and internal organizational conflicts of the military establishment. The explanation of military interventionism has to do with political-structural and institutional weaknesses of regimes and of states. The most conspicuous indicator of political and institutional instability is regime illegitimacy and the inability to secure political support through political channels.

(b) The military interventionists are on the whole a few conspiratorial officers who do not work in the open; on the whole they are not "progressive" if compared with their civilian counterparts, allies or adversaries; they are not a new middle class of progressives, for they are neither cohesive nor sustaining; at best they represent traditional middle class orientations, however corporative, technocratic and technologically advanced some of them might be (especially in Latin America); they are not revolutionary and are at best reluctant reformers; and some of them (especially in sub-Saharan Africa) are no more than petty tyrants and kleptocrats.

(c) They are certainly a ruling class, not a revolutionary or progressive social class. They are a self-appointed political elite free of class obligations in the sense that, even if they are a traditional middle class, they are not committed to champion the values and aspirations of the middle class while in uniform. They are certainly not the surrogates of this or any other class. They are a ruling elite in the sense that they are potential interventionists and serve as a major source of support for praetorian regimes.

EGYPT

It is not often that students of bureaucratic, military or political behaviour have the opportunity to examine the inner workings of the minds and perceptions of their subject of inquiry. The rare chance to study the praetorian military type at close range came to me recently (in December, 1977) during the euphoric days of the Sadat-Begin entente cordiale when I was invited as a special guest lecturer to Egypt's Military College, the Nasser Academy. The event was unique from many points of view. I was the first Israeli ever to address a forum of senior and ranking officers of the Egyptian military. I was also the first student of military praetorianism to meet and have extensive discussions with the praetorians themselves. I was able to spend time with different groups of the Egyptian military for one intensive day, and over a period of several days I met privately with the leading figures of the Egyptian military as well as with influential but less prominent officers. I had many discussions with those few that I have written about, the potential interventionists or (in other circumstances and countries) the coup makers. Indeed, it is this group that serves as the basis for political support of the Sadat regime. This was a field trip in praetorianism for me.

Although the subject matter of my lecture was an analysis of civil-military relations in Israel and the politics and strategy of Israel's defense forces, I nevertheless pursued the inquiries related to my concepts of praetorianism. My "researches" and inquiries were motivated by a deep sense of curiosity and obligation to my academic discipline. The initial confrontation with "five" praetorians in action began with my lecture, which was attended by some 600 officers; of this number there were close to 70 generals, together with a dozen of Egypt's most senior generals. The topic was a convergence of my intellectual and academic interests: civil-military relations. Although I lectured on Israel and a type of military and civil-military relations totally different from the praetorian, the topic dealt with the major subject of concern to the praetorian military—politics. It is especially national security policy—foreign affairs and military strategy—that delineates the praetorian military's chief input: the military's role in the use of force and in society and politics.

Though the generalizations I make are based on a fairly brief visit, and despite the fact that interviews with key and senior officers were in depth, I am nevertheless aware that some critics could call my observations incomplete or impressionistic. Still, I have worked in this field for over two decades and I can defend my diagnoses, both theoretical and applied. Nasser Academy is, in a way, as are other military and war colleges, a laboratory for the preparation, guidance, and orientation of the nation's military elite and served as such for my research as well. True, my meeting with Egypt's praetorians was not a preconceived, methodologically oriented, mechanistically inclined sociological data-gathering excursion, but was rather an opportunity for insight into the mind and the structure of the praetorian in a praetorian state.

Unquestionably, Egypt is a praetorian state. The absence of class cohesion, political community and sustained collective action (except for sporadic riots and demonstrations, all obviously types of collective behaviour), of group activity and of political aggregation, was conspicuous. The ideological poverty of the Arab Socialist Union party, the lethargy and rigidity of the enormous bureaucracy, all point to praetorian conditions. That Sadat's regime depends solely on the military establishment and political police, the malleable bureaucracy and the dependable services of the scribes of *Al-Ahram* and other Egyptian papers, lends further support to theses I have established in the past two decades on the praetorian syndrome and the interventionist praetorian army. The most conspicuous aspect of the Egyptian senior officer class and its military establishment in general is its high corporate orientation and dedication to professionalism. General Abdal-Ghani Gamasi, the then Minister of War, Commander in Chief of the Armed Forces and Egypt's most senior officer is a political figure who is averse to politics. At least that is his claim. A graduate of the military academy in 1939 and a contemporary of Nasser and the thirteen officers and July 1952 coup makers (graduating between 1936-1940), Gamasi was not one of the coup makers. He was never a member of the thirteen Free Officers or any of the other politicized officer groups so prevalent in the Egyptian army between 1936 and 1952.

General Gamasi, a very strict disciplinarian, valiant soldier and the architect of the successful Egyptian canal crossing in October 1973, is highly aware of his and the military establishment's influence and power. He told me that the strategy of the Egyptian military between 1967 and 1973 (while he served as chief of the Armed Forces Training, Chief of Operations, and deputy Chief of Staff respectively) was clearly political. Its object was to cross "the Canal of Shame" and to break Israeli political intransigence; this they did. The strategic goal was accomplished by two Israeli-Egyptian troop separation agreements between October 1973 and September 1975.

The Egyptians, according to Gamasi, built a state within a state in the form of a highly professional and well trained and drilled army whose purpose was strategic, not to conquer Israel. They had given up Nasser's war *à outrance* but decided to shake up the political stability Israel had achieved in the occupied territories and its "Finlandization" of the international community. For that purpose Egypt mobilized all its human, material, economic, intellectual and psychological resources and built the best Egyptian Army since 1948, whose strategic purpose was limited but whose Clausewitzian orientation was brilliant—to achieve political aims by a military surprise attack. "We have advanced in Sinai and retreated in Egypt" said Gamasi in an interview. The price Egypt paid for the October War was monumental. Its modernization was crippled and its demographic ills and wild population growth neglected, as were land reclamation, industrial modernization, and management development. The October War (known in Egypt as the Ramadan War and in Israel as the Yom Kippur War) was Egypt's crowning political achievement after the evacuation of British forces from the Suez in 1952. Cairo is full of October symbols. There is an October bridge, there are October coins, streets and mementos, an October magazine, and October monuments laid along the military road between Cairo and Ismailia. The October achievement is guarded like a jewel. Senior officers and graduates of the Nasser military academy deny that the military of 1977 has a political purpose similar to that of 1973. They expressed a sincere desire to opt out of the next Arab-Israeli Wars.

Nevertheless, their professional concern, the corporate defence of the military establishment, the great care with which they defend the military organization from politicization do in fact occur in the same organization which also serves as the *main* and *single* political source of support for the Sadat regime. And in that sense it is a praetorian military par excellence. It has no immediate goals of intervention but it serves as the regime's praetorian guard in two ways: to protect the regime from other sources of potential political power (as in the case of ASU in 1971); and to serve on the regime permanent and continuing notice of its fidelity—as long as the regime *satisfies* or does not *violate* the aspirations and goals of the military. Thus professional and politically objective aspirations are deeply rooted in policy and political orientations. This is true in nonpraetorian states as well. The difference is that the military in praetorian states is the *only* source of political support and regime legitimation. In that sense, of course, the apolitical stance of General Gamasi, and now Generals Ali and Mubarak and their fellow officers, is admirable. Though composed of dedicated professionals, the military nevertheless acts at least as a veto group and at most as a potential interventionist. Interventionism, as I have demonstrated in two decades of writing, is a most subtle political phenomenon. Interventionism does not mean a permanent and relentless effort on the part of the military to dominate the polity continously, but rather to serve as its praetorian guard, protecting regimes and states from undesirable opposition, rulers and rivals. But the military is in a position to intervene whenever it feels or suspects that a ruler or a regime might violate its conceptions of society, military and even politics. Sadat and the Egyptian military so far show similar values, aspirations, goals and orientations. These guarantee the preservation of Sadat's regime, Sadat's personalism and the military's corporatism. The guarantors could also become the violators of praetorian rule. Praetorianism is never completely static and praetorian states and regimes are always at the mercy of their guardians—the praetorian army.

CHAPTER 1

The Praetorian Army
and the Praetorian State

The philosophy of the revolution's purpose is like that of a patrol. To patrol is the true purpose of the [Egyptian military] in the annals of Egypt. . . . We now are to fight the greatest of our wars: the liberation of our fatherland from all its chains.

Gamal Abdel Nasser, *Falsafat al Thawra (The philosophy of the revolution)*, translated by Amos Perlmutter

Considered a deviant phenomenon before 1945, instances in which the military played an increasingly active role in politics became widespread after World War II. An army-dominated government was considered unnatural not because it was perceived as a new phenomenon—it had been recognized by political philosophers from Machiavelli to Mosca—but because some social scientists did not believe military rule was as worthy of study as civilian rule. This prejudice had a variety of causes, ranging from ignorance to antagonism toward war and the military profession. In the 1930s, for example, military government was identified as the ultimate type of totalitarianism.[1]

In the nineteenth and twentieth centuries military political interventionism was prevalent. Coups and counter coups occurred in all Latin American republics, in most independent Arab states, in most African states, in several Southeast Asian polities, in Pakistan, and in Greece and Portugal.

These events confirm the historical and political fact that when civilian government is neither effective nor institutionalized the executive is unable to control the military. The collapse of executive power is a precondition for praetorianism. Under praetorian conditions, many civil-military combinations become possible: the army can take over the government with or without the consent of civilian politicians, on their behalf or against them, with the aim of replacing one civilian group with another or with the aim of eliminating rivals in the military.

Frederick Mundell Watkins's classic definition of praetorianism appeared in the 1933 edition of the *Encyclopedia of the Social Sciences*: "Praetorianism is a word frequently used to characterize a situation where the military class of a given society exercises independent political power within it by virtue of an actual or threatened use of force." There is an essential distinction between historical and modern praetorianism.

HISTORICAL PRAETORIANISM

The Roman Praetorian Guard, the prototype of historical praetorianism, was a small military contingent in the imperial capital that preserved the legitimacy of the empire by defending the Senate against rebellious military garrisons. The influence of the Roman Praetorian Guard was based on three factors: its monopoly of local military power, the absence of definitive rules of succession, and the prestige of the Roman Senate. Though there was no hard and fast rule concerning selection of the princeps, the Senate's decree made him a legitimate ruler acceptable to the provincial armies; and the Praetorian Guard, the sole resident military force, was able to impose its candidate upon the Senate. Thus it was able to manipulate a widely subscribed concept of legitimacy and to attain a degree of political influence disproportionate to its size and military resources. Only when the provincial armies stumbled upon the secret that emperors need not be made in Rome did the legitimizing powers of the Senate as well as the strength of the Praetorians disappear.[2]

Patrimonialism and Praetorianism in Advanced Agricultural Societies

In Weberian theory, patrimonialism is defined as domination by *honoratiores* (honorable men, noblemen). It is a type of authority exercised in the manorial or patrimonial group (a more advanced unit than the patriarchal household, which is a relatively small unit based on blood ties). Patrimonialism is manifested in the decentralization of the patriarchal household and the extension of landholding, empire building, and "extrapatrimonial" recruitment (that is, recruitment not based on kinship). In this prebureaucratic political system, the ruler's staff is recruited only to ensure subordination to patriarchal rule, extended in "extrapatrimonial" recruitment to relations based on feudal, bureaucratic, or merely personal rulership. In patrimonialism, as in the patriarchal system, dependent relationships are based on loyalty and fidelity. The chief obligation of the subject is the material maintenance of the ruler. Patrimonial conditions give rise to political domination, for both the military and judicial authorities "are exercised without any restraint by the master as components of his patrimonial power."[3]

Whereas military authority and security arrangements are on an ad hoc basis in patriarchal types of domination, in a patrimonial state the military becomes a permanent establishment as the process of financial rationalization develops. Among the most important tributes which the patrimonial ruler extracts from his subjects are provision of troops or taxes to pay for mercenaries. Patrimonial states have recruited from the following sources: patrimonial slaves, retainers living on allowances (the *coloni* type); slaves completely separated from agricultural production; janissaries and mercenaries, supported by levies from the population but recruited from alien tribes or religious groups (Bedouins, Christians); or manorial peasants substituting military for economic service.[4]

The relationship between the patrimon and his conscripts has two pure forms, clientship and slavery, and various combinations. In the Ottoman Empire, for example, janissaries were recruited from aliens and pariah castes (Druze, Alawi, Kurds), while a "citizen" army was recruited from the peasants. The feudal armies of Western Europe, as an outgrowth of increased economic rationalism (with its need for organization, accounting, and planning), developed a group of privileged honoratiores, using peasant soldiers and military technology. As training became crucial, however, the relationship between patrimonial authority and the military was altered. The patrician no longer handled military affairs directly. With the development of military professionalization, it became possible for the military establishment to be used against the patrimonial authority's own political subjects. If a patrimon's political authority rested solely on threats—on the army or "coercive compliance"—his power to dominate might collapse. The Weberian term for the disintegration of the patrimonial system was "Sultanism"; its modern equivalent in social science theory is praetorianism.[5]

Patrimonial power was particularly susceptible to military domination in advanced agrarian societies (historical bureaucratic empires) that had large mercenary armies. "Native or foreign, once regularly organized mercenaries have become the preponderant force in a country, they have normally tried to force their rule upon the rest of society." If the military was not subdued, it became institutionalized as an autonomous group, and with every gain in professionalism its political importance increased. Then when legitimate authority faltered, the military could supplant it and fill the gap. For example, in the Ottoman Empire, the ruling institution became identical with the army during and after the reign of Suleiman the Magnificent in the sixteenth century; the janissaries remained the chief instrument of the sultan until 1827. Gradually they became a formidable and complex bureaucracy, and the introduction of firearms and cavalry increased their effectiveness. As praetorian values were routinized in the new technical units, they ensured the cohesiveness and political loyalty of all branches of the janissaries, the upholders of legitimacy.[6]

The Imperial-Colonial Legacies

In the European colonies during the nineteenth and twentieth centuries, the military was specifically oriented toward external conquest and dominance. External domination provided a vocational ideal, which was expressed in such organizations as the civil and military services in British India, the French Foreign Legion, the French Equatorial Army (the "Africans"), and the Spanish army in Morocco and South America. The values of the system were embodied in "civilisation française", Kipling's "white man's burden", and the missionary zeal of General Lyautey (a military administrator of French Africa). The concept of "civilisation française" was developed by the military who administered and in fact dominated French imperial policy in Africa and who were dedicated to the expansion of the empire.[7] The mission-oriented military was prone to become interventionist, particularly in the French and Spanish colonies.

This military type represented "the extreme in separation between a military organization and its supporting society". The basis of recruitment was particularistic: the aristocracy served as officers and the minorities as common soldiers. "Officers regard [ed] themselves as agents of a spiritual force, civilization, and view [ed] their service as a mission as well as a profession."[8] Soldiers were recruited from the imperial power's periphery or from the "native" population of the colonies, a procedure that was designed to safeguard imperial rule and loyalty. These natives were generally drawn from ethnic, cultural, and religious minorities (Druze, 'Alawi, and Kurd in the Arab East; Ghurka and Goumi in India; non-Moslems and members of small tribes in French Equatorial Africa). The imperial officer, who was expected to be a model for his colonial subordinate, might gain the reward of political domination through his subordinate capacity for leadership. For the colonizer (the imperial officer), soldiering and service in the empire were either the crucial test of an aristocrat or rungs on the climb up the social ladder for the middle class. The imperial officer was slavishly emulated by his subordinates and this model had considerable influence on modern Arab and African praetorians.

MODERN PRAETORIANISM

In developing polities the military functions somewhat as it did in the patrimonial states, serving as a center for political turmoil, political ambition, and threats to legitimate authority.

But modern praetorianism differs from the patrimonial model in two respects. First, the patrimonial military represented and defended legitimacy, but the modern military *challenges* legitimacy and offers a new type of authority.[9] Second (though less important), in historical praetorianism the authority relationship between the military establishment and political order is based on a traditional orientation, but in modern praetorianism authority relationships are based on a legal-rational orientation.[10] Modern praetorianism is the praetorianism of the professional soldier.

A modern praetorian state is one in which the military tends to intervene in the government and has the potential to dominate the executive. Among its characteristics are an ineffective executive and political decay.

The political processes of the praetorian state favor the development of the military as the core group and encourage the growth of its expectations as a ruling class. The political leadership of the state (as distinguished from its bureaucratic, administrative, and managerial leadership) is chiefly recruited from the military or from groups sympathetic to it. Constitutional changes are effected and sustained by the military, which plays a dominant role in all political institutions.

A modern praetorian government is most likely to develop when civilian institutions lack legitimacy; that is, they lack electoral support and effective executive power.* Such governments have often arisen from the ashes of weak republics. The most conspicuous examples have been the nineteenth-century nationalist polities in Spain and Latin America. Spain was the best model of praetorianism in the

---

*Above all, in illegitimate regimes belief in the stability, credibility, or effectiveness of established authority is lacking. In the Weberian sense, illegitimacy is lack of orientation toward authority. In modern praetorian regimes, the incumbent authorities do not derive their power simply from constitutional and fundamental laws, as Weber would have it. Rather, legitimacy is both a principle of authority and the orientation toward securing political electoral support. Thus, the praetorian condition is identified with the absence of electoral and political support procedures necessary for the establishment of authority.

nineteenth century. Its regime was the handiwork of disgruntled civilians and power-seeking politicians, all groping for ways to dominate central political power. Lacking popular support, liberal and progressive politicians viewed the army as a vehicle of hope and liberation, the instrument for gaining power and establishing an effective executive. In seeking military support, however, they threatened the very constitutional and political practices to which they were dedicated. Furthermore, when army officers entered politics, they adopted political behavior (that is, they aspired to rule), thus gradually losing their hold over the army. Their strength was challenged by rivals within the military: professionally oriented officers dedicated to the separation of the military and political spheres; politically oriented officers, dissatisfied with their own lack of power or status; a branch, section, or service discontented with its position within the military; or peripheral and fratricidal elements. Officers turned politician were also hurt by the civilian governments' failure to supply generals with armies, by soldiers' revolts, or by defeat in war.

In the twentieth century a developing country is ripe for praetorianism when the civilian government fails in its pursuit of such nationalist goals as unification, order, modernization, and urbanization. Various types of praetorianism probably represent specific stages of development. By the 1970s, for example, praetorianism often appeared in states that were in the early and middle stages of modernization and political mobilization.[11] Generally the army is propelled into political action in underdeveloped states when civilian political groups fail to legitimize themselves. The army's presence in civilian affairs is often an indicator of the existence of a corruption that is not expected to disappear in the near future. Modern praetorians are most likely to specify the "betrayal" and "corruption" of civilian politicians, parties, and parliaments as the reason for military intervention. Gamal Abdel Nasser, for instance, stated that the army must patrol society and that military rule is rule by order, shorn of "complicating" (that is independent) political structures and institutions. On the other hand, military intervention may occur when a state's material improvements are not appropriate to its corporate perspectives or when traditional institutions have been unable to produce such gains. Or it may be that, because of the traditional orientation of the people, modernized elites have proved incapable of establishing political institutions that would sustain the momentum of social mobilization and modernization.[12] Whatever the cause, in the ensuing disorganization both economy and ideology suffer setbacks.

TYPES OF MODERN MILITARY PRAETORIANISM

There are three forms (or subtypes) of military praetorianism: autocracy, oligarchy, and authoritarian praetorianism. Autocracy is a simple military tyranny, military rule by one man. In this system, unchecked personal authority is embodied in the single supreme ruler. The second subtype, military oligarchy, is government by the few. The executive is composed primarily of military men. The only intrinsic difference between the military oligarchy and the military autocracy is the number of rulers.

Authoritarian praetorianism, the third subtype, is characterized by military-civilian fusionist rule. Governmental authority, although unchecked politically, is nevertheless a coalition of military and civilian governing with little or no external political control. In the military autocracy the supreme ruler is always a military officer. In the military oligarchy the chief executive is either a former military man, now a civilian, or a civilian whose support comes exclusively from the military. Such a system cannot survive without the support of the military establishment. An authoritarian military regime is almost exclusively composed of military, bureaucrats, managers, and technocrats who restrict political support and mobilization. The majority of the authoritarian military executive body may be composed of military men or civilians, and the head of the government is not necessarily a military man. In fact, he may not possess military skills.

The major source of support in all military praetorian subtypes is the military establishment. In the military autocracy, electoral exercises are not even contemplated. A military oligarchy spends considerable effort to create a facade of electoral support and calls infrequent elections. The authoritarian military regime seeks external (in relation to the military) political support and is sincere in the exercise of restrictive elections, even if the choice is limited to the military-supported executive. However, this type of regime might tolerate political institutions and structures on the national level that are not necessarily oriented toward military rule (for example, parliaments, parties, and pressure groups).*

SOCIAL CONDITIONS CONTRIBUTING TO PRAETORIANISM

The following conditions in a society may contribute to the rise of praetorianism: structural weakness or disorganization; the existence of fractricidal classes, including a politically impotent middle class; and low levels of social action and of mobilization of material resources. The presence of some of these conditions does not necessarily lead to army intervention, however. Conversely, intervention may occur even though some conditions are missing.

In a state that lacks social cohesion, personal desires and group aims frequently diverge. The formal structure of the state is not buttressed by an informal structure; institutions do not develop readily or operate effectively; social control is ineffective; and channels for communication are few. Furthermore, there are no meaningful universal symbols to bind the society together. This syndrome is typical of a state in which the traditional patterns of social cohesion have broken down and have not yet been replaced by new patterns.[13] It may also accompany the emergence of new patterns of social cohesion in an unstable traditional society. Only a group separated from the society—a revolutionary organization, a party, a bureaucracy, or the army—can destroy such a

---

*Analysing the military regime in Brazil in 1973, Juan Linz commented: "Power basically remained with the armed forces, except for economic policy making, which is shared between the military, selected technocrats, and, to a lesser extent, businessmen. Institutions outside the armed forces have been created and disregarded constantly, leaving the military with ultimate power" ("The Future of an Authoritarian Situation" in *Authoritarian Brazil*, ed. Alfred Stepan [New Haven, Yale University Press, 1973] p. 235).

syndrome of social and economic disorganization. If the ruling civilians lack political experience and symbols of authority, military personnel may be able to manipulate the symbols of their institution to rule and to introduce some social cohesiveness. Although military leaders tend to be less articulate and sophisticated than civilian leaders, such attributes as impartiality and courage can make them more effective. They are better able to communicate with the people because they can elicit a psychological response on the symbolic level. Furthermore, they may be expected to overcome the syndrome of social disorganization to the extent that they maintain some distance from the divisions within the politically active population.

The second condition that promotes praetorianism is the existence of social classes that tend to be fragmented and incapable of mounting unified action even to achieve benefits for a particular sector. Although similar differences existed within classes during the developmental process in Western Europe or North America, such divisions are particularly acute in the under-developed countries of the twentieth century, where social and economic changes have been rapid and many stages of development have occurred simultaneously. In addition to the natural polarization between the wealthy few and the many poor in such countries, there are marked gradations and variations (leading to conflicts) within all three social layers—bottom, middle, and top. The top group is usually divided between traditionalists and modernists, mostly landowners who have adopted modern technology. The group at the bottom is also divided—in the case of under-developed countries, between the urban worker elite and the less privileged laborers.

Large foreign-owned industrial enterprises may give urban workers special benefits, such as high wages. Therefore this elite group of workers is little inclined to suffer the deprivations that political action designed to help its less privileged brethren may entail. Yet, it is precisely these workers, who are concentrated in large enterprises, who could be most easily organized for revolutionary action.[14]

This phenomenon has appeared throughout the under-developed world in the twentieth century. The urban workers in the large enterprises may be quite well off, as they were in pre-revolutionary China, while the conditions under which the masses of workers live are nearly subhuman. In Cuba, too, "permanently employed skilled and semi-skilled workers tended to develop a stake in the existing political and economic order. Even those not organized into unions had their interests carefully protected by labor laws. Although they themselves might be denied opportunities for upward social mobility, skilled workers and those at the foreman level were in a position to provide their sons with an education that would enable them to move ahead."[15]

The absence of a strong, cohesive, and articulate middle class—the class that historically has acted as the stabilizer of civilian government during modernization—is another condition contributing to the establishment of a praetorian government. The middle class in most praetorian states is small, divided, and politically impotent. In most states of the Middle East, for example, it represents no more than six per cent, and never more than ten per cent, of the population. Unlike the middle class in the West during industrialization, this class in the Middle East is composed of either bureaucrats or self-employed small businessmen; it rarely includes employers.[16] Since its members occupy different types of economic status, their economic interests diverge, as do their political interests. In Latin America (Argentina and Brazil, for instance) the middle class is relatively large and cohesive, comprising between ten and twenty per cent of the population, and sometimes more. And since it has a high percentage of politically active members, it could be the precipitator of military intervention since it requires military help to come to power or to retain power if it fails to win electoral support. In the Middle East, on the other hand, the military does not intervene on behalf of the middle class, or any class, for that matter. Thus, there is no conclusive evidence of a causal relationship between the military coup and the middle classes.

The next social condition for praetorianism is a low level of group social action and of mobilization of material resources. A state in the transitional stage of modernization not only lacks a commonly valued pattern of action but also lacks common symbols that aid mobilization for social and political action. The organization that is theoretically the most encompassing—the government—is supported by only a few divided sectors of inchoate social groups. The government thus has difficulty in obtaining support for its activities. Its programs are subverted and development projects fail. This failure in human mobilization results from the differences in the values of groups and members of society. Material resources, needed by the government as much as human resources, are also withheld. Industrialists disguise their profits to cheat the tax collector; bureaucrats take bribes; peasants hoard. The withholding of resources may take many forms, but the result is always the same: the government's development programs are subverted and its ability to remain in power without military support is jeopardized.[17]

MILITARY PRAETORIAN REGIMES: A POLITICAL EXPLANATION

To explain the political conditions for praetorian interventionism, I propose this axiom. *The praetorian army tends to replace weak and unstable political groups and regimes.* The motivation of the military to intervene is clearly political, even if it is triggered by non-institutionalized social conditions.[18]

Several hypotheses that can be derived from the literature attempt to explain the cause of military coups and praetorianism. Some hypotheses are sufficient; most others are conjectural and/or insufficient.

William Thompson, for instance, examines several hypotheses and causal inferences in the literature relating to military coups and regime replacement. According to him the dominant hypothesis concerns the pull of the system; that is, "much of indirect theorizing on military coups is concerned with the question of regime vulnerability. It is by far the dominant concern in the 'military politics' literature."[19] Since I concur that regime vulnerability is the major, if not the single, condition that propels the military into politics, it is necessary (especially in view of several of Thompson's valid criticisms) to distinguish between sufficient and insufficient explanations for the pull of regimes by military coups.

Insufficient Explanations

1. *The decline of authority.* Almost every student of the military in politics has proposed the decline of authority as an explanation or a cause of military coups. Although the literature is replete with empirical and other "proofs", the fact remains that not *all* declining authorities were pulled down by military coups. Most changes of regimes are neither designed nor initiated by the military. Nevertheless, I propose Portugal and Spain (1975); the People's Republic of China (1949); and the USSR (1917) as cases in which the decline of authority did not make the army overthrow the system. Instead the army did so only as an *instrument* of the regime (China, USSR) or in *coalition* with an established political party or group (Portugal). The fact that all Eastern European regimes (with the exception of Czechoslovakia and, partially, Yugoslavia) were pulled down by military coups between 1919 and 1939 and the new regimes were imposed by native Communist parties and the USSR after 1945 clearly demonstrates the insufficiency of this explanation. Decline of authority only explains the praetorian nature of the political system, that is, regime vulnerability may be exploited by *any* organized political force, including the military.[20]

2. *Historical legacies, failure of democracy.* Thompson also clearly demonstrates that explanations such as historical legacies, the failure of democracy, and the disjointed system[21] are insufficient to explain the rise of military regimes. In my view, the explanation why the military and not another group replaces a "declining authority" does not stem so much from the military's political motivation (which does, indeed, exist) as it does from the *relative* power of the military in regimes whose authority has declined.

3. *The military middle-class coup.* The most pervasive and non-substantiated explanation for the military *in* politics is that it is the spear-carrier of the middle class: that the decline of authority is coupled with the absence of a strong, cohesive middle class. The literature is replete with claims of evidence linking the military and the middle class. Essentially, two arguments have been derived from the same hypothesis: first, that the military is the spear-carrier of the middle class, and

second, that in the absence of a cohesive or established middle class, the propensity for military intervention is high. Both propositions are false because:

a.   the military may intervene on behalf of one class, all classes, or no class at all.[22] There is no proof that it is the middle class spearhead.

b.   the political motivation of the military activists, even when it benefits the middle class, is not necessarily generated by the *politics* or *ideology* of the middle classes.

c.   when they lack political power the middle classes search for allies. This is a logical political strategy for any group that seeks political power. In Latin America, for instance, many coups occur that could be properly called "working class coups". Such coups take place because the military finds alliance with labor unions politically rewarding, not because it possesses working-class consciousness. Historically some Latin American militaries have allied with the *caudillo*, some with the aristocracy, some with the liberals.

Various activist officers have "represented" different classes and sought such disparate allies as aristocrats, autocrats, anarchists, syndicalists, and Maoists. The soldiers of the Ottoman and the Austro-Hungarian empires were no more dedicated to a specific class than the modern Arab.[23]

Sufficient Explanations

Let us now turn to the dynamics of military coups. Again, there are interesting derivations from the proposition that coups are political actions of the military designed to replace rival groups and regimes with their own regime or one dominated by them.

1.   My proposition, based on the literature, is that the military group replaces an existing regime:

a.   when the military is the most cohesive and *politically* the best organized group at a given time in a given political system.

b.   when no relatively more powerful opposition exists. The Turkish army between 1961 and 1963 feared to intervene because of the retaliatory capabilities of the country's political parties. For more than a decade, the Egyptian Free Officers groups hesitated to intervene for fear of a combination of forces between the Egyptian court and Great Britain.[24] Some of Hitler's generals, especially the conservatives, planned four coups between 1938 and 1944. Nevertheless, most officers objected to the coups for fear of Hitler's popularity and Nazi-SS retaliatory power. Only in 1944, less than a year before the final defeat, did the military execute an abortive coup.

2.   Military coups and military intervention are conducted by:

a.   political activists in the military organization.
b.   members of political clubs, conspiratorial cabals within the military organization;
c.   officers with present or future political ambitions; and
d.   officers who do not consider the military as a life career. Political skill and commitment are more significant characteristics of coupmakers than age, rank, and seniority.[25] The argument that coupmakers are, on the whole, young, junior officers does not hold.

3.   Officers may be politicized as a result of:

a.   infiltration of their ranks by politically or ideologically committed officers or civilians who seek collaborators for a "civilianistic" coup;
b.   a new weltanschauung, such as fascism, socialism, or communism; or
c.   events—the anticolonial struggle, the coming of independence, economic disaster.

4.   Military coups are organized by:

a.   a coterie or a loose coalition of the political activists and their allies organized to negotiate their political role within the army, if possible, but if not, by means of the coup. A grievances coup (that is, one based on demands for better wages and working conditions) is a limited political action in the sense that such negotiations do not involve requests for political power and influence (the AFL-CIO president does not attempt to negotiate himself into the presidency of the United States); or
b.   a tight conspiracy composed of a few officers. On the whole coups have clandestine *political* support from outside the military. In addition, conspirators against established military regimes *must* join with politically influential individuals, interest groups, parties, or groups *outside* the army.[26]

5.   The decision to intervene, that is, to execute the coup, is a purely political decision that involves:

   a. political readiness
       i.   the maturation of the cabal
       ii. its political cohesiveness and commitment
       iii. the nature of its leadership
   b. political timing
       i.   strength of the authority to be replaced
       ii. the structure of coalition (with outside help)
       iii. political events

6. Coup legitimization, which begins as soon as the old regime is replaced, is a purely political action.

   a. The military, if it has acted alone, searches for political allies and kindred souls among the opposition and, if possible, among the disgruntled elements or opportunists of the deposed regime.
   b. If the coup is the product of a coalition, the political struggle between the military activists and their civilian allies is usually resolved when the military replaces or dominates the civilians.[27] (There are only a few exceptions, such as Portugal in 1975 and Turkey in 1971.)

THE PRAETORIAN ARMY

Political activity is contrary to the professional ethics and standards of the modern military, and the code of the professional army dictates that promotions be determined by ability, expertise, and education. Yet even in a nonpraetorian army such principles are not always accepted or observed. The link between professional and ruler precludes the certitude of professional non-interventionism. Character (that is, class) or political leanings often overrule expertise in the selection and promotion of officers. In some cases, professional standards may not exist at all, either because the army does not have a professional tradition or because the tradition has deteriorated. For example, in Argentina at the end of the nineteenth century, "institutional formal norms were never sufficiently enforced for the maintenance of discipline. Personal relationships and political affiliations remained major factors in the preservation of cohesion within the army and its control by civilian governments." In the imperial German army, as a result of emphasis on aristocracy and distrust of the bourgeoisie, character took precedence over intellect as a criterion for officer selection.[28]

An army becomes praetorian when a small group of officers, a few key activists, succeed in propelling the military into politics. This group is never more than five per cent of the total officer corps. In the most extreme form of praetorian army (the "ruler" type) the military establishes an independent executive and a political organization to dominate society and politics. The less extreme "arbitrator" type has no independent political organization and shows little interest in manufacturing a political ideology. To illustrate, the Iraqi military interventions in the late 1930s were carried out by an arbitrator army; those in the late 1950s, by a ruler army. The officers responsible for the first coup d'etat (October 1936), which was led by General Bakr Sidqi, eliminated moderate political leadership and transformed the government into a military dictatorship, but they had no political organization of their own. After Bakr Sidqi's assassination they were left leaderless and divided. The coup was followed by a counter coup, which was followed by several other military coups, until a civilian government was finally established in 1941. Although the army was a decisive factor in the political life of Iraq between 1936 and 1941, it could not serve as an effective and stabilizing alternative to the regimes and cabinets it toppled. Curiously enough, the political failures of the Iraqi army did not discourage Middle Eastern praetorian armies, including the Iraqi army itself. In 1958 another coup was staged by a ruler type of army. This time the army, under the leadership of Abd al-Karim Qasem, was more successful politically. It eliminated civilian politicians of both left and right, pruned its own ranks, and established a praetorian syndrome. By the middle 1970s, there seemed little chance of return to civilian rule.[30]

The actions of both types of praetorian armies—arbitrator and ruler—are affected by the internal structure of the army and the extent to which it has developed an identifiable political consciousness, political organization, and autonomy; by interaction between the army and civilian politicians and structures; and by the kind of political order the army wants to eliminate and the kind it wants to establish. Although the civilian and military spheres are treated here as independent variables in interaction and conflict, the military organization cannot be divorced from its social context. Initially, the political commitments and ideological positions of the military in the praetorian state are sustained either by the civilian politicians who encourage the army to enter politics or by the general sociopolitical context. After a certain level of political involvement has been attained, however, officers can begin to influence the positions taken by civilian politicians. This development occurs when a political group that originally infiltrated the army to avoid losing its support comes to share its goals. The more completely the army is immersed in politics, the greater is its desire to change the sociopolitical-context and the greater are the chances for political instability.

THE ARBITRATOR ARMY

This type of praetorian army has the following general characteristics: (1) acceptance of the existing social order; (2) willingness to return to the barracks after disputes are settled; (3) no independent political organization and lack of desire to maximize army rule; (4) a time limit for army rule; (5) concern with improvement of professionalism; (6) a tendency to operate behind the scenes as a pressure group; and (7) a fear of civilian retribution.

1. The arbitrator army accepts the existing social order and makes no fundamental changes in the regime or the executive structure.

In an under-developed country, where accepting the existing order often implies an anti-revolutionary ideology, the arbitrator army may be the instrument of conservative and anti-liberal forces. The Ottoman army was a conservative instrument before the coup of 1909, as was the Iraqi army in the 1920s.[31] The Argentine military establishment, which displayed an arbitrating orientation after the fall of Juan Peron in 1955, was anti-leftist and, specifically, after 1959, anti-Castro. Traditional Latin American caudillos have usually not attempted to change the social order.

2. The officers of the arbitrator army are civilian-oriented. Furthermore, at least in Latin America and Turkey, they are dedicated to protecting and preserving constitutional government. Even when civilian groups are not well enough

organized to set up a government, or when officers occupy positions in the government, the officers obey the instructions of civilian political groups. They do not inject their own viewpoint. They want to return to normality, which means acceptance of the status quo. This type of army expects to return to the barracks after political corruption has been eliminated and stability restored, for its officers are aware that they lack the skills to govern and they wish to avoid further political involvement.

The Chilean army of the 1924-33 period expected to return to barracks. Its officers participated in politics because civilian political groups had become disorganized, but the participation was limited and the professional norms of the military establishment were largely retained even during periods of fairly deep involvement. After returning to the barracks this type of army does not necessarily relinquish its political influence. In many cases it has continued to act as guardian of civilian authority and political stability. This is the essence of the Kemalist legacy in Turkey: the army serves as the guardian of the constitution. Until 1964 the army of Brazil played a similar arbitrator part.[32]

3. The arbitrator army has no independent political organization and makes no attempt to maximize army rule. General Nagib of Egypt, for example, who was recruited by Nasser and the Society of Free Officers in 1951 to head the list of Free Officers in the elections for the administrative committee of the Officers' Club, had no political organization of his own. He was not a charter member of the Free Officers, but was chosen from among three candidates to become the titular head of the 1952 coup. Lacking his own organization, Nagib was obliged to deal with the Free Officers' political organization, the Revolutionary Command Council (RCC).[33] Unfortunately for Nagib, his efforts to maximize civilian participation in the RCC cabinet and to oppose the policy of Nasser and the RCC to legitimize the military dictatorship failed, and he was ousted by the RCC in 1954.

4. The arbitrator army imposes a time limit on army rule and expects to hand the government over to an "acceptable" civilian regime, for it views prolonged rule as detrimental to its professional integrity. Therefore it encourages political

groups that are capable of establishing order, preserving stability, and guaranteeing that the new government will not retrogress. The existence of such organized civilian groups has a vital bearing on the army's decision to surrender its rule. When no such groups exist—that is, when there is a state of near anarchy—the arbitrator army, the only organized group in the state, may have to continue governing despite its civilian orientation and its desire to return to its own affairs. Where organized civilian groups do exist, the military as a whole withdraws from the government, although at times a key military figure may continue as chief of state. General Carlos Ibanez, for instance, was chief of state in Chile in the late 1920s and early 1930s, but the military institution as a whole was not politically involved.[34]

5. Professionalism and corporateness—the collective sense that arises from professional unity and consciousness—are closely related to the political attitude of the military, for unlike other professionals such as lawyers and physicians, soldiers depend upon the state for security. Both the praetorian military and the civil service are sensitive to political change, but the civil service is less affected by it because it has little physical power with which to threaten the regime. In an arbitrator army the officer corps (or important sectors of it) is strongly opposed to political involvement since it may destroy the professional military norms and expertise that provide security and predictability for the officer's career. This type of army tends to defend the existing regime in order to protect its own professional integrity. It may even intervene to defend the military against the threat posed by a disintegrating or unstable regime.

6. Because it fears open involvement in politics, the arbitrator army tends to operate behind the scenes as a pressure group. It influences civilian governments to respond to popular demands, thereby making it unnecessary for the military to intervene openly. However, the military's refusal to take responsibility for its actions creates a situation in which power is divorced from responsibility—a situation that may lead to instability. Moreover, since the arbitrator type of officer corps lacks cohesion, instability may result in factionalism or aggravate existing divisions. This condition may then

lead to a pattern of coup and countercoup in which the frequent changes in government are not accompanied by changes in policies but merely reflect personal rivalries. Most of the unsuccessful coups in Syria have been of this type. Civilians are usually involved in these personalistic cliques and attempt to use them for their own ends. Such entanglements may result in a vicious circle: civilian action tends to increase military cliquishness, and vice versa, because the combination of army and civilian motives blurs the separation of the army from the civilian socio-political context and results in the army's inability to change the political situation. This pattern has appeared in the Latin American sequences of coups d'etat (*cuartelazos*).[35]

7. The arbitrator army may be afraid of retribution from both civilian politicians and the civilian population. The presence of organized civilian groups may cause the military to fear the future actions of civilian politicians—dismissal of officers, demotion, or peripheral appointments and assignments. Such fears were apparent in General Gursel's attitude during the 1960-61 coup in Turkey and in Portugal in 1975-76.[36] If an army has become unpopular because it has initiated repressive measures, especially if its soldiers have been recruited from the native population, doubts about the civilian population's willingness to follow its orders may cause the army to withdraw because it fears mass violence as well as political retribution.

THE RULER PRAETORIAN ARMY

In its pure form this type of praetorian army has characteristics that are in direct opposition to those of the arbitrator type. It (1) rejects the existing order and challenges its legitimacy; (2) lacks confidence in civilian rule and has no expectation of returning to the barracks; (3) has a political organization and tends to maximize army rule; (4) is convinced that army rule is the only alternative to political disorder; (5) politicizes professionalism; (6) operates in the open; and (7) has little fear of civilian retribution. In practice, however, an army that displays most of the characteristics of the ruler type, including a well articulated ideology to which the officer corps adheres, may not actually rule. In such a case—the Peruvian army until 1972 for instance —the military presents a unified point of view and acts as the stabilizer of civilian governments that hold views similar to its own.[37]

1. Officers in developing countries challenge the legitimacy of the existing order, opposing both the political corruption of the traditional parliamentary liberal regimes and some of the modernizing authoritarian one-party systems. In these countries, traditional parliamentary politics and liberalism have become identified with status quo politics. The ruler type of praetorian army increasingly tends to abandon or convert existing institutions, ideologies, and procedures in favor of the institutions for modernization, industrialization, and political mobilization that are proposed by theorists of rapid growth. To nonconservative praetorians, the new theories are more suitable guides for altering traditional institutions than are the old "corrupt" liberal ideologies. However, these praetorians also reject as corrupt those radical-revolutionary civilian regimes that favor rapid modernization under a one-party system. The officers are not revolutionaries. Instead, they tend to be reformers, and any self-proclaimed conversion to revolutionary causes is likely to be much more superficial than their conversion to anticonservatism. Yet, in its reformist role, the army may be adamantly opposed to communism (to Castroism, in contemporary Latin America). In Peru, the military has generally opposed the local revolutionary party (APRA), but this has not prevented the army from adopting a reform orientation since 1973.[38]

The ruler army has at least three subtypes that reject the existing order and challenge its legitimacy: the antitraditionalist radical army, the antitraditionalist reformer army, and the conservative, antiradical army. The term "antitraditionalist" indicates opposition to traditional institutions such as the Sharia (Islamic canon law) and patrimony; "radical" means opposition to party or liberal organizations (parliamentary institutions, multiparty systems, democratic elections); and "reformer" refers to the acceptance of reform parties and parliamentary politics. These types can be placed on a left-right continuum in relation to the political order. Examples of the antitraditionalist radical army are the regimes of Abd al-Karim Qasem in Iraq (1958-63) and Juan Peron in Argentina (1945-55); the military regimes of Gamal Abdel Nasser in Egypt (1952-70); Houari Boumedienne in Algeria (1965-1978); most Syrian and Iraqi regimes since 1963; Portugal (1975); and General Suharto in Indonesia (after 1965). The antitraditionalist reformer army is represented by Mustafa Kemal (Ataturk) of Turkey (1919-23), Ayub Khan of Pakistan (1958-70), the Peruvian army (1968-75). The conservative, antiradical army is exemplified by the anti-Castro, anti-communist military rulers of Brazil and Argentina since 1966, and the regime in Iran 1978-9. The ruler army chooses the new political order as a reaction to the order that it has replaced. In other words, the ideology of the praetorian army depends on the nature of the ideology it has rejected. Choice here is rather limited; the final selection will depend upon what means the army takes to transform society into "something else," most often into something initially unknown to it. It took Nasser a decade, for instance, to opt for Arab socialism; in that period it was clearer to him what political system to destroy than what political system to create. Nasser was more leftist than the Wafd, just as Ayub Khan was more radical than the old Muslim League party. Boumedienne was to the right of Ben Bella, and Suharto to the right of Sukarno. Sadat moved to the right of Nasser. The Syrian 'Alawi are more radical than the mainstream Sunni Ba'th officers; the Portuguese army is more radical than Salazar.

In Pakistan, Ayub Khan's "basic democracy" developed as an alternative to the regime it replaced. Although the Pakistani army, an offshoot of the British Indian army, had kept aloof from politics, the need for reform and modernization enhanced its propensity for institutional autonomy and made a temporary ruler of Ayub Khan, who had been dedicated to military professionalism and maximizing civilian rule. Imbued with the British civil service tradition, he chose to blend a very modified version of British bureaucracy with the "military mind" and political reality of Pakistan—a coalition of bureaucracy and the military. The resulting mixture of traditional values and professionalism (both bureaucratic and military) created the concept of "basic democracy"—the ideology of the Pakistani army after 1958. In Algeria, Houari Boumedienne did not abandon Arab socialism but merely reduced its ideological intensity and commitments. In the process he became an antiradical type of ruler. Although by the middle 1970s he had not adopted an ideology of his own, by eliminating Ben Bella's legacy he had moved toward the modernization of Algeria without Ben Bella's radicalism. In Indonesia, after the 1965 Communist coup, the army liquidated the old regime; Sukarno's "guided democracy" had radicalized it. The political evolution of the Indonesian army indicated that, even if it did not offer an alternative ideology, it might proceed along the lines of a modified guided democracy without the vehemence, the radicalism, and the messianism that had marked the reign of President Sukarno.[39]

2. The ruler army has no confidence in civilian rule and makes no provision for returning to the barracks. This attitude may be a consequence of the development by an important sector of the officer corps of an independent political orientation opposed to the ruling civilian groups. Alternatively, civilian disorganization may have reached the point where progressive elements are unable to put their programs into effect. By the time military intervention occurs, civilians have already manifested their inability to control the situation. Civilian failure prompts the officers to feel that they should occupy formal positions in the governmental structure. In Egypt, for example, officers blamed civilians for the Palestinian crisis and for the Cairo riots of January 1952; they did not even trust those civilians—such as the more radical members of the Wafd or the Muslim Brotherhood—who subscribed to political philosophies similar to their own. In the early 1950s, after a number of years of civil war, the Colombian army led by Rojas Pinilla lost confidence in civilian rule, took control of the government, and implemented a Peronist type of developmental program. When this change occurred, only part of the army shared Rojas Pinilla's orientation, but afterwards the army showed an inclination to adopt developmental ideologies based on

technological and evolutionary change. By the middle 1970s the army still had no confidence in civilian rule and it seemed likely that it might again take over the government of Colombia. The military of Argentina, Brazil, and Peru also lost confidence in civilian ability to maintain constitutional rule under the pressure of social mobilization.

3. The ruler army has an independent political organization, and it attempts to legitimize and maximize its own rule. Considering itself the one elite group capable of governing, it usually tries to ensure the indefinite continuation of army rule by taking advantage of the lack of political and social cohesion and by strengthening its authority. Legitimizing itself through the creation of a radical-nationalist party, the ruler army manufactures or incorporates an ideology to support its organization. In Syria, for example, Adib Shishakly founded the Arab Liberation Movement in 1952 to legitimize the military dictatorship he had established in 1951.[40] Since then military coups in the Middle East have followed the precedent of establishing a Revolutionary Command Council to legitimize army rule and eliminate civilian and army opposition. While the formation of a RCC does not guarantee a coup's success nor ensure that it will attain legitimacy, it does give the army independence in political action and a means of circumventing whatever strong civilian organizations exist. Where such groups do not exist, the RCC serves to preserve the military dictatorship.

Legitimization of the army as the guarantor of stability and progress does not necessarily imply that its rule will be permanent. In Turkey, the Kemalist legacy served as a watchdog to prevent the civilian regime from returning to corrupt practices. By civilianizing his regime under the auspices of the army, Ataturk also legitimized the army's role in politics as the defender and protector of the constitution and of republican and honest civilian rule; in effect, he maximized civilian rule by legitimizing the army as its sole protector. Nasser, on the other hand, gave a civilian role to political parties and bureaucracies created by the army. Although this practice maximized army domination, it might discourage a return to civilian rule after Egypt has achieved modernization.

An army need not have its own ideology or political organization in order to favor a ruler type of praetorianism; it can take over the established, popular, nationalist-radical party. When the army came to power in Iraq after the 1958 revolution, it participated in the struggle between the oligarchs and the new generation, and many military leaders were closely associated with various ideological groups. Nevertheless, instead of formulating its own distinct set of ideals, it merely carried out the programs of the civilian groups. Its most important step was to take over the Ba'th party and militarize it. In Syria a somewhat different relationship developed between the army and the Ba'th party. Though sharing a common political ideology, the two organizations did not hold the same view of army rule: the Ba'th advocated parliamentary rule, while the army preferred praetorianism. The February 1966 coup indicated the trend in favor of the army rule. An army faction took over the Ba'th party's left wing, signifying further attrition of Ba'thist and civilian groups in Syria. In this case, the ideology of a civilian party served to legitimize the rule of the army; the Ba'th party became a party in uniform.

In Indonesia the evolution of the army as a political organization strengthened its position as a ruler. The political consolidation of the army occurred when many officers, supporting Sukarno's "guided democracy" in order to keep political parties out of power and to weaken the Indonesian Communist party, were absorbed into the national elite. The army participated in civic action and boosted economic development to compete with the Communist party at the grass-roots level. When the Communists attacked the army, the army struck back, and after 1965 it was involved in dissolving the old order and establishing a new one under army rule.[41]

4. The ruler army is convinced that its regime is the only alternative to political disorder and thus does not set a time limit nor search for an acceptable civilian successor government. This attitude is illustrated clearly by Nasser's political philosophy. In *Egypt's Liberation: The Philosophy of the Revolution*, Nasser argues that "only the army" can ameliorate conditions in Egypt and that the army plays the "role of

vanguard" in the Egyptian revolution. This attitude also typified some of the extreme radical nationalists in the Iraqi army during the late 1930s, among them Salah al-Din al-Sabbagh, whose xenophobia and anti-imperialist convictions led him to believe that the army was destined to relieve Iraq and Islam of the yoke of external and internal oppressors.[42] In the Middle East most army leaders have tended to espouse the kind of military dictatorships established by Shishakly and Nasser. If an army there still acts as an arbitrator (as it does especially in Syria), it is due more to civilian opposition and intra-army rivalry than to the army's belief in civilian rule.

5.   The ruler army sacrifices professionalism to political expediency. Political considerations take precedence over expertise, internal organization, and career security, and a new set of norms is developed. Politicization may destroy professional concepts of status and rank, or in certain situations (for example, in Syria between 1963 and 1966), a low-ranking officer may be politically superior to an officer of higher rank. The Thai army, however, is a striking exception to the thesis that a ruler army's political involvement diminishes its professional integrity. Since 1932 the officers of the Thai army, which is rooted in the traditional bureaucracy, "have led the ruling group, dominated the institutions of government, and set the style of Thai politics." Apparently the professional norms of the officer class can survive in a country where politics and social structure are bureaucratic.[43]

6.   The ruler army operates in the open because it wants to use military symbols to gain support for its programs and activities. A peculiar combination of both traditional and modern components, the military may be quite acceptable to a population for whom it represents a technologically advanced organization. For the traditionalists, the military symbolizes heroic leadership and honor, even though its officers may be "experts" and managers. "The great stress placed on professionalism and the extremely explicit standards for individual behavior make the military appear to be a more sacred than secular institution."[44]

7.   By the time the ruler type of praetorianism has developed, the army already exercises so much power that it

does not need to fear civilians. In Egypt, for example, the emergence of the army as ruler took place after an extended period of disorganization—growing violence in urban areas and the manifest failure of civilians to maintain order or implement development programs. Furthermore, the civilians were considered incapable of defending Egypt against imperialist powers.

Military government is government by surrogate. A praetorian government is one that secures political support without legitimacy. It is a military stewardship on behalf of absent executive and civilian political groups, and it results more from the inefficiency of civilian political organizations than from the political aptitude of the military interventionists. On the whole the military usurpers prove to be even greater simpletons in exercising political power than their civilian predecessors. In the absence of organized, politically articulate groups, officers who are untrained and unsuited for politics attempt to manipulate power to serve a variety of noble causes, including the elimination of corruption and avarice and saving the nation from foreign aggression or domination (and such threats have often been invented by the politically minded military itself). After entering the political arena, these officers have produced patriotic slogans, ideological pronunciamentos, and promises, rather than practical reforms, revolution, or counter-revolution. Tanks have replaced cavalry, the television station the pronunciamento, and the revolutionary command council the civilian executive. But praetorianism is still government from the turrets. Army control has become the rule, civilian control the exception. Patrolling used to be the function of civilian guards. Now it has become the exercise of praetorians in mufti.

NOTES

1. Harold D. Lasswell, "The Garrison State," *American Journal of Sociology*, 46 (January 1941), 455-58.
2. I am grateful to M. D. Feld of Harvard University for this analysis.
3. Max Weber, *Economy and Society*, ed. Guenther Roth and Claus Wittich, 3 vols. (New York: The Bedminster Press, 1968), 3:1006-69. The quotation is from p. 1013.

4. *Ibid.,* pp. 1015-17.

5. *Ibid.,* pp. 1020, 1013.

6. Gerhard Lenski, *Power and Privilege* (New York: McGraw-Hill, 1966), p. 243 (source of quotation); Albert H. Lybyer, *The Government of the Ottoman Empire* (New York: Russell & Russell, 1966), pp. 47-62.

7. M. D. Feld, "A Typology of Military Organization," in *Public Policy,* ed. Carl J. Friedrich and Seymour E. Harris (Cambridge, Mass.: Harvard University Press, 1958), 8:8.

8. For quotations see *ibid.,* pp. 8, 10.

9. Weber recognized that praetorianism might threaten legitimacy in the patrimonial state when the military was an alien professional establishment or when it represented a citizen army, but his analysis does not explain the process of political legitimation and the structural sustenance of praetorian rule. He saw praetorian domination as patrimonial or traditional rather than as an independent type of authority orientation. See S. N. Eisenstadt, *The Political Systems of Empires* (New York: The Free Press, 1963), pp. 172-73: and Weber, *Economy and Society,* 3:1006-69.

10. In the caudillismo case, personalism and violence united to seize the disintegrating patrimonial state apparatus. In the name of republicanism (in Latin America) and liberalism (in nineteenth-century Spain), caudillismo became the driving force of the nation. On personal, patriarchal, and patrimonial types of domination, see Weber, *Economy and Society,* vol. 3.

11. David C. Rapoport, "Praetorianism: Government without Consensus" (Ph.D. diss., University of California, Berkeley, 1960), pp. 14-15, defines praetorianism as a constitutional form of "government without consensus." Rapoport's thesis provides an outstanding theoretical discussion of praetorianism. Although I follow his definition, I emphasize the descriptive aspects of the subject and forgo discussions of constitutionalism, consensus, and authority, which he covers at length. This part of my book has been directly influenced by the works of Samuel P. Huntington, especially his essay "Political Development and Political Decay," *World Politics* 18 (April 1965); 386-440. For some time, he and I have carried on an intellectual dialogue. Hopefully, the result has been a more positive approach to a theory of civil-military relations in developing polities. Especially excellent is Huntington's chapter, "Praetorianism and Political Decay", in *Political Order in Changing Societies* (New Haven: Yale University Press, 1968), pp. 192-263. He argues there that the concept of praetorianism becomes a useful tool to explain the relationship between political development and modernization. In my view Huntington's analysis of the role of political decay in modernizing polities becomes most crucial in the case of praetorianism.

12. Huntington's central thesis in *Political Order* is the gap hypothesis, the idea that modernization breeds both political instability and praetorian order (pp. 32-33, 53-56). See Gino Germani and Kalman H. Silvert, "Politics, Social Structure and Military Intervention in Latin

America," *Archives europeennes de sociologie* 2, no. 1 (1961): 62-81. Analysis of the breakdown in modernization is found in S. N. Eisenstadt's extensive studies of the relationships among traditionalism, modernization, and change. See especially his "Breakdown of Modernization", *Economic Development and Cultural Change* 12 (July 1964): 345-67; "Political Modernization: Some Comparative Notes", *International Journal of Comparative Sociology* 5 (March 1964): 3-24; *Modernization: Protest and Change* (Englewood Cliffs, N.J.: Prentice-Hall, 1966).

13. Talcott Parsons, *Structure of Social Action* (Glencoe, Ill: Free Press, 1937), p. 377.

14. See Nadav Safran, *Egypt in Search of Political Community* (Cambridge, Mass.: Harvard University Press, 1961), p. 2.

15. Wyatt MacGaffey and Clifford R. Barnett, *Cuba* (New Haven: Yale University Press, 1962), p. 144.

16. Morroe Berger, "The Middle Class in the Arab World," in *The Middle East in Transition,* ed. Walter Lacqueur (New York: Praeger, 1958), pp. 63-65.

17. See Eisenstadt, *Political systems of Empires,* esp. chaps. 6 and 7. For Eisenstadt, the promotion of "free resources and [the] freeing [of] resources from commitments to particularistic-ascriptive groups" (p. 119) is one of the conditions for the creation and maintenance of autonomous political institutions.

18. Huntington, *Political Order,* pp. 192-98; Amos Perlmutter, "The Arab Military Elite", *World Politics* 22, no. 2 (January 1970): 284-300; Amos Perlmutter, "Israel's Fourth War, October 1973: Political and Military Misperception", *Orbis* 29 (1975): 434-60; S. E. Finer, *The Man on Horseback: The Role of the Military in Politics* (London: Pall Mall Press, 1962), *chap.* 5.

19. William Thompson, "'Explanations of the Military Coup", (Ph.D. diss., University of Washington, Seattle, 1972), pp. 81-124.

20. R. L. Gilmore, *Caudillism and Militarism in Venezuela, 1810-1919* (Athens: Ohio University Press, 1964); E.J. Hobsbawm, *Primitive Rebels* (New York: Norton, 1959); M. Janowitz, *The Military in the Political Development of New Nations:* An Essay in Comparative Analysis (Chicago: University of Chicago Press, 1964); G. W. Grayson, "Portugal and the Armed Forces Movement", *Orbis* 29 (Summer 1975): 335-78; M. C. Needler, *Political Development in Latin America: Instability, Violence, and Evolutionary Change* (New York: Random House, 1968), pp. 157-63;

21. Thompson, "Explanations of the Military Coup", pp. 82-97.

22. *Ibid.,* pp. 99-103. See also M. Halpern, "The Problem of Becoming Conscious of the Salaried New Middle Class", *Comparative Studies in Society and History,* Vol. no. 12, 1 (January 1970); Morroe Berger, "Military Elite and Social Change: Egypt Since Napoleon", Research Monograph no. 6 (Princeton University: Center for International Studies, 1960); J. Nun, "The Middle Class Military Coup", in *The Politics of Conformity in Latin America* ed. C. Veliz (London: Oxford University Press, 1967); L. North, *Civil-Military Relations in Argentina,*

Chile, and Peru, Politica of Modernization Studies (Berkeley: Institute of International Studies, 1966); Huntington, *Political Order;* R.D. Putnam, "Toward Explaining Military Intervention in Latin American Politics,"*World Politics,* vol. no. 20, 1 (October 1967); M. Halpern, *The Politics of Social Change in the Middle East and North Africa* (Princeton, N.J.: Princeton University Press, 1963); E. A. Nordlinger, "Soldiers in Mufti: The Impact of Military Rule upon Economic and Social Change in the Non-Western States," *American Political Science Review,* Vol.no. 4 (1970); Amos Perlmutter, "The Myth of the Myth of the New Middle Class: Some Lessons in Social and Political Theory," vol. no. 12, 1 (January 1970); and Amos Perlmutter, "The Arab Military Elite."

23. R. A. Hansen, "Military Culture and Organizational Decline: A Study of the Chilean Army," (Ph.D. University of California, Los Angeles, 1967), pp. 127-165; Robert A. Potash, *The Army and Politics in Argentina: 1928-1945,* (Palo Alto, Calif.: Stanford University Press, 1969), pp. 182-200; pp. 46-48; June Hahner, *Brazilian Civil-Military Relations, 1889-1898,* (Ithaca, New York: Cornell University Press, 1966), p. 4; Eliezer Be'eri, *Army Officers in Arab Politics and Society* (New York: Praeger, 1970); H. A. R. Gibb and H. Bowen, *Islamic Society and the West,* vol. 1, pt. 1, (London, Oxford University Press, 1950); J. Rothschild, *Pilsudski's Coup d'Etat,* (New York; Columbia University Press, 1966).

24. U. Dann, *Iraq under Qassem: A Political History, 1958-1963,* (New York: Praeger, 1966); *The Army and Politics in Argentina;* Potash, Itamar Rabinowitz, *Syrian Army and Ba'th Party, 1963-1966: Army-Party Symbiosis,* (Tel Aviv, Israel, Universities Presses, 1973); A. Stepan, *The Military in Politics: Changing Patterns in Brazil* (Princeton, N.J.: Princeton University Press, 1971); W. F. Weiker, *The Turkish Revolution,* "The Army and the Founding of The Turkish Republic," *World Politics,* vol. 11, no. 4 (July 1959); Anwar al-Sadat, *Revolt on the Nile,* (New York: John Day, 1957).

25. Gienen, "Public Order and the Military in Africa"; E. Lieuwen, *Arms and Politics in Latin America,* rev. ed. (New York: Praeger, 1961); Finer, *The Man on Horseback;* L. N. McAlister, "Civil-Military Relations in Latin America," in *Dynamics of Change in Latin American Politics,* ed. J. D. Martz (Englewood Cliffs, N.J.: Prentice-Hall, 1966); pp. 5-36; Potash, *The Army and Politics in Argentina,* pp. 182-237; Majid Khadduri, *Independent Iraq: A Study in Iraqi Politics, 1932-1958,* 2d ed. (London: Oxford University Press, 1960), pp. 76-80.

26. Khadduri, *Independent Iraq;* Thompson, "Explanations of the Military Coup," pp. 161-67; Ruth First, *The Barrel of a Gun: Political Power in Africa and the Coup d'Etat,* (London: Penguin Press, 1970); P. J. Vatikiotis, *The Egyptian Army in Politics: Pattern for New Nations,* (Bloomington: Indiana University Press, 1961); Carlos A. Astiz, *Pressure Groups and Power Elites in Peruvian Politics* (Ithaca, New York, and London: Cornell University Press, 1969); Luigi R. Einaudi, "Peru," in Luigi Einaudi and Alfred Stepan, *Latin American Institutional*

Development: Changing Military Perspectives in Peru and Brazil, (Rand R-586-DOS, April 1971), pp. 1-70; M. Lissak, "Modernization and Role Expansion of the Military in Developing Countries," *Comparative Studies in Society and History,* vol. 9, no. 3 (April, 1967); "Public Order and the Military in Africa"; North, *Civil-Military Relations.*

27. See Irving Louis Horowitz, "The Military in Latin America," *Elites in Latin America,* ed. Seymour Martin Lipset and Aldo Solari (London: Oxford University Press, 1965).

28. Martin Kitchen, *The German Officer Corps,1890-1914* (London: Oxford University Press, 1968), pp. 28-32.

30. Khadduri, *Independent Iraq,* pp. 76-80; Uriel Dann, *Iraq under Qassem* (Jerusalem: Israel University Presses, 1969).

31. Khadduri, *Independent Iraq,* pp. 78-80; North, *Civil-Military Relations,* pp. 1-10.

32. North, *Civil-Military Relations,* pp. 34-37. In Turkey the transformation of the army rebels of 1960-61 into permanent senators illustrated once again the persistence of the Kemalist legacy, at least as of 1976. Charles Simmons, "the Rise of the Brazilian Military Class, 1840-1900," *Mid-America* 39 (October 1957): 227-38.

33. Lacouture and Lacouture, *Egypt in Transition,* pp. 144-145; Eliezer Be'eri, *Ha-Kzuna ve-Hashilton Ba-Olam ha-Aravi* (The Officer Class in Politics and Society of the Arab East) (Tel Aviv, Israel: Sifriat Poalim, 1966), pp. 74-80; Shimon Shamir."Five Years of the Liberation Rally," *The New East (Hamizrah Hehadash)* 8, no. 4 (1957): 274.

34. North, *Civil-Military Relations,* pp. 34-37.

35. Huntington, *The Soldier,* chap. 3, pp. 29-79. See George Blanksten, *Ecuador: Constitutions and Caudillos* (Berkeley and Los Angeles: University of California Press, 1951), pp. 51-54, for a discussion of the "vicious circle" phenomenon. For Latin American cases of this type, see McAlister, "Civil-Military Relations in Latin America."

36. See Weiker, *The Turkish Revolution,* for a complete discussion of this event.

37. North, *Civil-Military Relations,* pp. 52-57.

38. Huntington, *The Soldier,* pp. 93-94, discusses briefly the conservatism of the professional officer. He is dealing with nonpraetorial states, however. See Richard Patch, "The Peruvian Elections of 1962 and Their Annulment," *American Universities Field Staff Reports,* West Coast South America Series, vol. 9 (September 1962), p. 6.

39. Huntington, *The Soldier,* pp. 83-85. The basis of military power in Pakistan was the rural elite and the urban rich. For a parallel analysis that emphasizes the role of the army as the bearer of explicit political norms and images, see Lissak, "Modernization and Role Expansion," pp. 240-255. On Indonesia see Lev, "The Political Role," pp. 349-64.

40. Patrick Seale, *Struggle for Syria: A Study of Post-War Arab Politics: 1945-1958* (London, Oxford University Press. 1965). pp. 124-31.

41. Majid Khadduri, "The Role of the Military in Iraqi Society," in *The Military in the Middle East,* ed. Sydney N. Fisher (Columbus: Ohio

State University Press, 1963), p. 47. I am indebted to Daniel S. Lev for most of the points made here on the Indonesian army. See Lev, "The Political Role," pp. 360-64.

42. Gamal Abdel Nasser, *Egypt's Liberation: The Philosophy of the Revolution* (Washington, D.C.: Public affairs Library, 1955), pp. 32-33, 42-45. See F.L. Carsten, *The Reichswehr and Politics 1918-1933* (Oxford: Clarendon Press, 1966); Khadduri, *Independent Iraq*, pp. 200-06. See also Col. Salah al-Din al-Sabbagh, *Fursan al-Arabiyyah fi Iraq* (The Knights of Arab-hood in Iraq, Damascus, 1956), pp. 29-30.

43. David A. Wilson, "The Military in Thai Politics," in *Role of the Military*, ed. Johnson, p. 253 (quotation), pp. 268-69; Fred W. Riggs, *Thailand: The Modernization of a Bureaucratic Polity* (Honolulu: University of Hawaii Press, 1966).

44. Lucien W. Pye, "Armies in the Process of Political Modernization," in *Role of the Military*, ed. Johnson, p. 75.

CHAPTER 2

The Birth of a New Class

By Manfred Halpern

INTRODUCTORY NOTE

Manfred Halpern has been a pioneer in modern Middle East studies and has been responsible, among others, for shifting the emphasis in the field from the historiographers and linguists and helping to set up a new social science approach for the analysis and interpretation of social, economic and political events in the Middle East. Nevertheless, Halpern's approach represents the dominance of what Robert Packenham clearly identifies as the liberal approach to the politics of developing countries: an effort to demonstrate on unconvincing evidence that the indigenous and rising middle classes and the salariat in developing countries have become the central political force that is not only behind the rise of the new elites in the modern Middle East, but also guarantees the foreign policy of liberal and imperial America. Thus the new middle class becomes an analytic concept as well as an empirical phenomenon of considerable importance in explaining the politics of social change in the Middle East and North Africa. The new middle class is a formula, a liberal American prescription for the rule of its own surrogates in the area.

I have strongly dissented from this liberal and rather imperial view. This led to a serious academic controversy which the reader will no doubt identify in our polemics. I include this debate in its entirety in view of both its intensity of commitment and the

*divergent approaches Professor Halpern and myself have charted
to explain the political behavior of modern Middle Eastern elites
in Arab praetorian states. My insistence on the praetorian
explanation of Arab elite behavior (the new middle class) has
led me to both considerable revision of the liberal approach and to
another and in my view more fruitful explanation of civil-military
relations in secular and praetorian Arab politics.*

The traditional Middle Eastern elite of kings, landowners,
and bourgeoisie is declining in power or has already yielded
its place. Workers and peasants are only beginning to enter
the realm of politics. As for a middle class, the consensus of
observers is that it barely exists. "Nationalism" and "social
change" are nothing more than abstractions. Who shapes
politics and makes the fundamental decisions in the Middle
East and North Africa?

Two different answers are usually given. Individual personalities and small cliques, reply many Western policymakers.
A "new indigenous intelligentsia . . . rootless [and] possessing
no real economic base in an independent native middle
class",[1] is the explanation increasingly being accepted by
social scientists. Here we shall argue that both these views
overlook the emergence of a new social class in the Middle
East as the principal revolutionary —and potentially stabilizing—force.

In our unproductive search for middle classes in underdeveloped areas, the fault has been in our expectations. We
have taken too parochial a view of the structure of the middle
class. A study of both Western and non-Western historical
experience suggests that the British and American middle
classes, which have commonly been considered prototypes,
were actually special cases. Moreover, with the growing scope
and scale of modern enterprises and institutions, the majority
of the middle class even in the United States and Great
Britain is no longer composed of men whose independence is
rooted in their possession of productive private property.
Bureaucratic organization has become the characteristic
structure of business (or charity or trade unions) no less than

of government, and the majority of the middle class is now salaried. They may be managers, administrators, teachers, engineers, journalists, scientists, lawyers, or army officers. A similar salaried middle class constitutes the most active political, social, and economic sector from Morocco to Pakistan.

Leadership in all areas of Middle Eastern life is increasingly being seized by a class of men inspired by non-traditional knowledge, and it is being clustered around a core of salaried civilian and military politicians, organizers, administrators, and experts.[2] In its style of life, however, this new middle class differs from its counterpart in the industrialized states. The Middle East moved into the modern administrative age before it reached the machine age. Its salaried middle class attained power before it attained assurance of status, order, security, or prosperity. In the Middle East, the salaried new middle class therefore uses its power not to defend order and property but to create them—a revolutionary task that is being undertaken so far without any final commitment to any particular system of institutions.

This new salaried class is impelled by a driving interest in ideas, action, and careers. It is not merely interested in ideas: its members are not exclusively intellectuals, and, being new to the realm of modern ideas and eager for action and careers, they may not be intellectuals at all. Neither are they interested only in action that enhances their power: they also share a common commitment to the fashioning of opportunities and institutions that will provide careers open to all who have skills. This involves them in actions quite novel to their society, and hence also distinguishes them from previous politicians. They are not concerned merely with safe careers. They know that, without new ideas and new actions dealing with the backwardness and conflicts of their society, careers will not open or remain secure. The men of this new class are therefore committed ideologically to nationalism and social reform.

Obviously, there is also a part of the new middle class that has neither deep convictions nor understanding. In contrast to the dominant strata of its class, this segment excludes itself from the process of making political choices, and hence does not alter the present analysis. It is also true that some members of the new middle class are interested only in ideas (hence inspire and clarify, or merely stand by), only in action (hence rise spectacularly and fall), or only in safe careers (hence merely serve). Among the last, clerks especially compose the largest yet relatively most passive segment of the new middle class. Our analysis focuses on men interested in ideas, action, and careers because such a description fits the most influential core of this group.

There are also opportunists among them but, by now, of two different kinds which are often confused by those who are taken advantage of. There is the politician who, largely for the sake of satisfying the aspirations of his new middle class constituency and so also staying in power, takes advantage of whatever opportunities may offer, east or west, at home or abroad. There is also the free-floating opportunist—Stendhal's novels describe him very well for a period in French history when values and institutions were similarly in doubt—who represents no one but himself, but represents himself exceedingly well, being loyal only to the art of survival. Some sell their skills as political brokers; some come close to selling their country. In the twentieth century it has become essential, however, to be able to distinguish between those, however perverse they may appear, who are out to gain greater elbow-room for the new middle class they represent and those, however smooth, who also make deals because they can fashion no connections unless they continually sell themselves.

In the Middle East, this salaried new middle class assumes a far more important role than the local property-owning middle class. Although the latter is about as numerous as that portion of the new middle class which is actually employed,[3] it has far less power that the salaried group. Neither in capital, organization, nor skills do the merchants and middlemen control anything comparable to that power which can be mustered by the machinery of the state and hence utilized by the new salaried class. In this part of the world, no other institutions can mobilize as much power and capital as those of the state. By controlling the state in such a strategic historical period, this new salaried class has the capabilities to lead the quest for the status, power, and prosperity of middle-class existence by ushering in the machine age.[4]

In the West, a variety of organizational structures and devices—both governmental and private—have gradually made individual entrepreneurship a rare commodity. Stock companies, subsidies, insurance, tariffs, as well as large governmental, business, and union bureaucracies have served, among other things, to reduce individual risk and enlarge institutional predictability. The pressures that make for organization and organization men are much more desperate in the Middle East. In most of the countries of this region, there are few important jobs in the modern sector of the economy available outside the large organizations and institutions that constitute, or are guided by, government. Those who cannot get into them or cannot hold on to them usually count for little, and often cannot make a living. For most there is little hope for safety or prosperity in separate personal endeavors. Indeed, more organization is urgently needed for aggregating separate interests, bargaining among them, and executing a common will.

The intelligentsia, that is, those with knowledge or awareness to see that a social and political revolution is in progress, form the largest and politically most active component of the new middle class. But they are not the only component of this class. Some members of this new class are already middle class in their pattern of consumption but still searching for ideas (hence new in a society once sure of its truths). Others are interested only in ideas about means and not, like the intelligentsia, also about ends, and the concern for truth of the intellectuals does not interest them. The intelligentsia, however, is the predominant force of this class, in part because its knowledge inescapably exposes the weakness or irrelevance of tradition. Just as in Russia in the nineteenth century, however, the intelligentsia is more rebellious than self-confident. Its thought is "by its very nature unspecific, unformulated, unfixed . . . sensitive to every intellectual wind from Europe, alert to the changing history of both Russia and the West. For all their dogmatism at every stage, some of the most energetic minds of the intelligentsia passed from one ideological stage often to its extreme opposite in their insistent search for a total system which should somehow resolve all the largest questions of national destiny."[5]

They are new men. They are often the very first in the history of their family to be literate. They often discover their best friends at school or in a political movement, not among kin or established brotherhood or faction. They are the first to trust strangers on grounds of competence or shared ideology.[6] They are ready to trade new dogmas for old. They are also the first publicly to confess their uncertainties. Until Gamal abd al-Nasser no Egyptian politician had begun a statement of his philosophy with the confession: ". . . I feel that I stand before a boundless world, a bottomless sea—and a trepidation restrains me from plunging into it since, from my point of vantage, I see no other shore to head for."[7]

In Russia the intelligentsia was often known as the *raznochintsy*, the "men of varied ranks," on the justifiable recognition that they sprang from all classes, but also on the unwarranted conclusion that they therefore belonged to none. To make this assumption about the Middle East is to suppose that the classes from which they come, in contrast to the one in which they are now gathering, are solid and neatly distinguishable in their relationship to each other and their role in society. That is not the case, and one of the principal reasons in the Middle East as it was in Russia for the departure from their previous classes of men eager for ideas, actions, and careers is that these classes can no longer maintain their customary relationships to each other, or play their traditional role in what is becoming a modern society. It is their new role that defines their class membership, not the accident of their birth in a particular traditional social class. "The French expression '*sorti du peuple,*' like the English 'sprung from the working class' does in fact indicate both origin and breach with them."[8]

In the Middle East (as in other rapidly changing, underdeveloped societies) the new intelligentsia acts in behalf of the older ruling classes only until it is strong enough to win control of the government. When this occurs, however, the intelligentsia no longer remains socially unattached but acts in the interests of the new middle class of which it is an integral part. It cannot preserve the privileges of the older ruling classes if it hopes to propel any Middle Eastern country into the modern age. Similarly, it cannot offer the immediate rewards sought by workers and peasants, because its plans for the modernization of the country call for mobilization of the underlying population for new roles and productive sacrifices.

In the Middle East, as in Russia, the new middle class springs largely, though not exclusively, from groups that had not hitherto been important, and hence had more reason and less deadweight to take advantage of new knowledge and skills. Le Tourneau's description of North Africa could readily be applied to the rest of the Middle East. One can still find among the middle class, he points out, "a good number of members of the old leading families, the ruling aristocracy, the trading bourgeoisie, or even, but in lesser proportion, intellectuals of a traditional kind". Since the turn of the century, however, "things have changed, and young men from the hinterland now form the essential backbone of the middle class". The political parties reflect this change:

> The Democratic Union of the Algerian Manifesto has as leader a pharmacist from Setif, M. Ferhat Abbas [until recently Premier of Algeria's Provisional Government]; his principal lieutenants are doctors, lawyers, and teachers among whom almost no one is a descendant of a "grande famille" of earlier days. The same holds true for the Tunisian Neo-Destour, whose leader, M. Habib Bourguiba, is a lawyer born to a humble family of the Sahel, and for the Moroccan Istiqlal, whose governing committee is, in large part, composed of former students of the Moslem College of Fez.[9]

In Egypt, Nasser illustrates the type perfectly: the son of a postmaster, he graduated in 1938 from the first class of the Egyptian Military Academy that had admitted students from other than the upper classes. He was among the first to take advantage of a new avenue to knowledge and status. Such men are not merely strays or a stratum of spokesmen for other classes but the creators of a new class system more appropriate to the new tasks and relationships of the emerging modern age in the Middle East.

The new middle class itself does not define or crystallize its character from the very outset, but only as its various strata come to intervene in the process of modernization and assume additional roles in it. It originates in the intellectual and social transformation of Middle Eastern society, not as a homogeneous socio-economic class but as a secularized action group oriented toward governmental power. After capturing political power, it also attains hold of its own economic base. By controlling government in the Middle East, it also comes to own or control the countries' largest and most significant means of production. It becomes a salaried middle class with the power to decide its own salaries and responsibilities. The attainment of salaried status by this stratum of the middle class in turn also legitimizes the drive for the same status by the remaining would-be salaried middle class and usually gives that demand priority among political problems.

Unlike the traditional elite of landowners and trading bourgeoisie or the tradition-bound artisans or peasants, it is thus the first class in the Middle East that is wholly the product of the transition to the modern age. Unlike the emergent new generation of peasants and urban workers, it is already powerful and self-conscious enough to undertake the task of remolding society.

The new middle class has been able to act as a separate and independent force because: (1) prior to its seizure of power, it is freer than any other class from traditional bonds and preconceptions, and better equipped to manipulate armies and voluntary organizations as revolutionary political instruments; (2) once it controls the machinery of a modernizing state, it possesses a power base superior to that which any other class in the Middle East can muster on the basis of prestige, property, or physical force; (3) it is numerically one of the largest groups within the modern sector of society; (4) it is, so far, more obviously cohesive, more self-conscious, and better trained than any other class; (5) its political, economic, and social actions, in so far as they come to grips with social change, are decisive in determining the role other classes will play in the future; and (6) it has shown itself capable of marshalling mass support. Wherever the salaried new middle class has become dominant in the Middle East, it has become the chief locus of political and economic power and of social prestige. There are few classes anywhere in the world of which this much can be said.[10]

Thus there can rise to power a Nasser as "Saladin in a Grey Flannel Suit,"[11] greeted as hero or devil, but conceivable in these dimensions largely because he symbolizes and represents a whole class—a class which is the principal actor of the age. Those who disagree with his policies or methods may continue to think of him as devil, but they at least must recognize that this kind of devil cannot be exorcised. As the representative of a particular policy, Nasser can be foiled. As the representative of a class, and this class is the product of the Middle East's movement into the modern age, his kind cannot be made to disappear by military intervention. To acknowledge the growing presence of such a class is also to deny the long-held Western myth that the passing of the remaining older ruling elites in such countries as Iran or Jordan would leave an internal social and political vacuum.

Conflicts within the New Middle Class

To seek to create a modern prosperous economy, a modern society, and a modern nation is a noble objective. However, the task itself involves painful decisions about who shall receive rewards, or shall no longer receive them, and who shall change position, and when and how. There are obviously different ways of eliciting sacrifices, sharing sacrifices, and establishing goals for which such sacrifices are to be made. There are, correspondingly, different ways of minimizing the antagonism of conflicting interests and values as the new middle class translates its objectives into the mission of the entire nation. It is also possible for nationalists representing the new middle class to hold different conceptions of the national interest in relation to foreign nations. What, then, determines these choices on the part of the new middle class?

The factors that readily come to mind—the burden of the past, available skills and resources and the awareness and opportunities to utilize them, differences in individual character and temperament, the force of ideas and the exigencies of particular local power constellations—are all relevant and important.[12] An elite in power, whatever the social class from which it springs, faces problems and temptations in the very business of maintaining itself in power which will often distinguish it from those who have the same hopes and interests but not the same responsibilities. Membership in a particular social class is by no means the sole determinant of policy decisions. Differences in political choices among members of the new middle class, however, also reflect differences among the strata of that class and the variant character of its class consciousness.

Such differences are real enough, but they usually become politically important only after the new middle class has achieved power. Earlier, all its members normally concentrate on the battle for power, mobility, and status in order to open up the controlling positions in society and administration. Soon after the triumph of the new middle class, however, it becomes apparent that there is simply not room for all of them—that some will be "in" and most will be "out." It also becomes clear that, although they are agreed on the need for the transformation of their society, they are not of the same mind as to what to do with their historical opportunity.[13]

Such differences, however, are never merely political, or merely social, or merely economic. All three realms are entwined—as, for example, in one of the most profound of all tensions within the new middle class—between those who are salaried and those who would be like them but are not. Only a minority of the Middle East's new middle class actually holds jobs and draws salaries. The rest either can find no jobs consonant with their skills and values, or else work for status quo regimes which deny this group status and power. It would be quite misleading to exclude the "would-be" new middle class from this middle class. Both components of the middle class possess modern rather than traditional knowledge, and both are eager for a forced march into the modern age. Both are striving for the status, power, order, and prosperity that ought to go with middle-class existence. They resemble each other in every respect except success. This would-be middle class will therefore enlist itself in any movement that promises the kind of education that creates modern skills, the kind of job that opens a career, and the kind of action that gives a mere career individual rewards and social importance.

The inclusion of this group among the new middle class may be unexpected to those who restrict themselves to the classical economic definition of classes. In areas like the Middle East, however, where a modern economy is still to be created, and where control over the state and the forces of social change is more potent than ownership of property, property relations alone cannot serve to define class relations. In the midst of a profound transformation of society, it would also be quite wrong to define a social class statically, in terms of occupation, or employment at a particular moment in time. Each class must be defined in terms of its political, social, and economic role in the process of social change. In the present instance, that means taking account of all who either already perform the role of a member of the salaried middle class or who are bent by revolutionary action, if necessary, to gain a chance to perform this role and no other.

How searing the difference can be between the new salaried class and the would-be middle class, whose basic orientation must be defined by middle class deprivations instead of middle class achievements, is illustrated by the situation in Iran. The Iranian example also demonstrates on how many levels that difference can recur, and how quickly the pressure of frustration can mount in the Middle East. In the 1920's and 1930's there were jobs in Iran for all who were educated, and there was only one cause of frustration. Status was still largely the fruit of traditional rank rather than individual accomplishment. "Those who had been educated abroad [and] had good family background and professed unquestionable loyalty to the political system . . . were given top administrative posts. . . . The graduates of the University of Tehran and other colleges (plus some high school graduates during the 1930's) were assigned less important government positions and formed the majority of the lower echelon of the civil service. They tended to come from families where the fathers had been merchants, guildsmen, and clergymen."[14]

Within a decade, the causes of discontent had multiplied enormously. Those members of the new middle class who had ideas and careers found their opportunities for status and action circumscribed. By the early 1940's, the "surplus of government employees was glaringly evident at all levels, [hence] the prestige of civil service jobs also dropped. . . . The duties proved to be routine and the job gave . . . no responsibility or sense of social participation." Inflation, the result both of planned and unplanned scarcities in the economy, took its toll. "The civil servant was no longer able to maintain his accustomed standard of living, and since then it has become necessary for him to take on a second job, equally uninspiring." He had also become socially isolated, "that is, he feels alienated from his family and he also senses the abyss that lies between him and the under-privileged, illiterate masses." He had also become more conscious of "the divergency of [his] interests with the upper-class elite whose mode of life is even more Western than [his]."[15]

But that is not all. Just at a time when the status of those members of the new middle class having careers is becoming increasingly insecure, they are also being exposed to the growing challenge of a would-be middle class demanding careers, status, and power. Approximately 18,000 students graduated from Iranian colleges between 1851 and 1958. A smaller number studied abroad. Yet in 1958 alone, 9,321 students were enrolled in the University of Tehran and more than 10,000 additional Iranians were studying in universities abroad.[16] There are few jobs open for them in the government, and even fewer in private business.

Yet a still larger number are waiting—waiting to get into schools in which there are no vacancies in order to wait for a job that does not exist. "Because the University of Tehran and the universities in the provinces can accept only a third of those who apply, competition is very keen, and family influence often plays a part in acceptance." But the number of those who actually apply is only a partial measure of frustration. "Looking at it one way, the present 20,000 (approximately) Iranian college students constitute only ten per cent of secondary school enrollment, and two per cent of the graduates of elementary schools." However, if we compare the number of college students with the potential college age group in the total population (some 1,760,000), or merely in the major urban areas (some 440,000), then the number of students who actually reach college is far below one per cent.[17] "There is sufficient evidence to indicate that this large college age group . . . constitutes for a non-technical society like Iran an unrestful group and a potential source of change."[18]

In Egypt there has occurred the same closing of opportunities during the past decade. In 1947, about a third of all Egyptians with primary education or above held government jobs. The entire educational system was designed largely to prepare students for the civil service and, until recently, salary and promotions depended on the type of school certificate, rather than on the nature of the work or the skill of performance. In 1953, about forty-one per cent "or forty-six per cent, depending on how closely one calculated," of total expenditures went for government salaries and wages.[19] Meanwhile, although a third of all Egyptian children of school age had no opportunity even for primary education, there were almost twice as many university students in proportion to the population as in industrialized Great Britain, and all would be clamoring for appropriate jobs. In Iraq between 1950 and 1955, about 10,000 Iraqis graduated from the Colleges of Law, Commerce, Arts, and Sciences, but only 1,250 of them found jobs in government and business.[20]

Partially overlapping the distinction between the working and jobless sections of the new middle class is the difference between the younger and older members of this class. "Youth" is not a passing phase in this region where half of all the people are under 20 years old, and where population grows so quickly and opportunities so slowly. In this situation men in their forties may still have almost all the naïveté of youth—being untouched by careers, status, and power—yet have none of youth's innocence, for they know what they have missed.

The plight of youth is obvious when the elite is recruited only from traditional classes. This plight is not resolved when the new middle class comes into its own. Initially, it grows worse. Those who have arrived often come to the top in their thirties (Ataturk, Nasser) or their forties (Kassim, Ayub). What they do can have more far-reaching results in the lives of their people than the actions of any preceding government.

Yet almost all of them become authoritarians who do not intend to relinquish the reins of power until they die. Nor do members of the leading echelon of administrators and directors in government, business, journalism, schools, etc. mean to depart before the particular head of state to whom they owe their position. The older group of nationalists often learned patience and perseverance in the long struggle for power when a foreign state could always be made to bear the blame for the postponement of success. The younger men now find no target for their frustration except their own ruling elite.

When youth wins out early and retires late, all the young men who mature for action thereafter are unlikely to be able to acquire a stake in the status quo and hence in moderation. When the age group that made the revolution lingers, yet does not increase the range of employment for those with talent, energy, and ideas, then the young are likely to remain radical (i.e., insist on going to the roots of the problem) or else extremist (i.e., using violence to substitute a dogmatic answer of their own). The characteristic extremism or radicalism of contemporary Middle Eastern student groups must therefore be taken more seriously than it might be in countries where one might smile comfortably at Clemenceau's jest that men who are not socialists at twenty have no heart, and men who remain socialists at forty have no head.

The sharp and often bitter competition among members of the new middle class, however, does not inhibit the acquisition of a common historical awareness that each of them suffers from the same burden of the past and the same frustrations of the present. In the very fact of their separate individuality lies the essence of their common fate.[21] Coming into being by influx from all social classes—uniting the Western-educated son of a landlord with the army-trained son of a postmaster—the new middle class is the first in Middle Eastern history for whom family connections can no longer help automatically to establish class membership. Also, being itself composed of new men, it is the first which cannot hope to rest on inherited status or existing opportunities. It is the first class for whom communication depends on successful persuasion of other individuals; it cannot base itself on the implicit consensus of the past. The new middle class is distinguishable from all other classes in the Middle East by being the first to be composed of separate individuals. It is therefore also the first class for which the choice between democracy, authoritarianism, and totalitarianism is a real and open choice.

The Relationship of the New Middle Class to Other Classes

The fact that the goals of the new middle class demand the mobilization of the entire society in no way implies that the role it assigns to others in its national design will correspond to the interests felt by other classes. Even the communists, whose ideology declares their dictatorship to be in the interests of the proletariat, cannot escape this clash of class interests. "It took some time until the lesson had . . . been learned; communism must cease to be 'proletarian.' . . . 'Revolution' no longer signifies 'liberation of the toilers' but 'all power to the planners.' "[22] No other rulers, at least in underdeveloped areas, can escape this conflict. If most Middle Eastern peasants and workers want more worldly goods, they want them for the sake of living well here and now; for the sake of gaining the prestige of offering larger dowries, of having more leisure. The contrast between postponing rewards and reaping them now is great enough, especially in a part of the world where scarcity and uncertainty have always loomed so threateningly, to create valid and deeply felt distinctions between political parties; indeed, between styles of life. Hence there is no reason to assume that the contradiction—even between those who demand immediate satisfactions for workers and peasants and those who claim to represent their "true" interests in the long run—can be "non-antagonistic."[23]

Such contradictions need not, however, become overtly antagonistic. This is not because nationalist ideologists deny that such conflicts are genuine, but because the sense of class interests is still blurred. The new middle class has only recently been emerging as a class, and tribal and family loyalties remain predominant among many of the peasants and workers. Although the disciplined organization of a majority of urban workers into trade unions in Morocco and

Tunisia within a decade or less demonstrates how quickly the Middle East is changing, the mobilization of peasantry and workers by the new middle class has scarcely begun in most countries of this region. Charismatic and nationalist identification between leaders and followers frequently creates much overlapping enthusiasm even when there are few overlapping interests. And peasants and workers are often content to yield much for concrete rewards, regardless of the political system that grants them—especially greater justice from the courts, more honesty from the administrators, more wells, more schools, more food. The Middle East is only beginning to enter the age of choice, and hence of experiencing the price of making friends and enemies among one's own people. Middle Eastern political and social stability, therefore, has scarcely yet been tested.

The new middle class is not the first class that has sought to take the leading role in modernizing the Middle East. There were individual rulers in the nineteenth century who recognized that the survival of their power, the prestige of their dynasty, and the security of their domain depended on the modernization at least of their army, bureaucracy, and trade. Mohammed Ali (in power 1805-1848) in Cairo, and Sultan Mahmud II (in power 1808-1839) in Constantinople were among the earliest such rulers. Later, when Middle Eastern empires were succeeded by independent states, the bourgeoisie and large landowners assumed this task, but once again limited their performance largely to what was required to enhance their own status and power. Hence trade and bureaucracy remained the principal foci of modernization. To reflect the participation of a somewhat broader group in politics, party cliques and quasi-parliamentary structures were developed. Since European influence in the Middle East was usually strong enough during this period to curb the army's growth, it was modernized only sufficiently to make it an adequate repressive force. There was little or no response to pressures for modernization from below, and no general commitment to deal with social change.

This older bourgeoisie was in its structure, interests, and relationships, and hence in its political role, quite different from the emergent new middle class. The former maintained itself in urban enclaves within a "feudal" society.[24] It never attained the strength to unite city and countryside into a single economic unit, or the courage to reshape that larger society which was, nonetheless, beginning to crumble around it.

Many of the small businessmen—the principal pillars of the propertied middle class—have tended here as elsewhere "to develop a generalized hostility toward a complex of symbols and processes bound up with industrial capitalism, the steady growth and concentration of government, labor organizations, and business enterprises, and the correlative trend toward greater rationalization of production and distribution."[25] Their interests therefore differ from those of a salaried new middle class accustomed to life in an organization, and their range of interests and their links with the new class are too limited in the Middle East to give them a leading role in shaping the direction of a society in upheaval.

In part, of course, even the salaried middle class is aware of itself only as an interest group with pragmatic, specific, and relatively short-run demands. It may concentrate on conspicuous consumption—acquiring Cadillacs, building steel mills regardless of their relative economic utility, or improving armies that are already strong enough to maintain internal security and protect the frontiers against all but the large industrialized powers. To allocate savings and scarce foreign exchange to the satisfaction of the immediate desires of the new middle class in this manner is no different from allowing them to be used by peasants for larger dowries—the conflict is then between interest groups, not between different orientations toward social change. The interest of one group is satisfied at the direct expense of another's.

It is quite apparent, however, that the pace and pain of social change had become too great by the second half of this century for the new middle class to avoid acquiring a larger historical consciousness of its role.[26] The new middle class has become the bearer of civic spirit on a national scale in the Midde East because it cannot translate its ideas into action or achieve careers or status unless it creates a nation of individuals linked by consciousness and material fact—a nation that economically, socially, and politically can survive social change. For almost every individual in the Middle East is now in motion, even those who are still standing still. Things are not the same for those who toil and die in traditional fashion if their neighbors now have modern implements to plant modern cash crops and can keep themselves healthy with modern medicines. When people come to be called traditionalists by their neighbors, the old spell has been broken.

The new middle class not only possesses the kind of empathy that allows its members to see themselves "in the other fellow's situation."[27] Even in traditional Islam, it was not infrequent for an artisan to become the leader of a religio-political rebellion, or for a soldier or tribal chief to become Sultan. Some could envisage playing such roles; others could not. What characterizes the new middle class in the Middle East is that it is the first that has the capacity to envisage new types of roles to be played in a new kind of world.

In the midst of a profound social transformation which it helps to shape and sharpen, this new middle class will, of course, not remain a stable or static element. In part it will give birth to new strata from within itself; in part it will be midwife to other classes kindred to it—namely those which are usually termed upper and lower middle classes. Indeed, these are already beginning to appear in their modern version.

Given the predominant role of the new middle class in the government, and hence in the social and economic development of the country, the modern upper middle class is very likely to develop to a considerable extent from among the ranks of the former. Even the members of modern professions, almost exclusively sons of landlords and the traditional bourgeoisie earlier in this century, are being increasingly drawn from the same broader ranks as the salaried middle class. If such social and economic development grows apace, the modern upper middle class of politicians, professional men, and administrators may well come to dominate society and give it a moderate orientation.

This upper middle class which starts, as it were, from scratch, may be joined by private entrepreneurs taking advantage of the new political stability and the economic foundations built by the government. It seems, however, rather rare for members of traditional bourgeois families to take advantage of their capital and connections to acquire new skills relevant to an industrial economy.[28] To have become rich in traditional fashion often shrouds incentives to the learning of modern skills. As for selfmade modern capitalists in the Middle East, much will depend on the ideology of the salaried middle class. In Egypt, even the most efficient large private enterprises have been nationalized for the sake of centralizing control over investments and distribution of benefits. In Syria, capitalists threatened by the same policies during 1961 allied themselves with opposition movements drawn from the would-be middle class and succeeded in installing a tenuous new regime pledged to a mixed economy.

Members of the traditional elite who are not landlords or traders have sometimes gained access more readily to the modern upper middle class. Sons of the traditional bourgeoisie in a number of Middle Eastern countries have transformed themselves into one of the most influential elements of the modern upper middle class by virtue of their training as officers in the army. Trained in modern technology and administration, and assigned a national mission, this group had the opportunity and incentive for a successful transition. Similar to them in origin and second to them only in power are many of the Western-trained members of the upper levels of the bureaucracy. And there are, it must be added, a number of kings who seem anxious to make the same transition—among them those of Afghanistan, Iran, Jordan, and Morocco. But be they general, bureaucrat, or king, they are likely to fail politically unless they can relate themselves to the aspirations of the new middle class. For they themselves number in no country of this region more than a few hundred. Even if some of them have independent incomes, nevertheless all are dependent upon civil and military bureaucracies without whose loyalty or cohesion they can no longer function at all.

The modern lower middle class is, in the Middle East, composed of two distinct groups. There are those whose "western education is limited, and more probably has been cut off at an early stage. Self-education seems to be a recurrent feature among them."[29] But there are also those in the lower middle class who, instead of being able to capitalize on a modicum of modern knowledge, suffer from a peculiarly modern disability. They are well trained, but in classic subjects (e.g., *Shari'a* law) or in the wrong language (e.g., Urdu, when English is essential to government and business). In any but the modern age, they would have been able to rise to a status equivalent at least to that of the modern middle class. Now they can only hope to eke out a lower middle class existence. In short, both components of the modern lower middle class in the Middle East consist of men who are frustrated in their social mobility. They are not like the traditional lower middle class, composed predominantly of small artisans and shopkeepers and minor clerks, most of whom implicitly accept their station in life.[30] They are not, like the middle and upper strata of the new middle class, capable of translating their ambition into reality. Hence, organizing their discontent is likely to offer a major potential for political action.

Prospects for the New Middle Class

Thus the character and terms of the struggle for power in the Middle East become clearer. The changes now under way in the social and political system appear to have three successive, though often overlapping, phases: first, the battle between the new middle class and the traditional ruling class; second, the drive by the successful new middle class to supply cadre for all five groups that compose the elite in modern society (political leaders, government administrators, economic directors, leaders of masses, and military chiefs);[31] and third, the struggles among strata within the new middle class for predominance, increasingly involving other new classes, especially uprooted peasants and workers.

In terms of these phases, it is apparent that the most important political struggle in the Middle East is no longer between the new middle class and the traditional ruling class. The new middle class has already come to power in almost all but the least developed and regionally least influential countries.[32] At this extraordinary moment when the traditional ruling class has been defeated and the peasants and workers have not yet organized themselves to make their own demands, politics has become a game played almost entirely within the new middle class. Thus, it is a political era resembling none that preceded it and probably none that will follow it, and one that is likely to prove particularly volatile and productive.

It will be volatile, in part, because politics within the new middle class will involve competition for a very limited number of powerful positions by persons who, even on behalf of issues, must often substitute the force of personality (itself still evolving) for the strength of established political parties. Compromises will be hard to arrange. Because the majority of the people are unrepresented, one of the most persuasive arguments for compromise among executive policy-makers in other countries—the anticipated reaction of a free legislature —will continue to be irrelevant. Disagreements among policy-makers in authoritarian regimes will usually mean ouster for one or the other.

Although repression of one faction of the new middle class by another faction is common, membership in the same class seems to make a difference. Rival movements are outlawed, but individual members—men with whom, after all, one went to school, worked in common clandestinity, and with whose ideas one may once have toyed oneself—are often allowed to write editorials or remain in the bureaucracy. And the more important opposition leaders are, with startling frequency, appointed to Embassies abroad, being jailed only if they insist on returning. The centuries of repression which the new middle class fought to end more clearly and courageously than anyone else are, at present, in disrepute. For the first time since the Middle Ages, and in contrast to recent status quo oligarchies such as the late Nuri al-Sa'id Pasha's in Iraq, the elite and the main opposition, both drawn from the new middle class, speak a mutually comprehensible language derived from a common experience. Thus a genuine political dialogue is at last in progress in the Middle East.

The vital question now—vital because the outcome affects

all aspects of society—is which segment of the new middle class shall predominate, what ideological orientation it will prefer, and what factors help or hinder the progress of competing factions.

The thrust toward revolutionary action on the part of the new middle class is overwhelming. It is itself the product of an unfinished and uncontrolled revolutionary transformation of society. It intends therefore to organize social change rather than become its victim. Even those who do not possess this broader vision, but who nevertheless would like to live in the same style as the average man in the more conservative industrialized nations, will have to upset the status quo much further before they can hope to enjoy the benefits of a stable new status quo. Unlike the great majority of the Western salaried middle class, this new class cannot afford to perpetuate the traditional norms and laws of society, even though it is already being threatened by the confusion of standards and the growth of extremism in its own ranks. The largest component of the new middle class in most countries, and the most rapidly growing, will be the young with few links to tradition or to the previous generation, with inadequate knowledge and skills, and with little chance of status or of any useful job. Both the burden of the past and the threat of the future impel the salaried middle class to become the principal revolutionary force, creating new standards and institutions relevant to a modernizing society.

There is no inescapable doom that revolutionary change must come through violence, however. One of the most remarkable, and remarkably neglected, phenomena of modern history is the near absence of violence that has marked rapid, structural changes in all those countries where, since 1950, the new middle class has come to power. In Egypt, for example, a landed ruling class was economically dispossessed, socially displaced, and politically overthrown. A new social class took its place, the greater part of the economy was nationalized or at least placed under effective state control, the legal basis of authority and the structure and functions of political institutions were fundamentally altered, and a religion-bound culture was secularized, all at the cost of less than twenty lives.[33] This is a remarkable performance in contrast to the French Revolution of the eighteenth century, or the Chinese and Russian Revolutions of our time.

The absence of violence alone, however, is not sufficient evidence of stability, or a clear sign that the fundamental revolution of Middle Eastern society has come to an end. The new middle class will be able to signal its conversion from a revolutionary into a stabilizing force only when it has succeeded in limiting the realm of politics to the domain of public authority, thus allowing the social, economic, and private business of men once again to become autonomous realms. That cannot happen until there is sufficient capacity and consensus for dealing with social change, and until political leaders need no longer convert all aspects of existence into issues of power.

In most countries of this region it is improbable, certainly within the next decade, that the new middle class will have succeeded in establishing firm economic, political, and psychological foundations for the growth of individuals and groups that can be autonomous in action yet share in a broad consensus of values. Instead, most of the governments will still be struggling to establish their own authority, and assure physical survival for their citizens. The status and prosperity that ought to accompany middle class existence is likely still to elude most of its members, and even the term "middle class" will retain ironic overtones. They will still be caught in the middle of time, between an age not yet quite dead and one not yet quite born. They will still be suspended between a traditional folk that is being uprooted but not yet sure what leadership to follow over the longer run, and a political elite, drawn at last from their own class but unable as yet to satisfy their aspirations. The new middle class will not be able to escape soon from the harsh struggle for the sheer biological and psychological necessities of life. Hence it will not soon escape from an age of revolution into an age in which both freedom and authority are assured.

The salaried new middle class possesses one advantage over all previous ruling groups. The tasks it must perform in order to create status, power, and prosperity for itself no less than the nation require the establishment of modern, integrating institutions which can mobilize the spirit and resources of the entire nâtion. At the same time these institutions, by their very nature, are also peculiarly adapted to control by the new middle class.

While it is almost inevitable in the present historical situation that the new middle class will acquire power, there is nothing inevitable about its orientation or its permanent success. Under the inspiration of particular personalities, ideologies, or environmental changes, this new ruling group may fractionalize more often than act in unison. Overwhelmed by pressure of sheer population, inadequate organizational skill, or lack of courage, it may not be able to cement a working relationship with the majority of the population—the peasants and workers. Yet unlike any of its predecessors, the new middle class has goals which depend for their success on popular support and participation, whether achieved by consent, authority, or terror.

Thus, the new middle class is faced with most extraordinary opportunities. If it fails to consolidate its authority by achieving sufficient internal cohesion and general social progress, and its factions are instead engaged in ruthless competition for the support of the rural and urban masses, the approaching future is bound to be one of fearful unrest.

NOTES

1. Morris Watnick, "The Appeal of Communism to the Peoples of Underdeveloped Areas," in *The Progress of Underdeveloped Areas,* edited by Bert F. Hoselitz, Chicago, 1952, pp. 158-159.
2. For example, when Tunisia became independent in 1956 under the leadership of the Neo-Destour Party, a party controlled almost entirely by the new middle class, the election for a Constituent Assembly rewarded this class in the following way: To fill 98 seats, the country voted for 18 teachers and professors, 15 lawyers, 11 civil servants, 5 doctors, 4 pharmacists, 2 journalists, 2 commercial employees, 1 engineer, 1 appraiser, 5 workers, 17 farmers, and 17 businessmen and contractors. By contrast, every Middle Eastern parliament prior to 1950, except that of Turkey, contained a majority of landowners and a minority of professional men and industrialists.
3. In this analysis, the term "new middle class" excludes the property owning middle class. However, it includes both those who are now drawing salaries and a far larger group—a "would-be new middle class" which resembles this class in every respect except that it is

unemployed. The "would-be" salariat is discussed in greater detail in the next section of this chapter.

From a different perspective, Professor Morroe Berger defines the middle class as including (1) "merchants and small manufacturers, self-employed, whose income and influence are not great enough to place them among the really powerful men in political or economic life" and (2) "independent professionals such as doctors and lawyers; employed managers, technicians, and administrative workers such as clerks and bureau chiefs; and the civil service." He concluded that, in 1947, these amounted altogether to about half a million persons in Egypt, 51 per cent of them merchants; that is, mostly small retailers. ("The Middle Class in the Arab World", in *The Middle East in Transition*, edited by Walter Laqueur, New York, 1958, p. 63.) Thus defined, the salaried middle class and the property-owning middle class together amount to about six per cent of the gainfully employed population or about three per cent of the total population in Egypt. If one also includes the agricultural middle class, as does Professor Hassan el-Saaty ("The Middle Class in Egypt", *L'Egypte Contemporaine*, April 1957, pp. 47-53), the total figure for Egypt in 1947 increases to sixteen per cent. The middle class is probably as large, or else smaller, in other Middle Eastern countries. By contrast, a new middle class composed of the salariat—whether employed or unemployed—must be estimated to number (no one has yet counted them) a far higher percentage. Aspiration is politically as relevant a criterion for such a census as education and position.

4. The present work is not the first to notice the emergence of this new class in underdeveloped areas. Professor T. Cuyler Young, drawing in part on his experiences as Political Attaché at the American Embassy in Tehran during 1951-1952, was the first to publish an analysis of the role of the new middle class in the Middle East in "The Social Support of Current Iranian Policy", *Middle East Journal*, Spring 1952, pp. 125-143. Professor John J. Johnson was the first to suggest that in Latin America "the urban middle groups are vitally, if not decisively, important in an area where one still commonly hears and reads that there is no middle class to speak of [and] where, in the view of traditional scholarship, individuals hold the center of the stage." *(Political Change in Latin America: The Emergence of the Middle Sectors*, Stanford, 958, pp. vii-ix.)

Between these two and the present essay, there are common intellectual links. In his preface, Johnson states that he "first became fully aware of the importance of the urban middle sectors in Latin American politics during the fifteen months in 1952-53 that [he] was with the State Department as Acting Chief of the South American Branch of the Division of Research for American Republics." At that time, a number of us in the Division of Research for Near East, South Asia, and Africa had contributed to an analysis in January 1952 of the causes of *Political Instability in the Middle East* which was to become a prototype for a series of such studies of other underdeveloped regions.

An evaluation of the role of the "urban middle sector" was one of the principal themes of that study.

If at least one of the collaborators of that 1952 study has changed his mind, and substituted "middle class" for "middle sector", it is because the latter term is finally too broad: Johnson includes within it the "poorly paid white-collar employee in government" as well as the "wealthy proprietors of commercial and industrial enterprises". Class is a term with peculiar advantages. The anthropological term "acculturated" includes those who have forsaken pottery for aluminum no less than those who have left Islam for communism. The parochially historical term "Westernized" defines only one portion of those who now make modern political choices. The sociological terms "traditional", "transitional", and "modern" designate way-stations in social communication and psychic mobility insufficiently related to conflicts over political ideology and power. The political term "elite" is often used to designate any dominating power group without concern for the social classes from which it may be drawn. Once the term "class" is freed from its ideological strait jackets and defined dynamically in terms of the evolving interests, opportunities, and behaviour of a class in the midst of the transformation of a *society*, and not merely of its *economy*, "class" may well continue to serve us as the most useful category for relating changes in social structure to changes in political power.

5. Herbert E. Bowman, "Intelligentsia in Nineteenth Century Russia", *The Slavic and East European Journal,* Spring 1957, p. 15.

6. Some of the men appointed to the cabinet by the Iraqi army conspirators of 1958 had until their appointment neither heard of the revolution nor met their new chiefs.

7. Gamal abd al-Nasser, *Egypt's Liberation: The Philosophy of the Revolution,* Washington, 1955, p. 17.

8. Maurice Duverger, *Political Parties: Their Organization and Activity in the Modern State,* London, 1954, p. 159.

9. Roger LeTourneau, "Le Développement d'une Classe Moyenne en Afrique du Nord," in *Development of a Middle Class in Tropical and Sub-Tropical Countries, Record of the XXIX Session Held in London from 13-16 September 1955,* Brussels, International Institute of Differing Civilizations, 1956, pp. 106-110. The group that split off from the Moroccan Istiqlal party under Mehdi Ben Barka's leadership in 1959, the National Union of Popular Forces, is even more clearly the product of a class shaped by modern secular education and the values of the new middle class.

10. Hence we cannot accept the Marxist idea that the intelligentsia, since it does not start from an economic base of its own, is unable to act in its own interest but must ally itself with one class or another. In areas like the Middle East, Soviet analysts have talked about a "national bourgeoisie", composed of local industrialists, merchants, and bankers, a "lower middle class" which employs little or no outside labor, an "intelligentsia" of students and clerks, even a "military intelligentsia."

(See Walter Z. Laqueur, "The 'National Bourgeoisie', a Soviet Dilemma in the Middle East", *International Affairs,* July 1959, pp. 324-441.) They have failed to perceive, however, the central role of the class which contains such men as Ataturk, Nasser, Kassim, and Bourguiba and which not only leads the nationalist revolution, but is the harbinger and architect of a decisive change in the social structure of the Middle East.

There are fundamental reasons for this failure of recognition. Perceptively, the Marxist philosopher Georg Lukaçs has noted: "In such periods of transition, society is not dominated by any system of production. . . . In these circumstances it is, of course, impossible to speak of the operation of any economic laws which would govern the entire society. . . . There is a condition of acute struggle for power or of a latent balance of power. . . . : the old law is no longer valid and the new law is not yet generally valid." He adds, "As far as I know, the theory of historical materialism had not yet confronted this problem from an economic perspective." *(Geschichte und Klassenbewusstsein,* Berlin, 1923, pp. 243 and 249.) As far as the present author is aware, this vacuum remains.

11. C.L. Sulzberger's phrase in *The New York Times,* March 26, 1958.

12. Not that we know by any means enough about how these factors operate. It would be most instructive to make a number of case studies, to examine, for example, the dynamics involved in the change by different age-groups in the control over large parts of the same political movement (e.g., from al-Fassi to ben Barka in Morocco's Istiqlal party); the change of outlook within the same family (e.g., the change from Abbas, father, recipient of the French Legion of Honor to Abbas, son, recent Premier of the Provisional Algerian Government in Exile); and the change within a single spirit (e.g., Edward Atiyah, *An Arab Tells His Story: A Study in Loyalties,* London, 1946) and contrast these with the fate of a party which remains under the control of a single age-group for several decades (e.g., the Wafd in Egypt), of a family which maintains its role as a mediator above political factions for several generations (e.g., the Shehabs of Lebanon), and of a man who never changed his mind (e.g., Nuri of Iraq).

13. At such a point, the intelligentsia may well split again and speak for different competing factions within the new middle class—another reason why it is not possible to use "intelligentsia" and "new middle class" interchangeably.

14. Reza Arasteh, "Education for Bureaucracy and Civil Service in Iran," an unpublished manuscript presented to the Faculty Seminar of the Program in Near Eastern Studies, Princeton University, May 1959, pp. 38-40. Arasteh has now enlarged upon this subject in *Education and Social Awakening in Iran, 1850-1960,* Leiden, 1962.

15. Arasteh, "Education for Bureaucracy and Civil Service in Iran," pp. 39-43.

16. By contrast, only 16,229 students were enrolled at various levels of the Koranic schools, once the only educational institutions. (Ernst A.

Messerschmidt, *Iran,* Cologne, 1953, p. 48.) The figures for the religious schools apply for 1952/53.

17. In the United States, 22 per cent of this age group goes to college.

18. Arasteh, "Education for Bureaucracy and Civil Service in Iran," pp. 17-28, *passim.*

19. Morroe Berger, "Civil Service and Society," an unpublished paper prepared for a Panel on Comparative Public Administration, Fiftieth Annual Meeting of the American Political Science Association, Chicago, September 1954.

20. *Al-Hawadith* (a Baghdad daily), September 17, 1955.

21. Some may concentrate on preserving their status, some on enlarging it, others on attaining it. Such competition, however, does not touch their class membership. Separate individuals, to amend only slightly a formulation by Karl Marx (*The German Ideology,* New York, 1938, p. 49), form a class only in so far as they play a common role in relation to social change, and have to carry on a common battle against another class or seek collaboration with it. Otherwise, they may be on hostile terms with each other as competitors.

22. G.L. Arnold, "Collectivism Reconsidered", *British Journal of Sociology,* March 1955, p. 12. The issue of antagonism between the planners and the workers had actually been raised decades before the Russian Revolution. As early as 1899, a Polish revolutionist named Waclaw Machajski had raised this point in *The Evolution of Social Democracy,* and in 1904, in *The Intellectual Worker,* he restated his thesis that the theory of socialism had not been worked on in the interests of the proletariat but of a new force, "the growing army of intellectual workers and the new middle class." Their revolution would produce a state capitalism in which the technicians, organizers, administrators, educators, and journalists would constitute the "great joint stock company known as the State, and become, collectively, a new privileged stratum over the manual workers." (Daniel Bell, "One Road from Marx: On the Vision of Socialism, and the Fate of Workers' Control, in Socialist Thought," *World Politics,* July 1959, pp. 491-512.)

23. Cf. editorial in *Peiping People's Daily* on "non-antagonistic contradictions," reprinted in *Pravda,* April 15, 1957.

24. This distinction between the role of the bourgeoisie and the middle class is also employed by G.D.H. Cole, "The Conception of the Middle Classes," *The British Journal of Sociology,* December 1950, pp. 275-290.

25. Martin Trow, "Small Businessmen, Political Tolerance, and McCarthy," *American Journal of Sociology,* November 1958, p. 274.

26. In Lebanon, however, there appears to be a peculiar obstacle to such a change: various religious and ethnic groups have become political interest groups, each entitled to a proportionate share of jobs in parliament, bureaucracy, and education.

27. The key concept defining transitional and modern man in Daniel Lerner's *The Passing of Traditional Society: Modernizing the Middle East,* Glencoe, 1958, pp. 49-54, 69-75.

28. See Bert F. Hoselitz, "Entrepreneurship and Economic Growth," *American Journal of Economics and Sociology,* October 1952.

29. Leonard Binder's description of the Pakistani lower middle class is probably applicable to the rest of this region [drawn from an unpublished manuscript delivered at the Dobbs Ferry Conference of the Social Science Research Council, 1957]·

30. In Turkey, where the modern age began earlier than in most of the Middle East, the mid-nineteenth century saw the appearance of the Young Ottomans, many of them minor bureaucrats, whose level of expectations had risen since they had become the Empire's new experts in communication and administration. Yet they lacked the lubricants of money and family status to advance themselves. At that point in history they allied themselves almost entirely with the ulema who were beginning to lose prestige with the growth of secularization. (See Şerif Mardin, *The Genesis of Young Ottoman Thought, A Study in the Modernization of Turkish Political Ideas,* Princeton, 1962.) In twentieth century Egypt, such men often allied themselves with the Moslem Brotherhood.

31. These five categories are drawn from Raymond Aron, "Social Structure and the Ruling Class," *The British Journal of Sociology,* March and June 1950, p. 9. Aron points out that "the fundamental difference between a society of the Soviet type and one of the Western type is that the former has a unified elite and the latter a divided elite" (p. 10). From that perspective, the Middle Eastern situation fits somewhere in between, since the elite is drawn from a single, small, and embattled class which strives for the unification of the elite but seldom succeeds for long in preventing clashes. The pressure for a unified elite in the Middle East, moreover, is based on historical exigencies (the availability of a large number of members of the new middle class for a small number of careers in the new institutions of society) and political expediency (the need for loyal supporters in an environment in which the majority does not yet share the outlook of the new middle class). Conformity to an ideological dogma which justifies the unification of the elite (for example under the guise of the "dictatorship of the proletariat") characterizes only the communists in the Middle East.

32. The displacement of the landowners and traditional bourgeoisie as the political elite does not necessarily imply their demise as a social class. Where such a demise of what was always a small group is in fact in progress, as in Tunisia, and where a strong egalitarian strain makes it difficult for any member of the new middle class to raise himself socially or economically high above his fellows, it may, strictly speaking, be wrong to speak of a *middle* class. Even here, however, "middle" still serves to define its aspirations and style of consumption, whatever its final destiny.

33. Two soldiers were killed during the brief fighting that accompanied Nasser's coup in 1952, eleven strikers were shot during riots or subsequently court-martialed and hanged in 1952, and six members of

the Moslem Brotherhood, as they might under the laws of any country, were sentenced to death in 1954 for having conspired to assassinate Nasser.

Where the toll of violence was greater, the causes so far lay largely either in the resistance of the entrenched rulers to the emergence of the new middle class (as in Algeria), or in a deep division within the new middle class (as in Iraq).

CHAPTER 3

Egypt and the Myth of
the New Middle Class

By Amos Perlmutter

Authors in recent literature on developing polities have been searching for a middle class that could and, some even argue, should assume primary responsibility for all phases of development: social, economic, and political. This middle class has been identified as the New Middle Class (NMC). In contrast to the "old" middle class, the authors maintain, the NMC will create leaders; is more numerous; possesses organizational skills; is honest; develops forward-looking "new men"; in short, is shouldering, and should shoulder, social and political change.

One of the spokesmen of these authors, Manfred Halpern, quotes T. Cuyler Young, who writes on Iran, and John J. Johnson, who writes on Latin America, as evidence for the existence of such a class in the Middle East as well as other areas. Halpern, unlike the authors he cites, delegates to this class the responsibility for modernization. He sees it as a source of stability, able to control and co-ordinate asymmetrical developments and the processes of modernization of social and political change.

Halpern, as do others, demonstrates empirically the rise of the NMC but also uses sociological and political developmental theories to demonstrate its potentials and its role. What for other authors has been merely empirical and "noticeable," Halpern lifts to the plane of political and social theory, making—theoretically at least—the rise and the responsibility of the NMC inevitable.[1]

In addition to demonstrating the emergence and predicting the future role of the NMC, Halpern analyses the political behavior of its various class strata and argues that its most cohesive stratum is the army.[2] He goes one step further; "As the army officer corps came to represent the interests and views of the new middle class, it became the most powerful instrument of that class."[3] In other words, in the absence of a cohesive new middle class, its most powerful instrument—the army—becomes the New Middle Class![4]

Halpern[5] quotes Johnson[6] as evidence that "the present work [Halpern's] is not the first to notice the emergence of this new class in underdeveloped areas."[7] Unmentioned, however, remains George I. Blanksten's severe criticism of Johnson's vague "middle sectors" concept:

> Everywhere [in Johnson's book] there are impressions, hints, suggestions of the nature of this change [political and social] . . . What *is* difficult is the task of raising the social scientist's awareness of the processes involved from the level of impression and suggestion to that of conceptualization and theory productive of reliable knowledge. Johnson refuses to accept this challenge, and consequently does not carry the middle sectors from the domain of impressionism to the world of testable theory.[8]

Halpern does express apprehension about possible failure of the NMC:

> The new middle class is faced with most extraordinary opportunities. If it fails to consolidate its authority by achieving sufficient internal cohesion and general social progress, and its factions are instead engaged in ruthless competition for the support of the rural and urban masses, the approaching future is bound to be one of fearful unrest.[9]

Thus, theoretically and empirically, if the NMC is not forthcoming, i.e., if it does not become cohesive or substituted for by the army, if it is fratricidally divided, developing polities would be pitted against "fearful unrest".

This paper does not dispute the theoretical and empirical assumptions that the absence of the new middle class is critical for any modernizing and developing polity. It challenges three of Halpern's fundamental assumptions and expectations in connection with the rise of the New Middle Class and its potentials:

1) The potential cohesiveness of the NMC.
2) The potential capacity of the NMC to bring about social change and political reform.
3) The extraordinary role which is assigned to the military in cementing the NMC and enhancing its political power.

This paper does support the contention, which is easily demonstrable, that the NMC "has become the chief locus of political and economic power and of social prestige".[10] Halpern, however, does not evaluate the returns to political development and social change of the NMC's rise in political power and social prestige of the army nor show that these are not gained at the price of political development, the cohesiveness of the NMC, and the integrity and resiliency of the army as its most powerful instrument.

We have chosen to challenge the NMC concept by focusing especially on Egypt, not at the expense of other Middle Eastern countries, but for the following reasons: (1) Egypt was the first province of the Ottoman Empire to undergo modernization (even before the Ottoman Empire itself began modernizing reforms). (2) The case made for Egypt concerning the relationships between the NMC and the army is analogous to *all* modernizing Middle Eastern countries where this class has arisen with the help of the army.

We thus offer a comparative dynamic explanation[11] of the role of the middle class and its relationship with the bureaucracy in modern Egypt. This type of analysis may help demonstrate why the search for the *New* Middle Class has been unproductive.

I. BUREAUCRACY AND MIDDLE CLASS IN MODERN EGYPT
(1805-1919)

The model of the middle class—with its linkage to social and economic stability, independence, ideological cohesiveness, and its leadership role in industrialization—was formed by the analysis of Western European development.

From Muhammad 'Ali's retainers through Isma'il's proxy bureaucratic entrepreneurs to the political retainers of the monarchy, the Egyptian salariat was not a middle class occupying a leadership position in any sense. In Egypt, the middle class did not develop—as it did in Europe during modernization and early industrialization—during periods of economic growth under Muhammad 'Ali's (1805-1849) and the beginnings of British rule (1882-1919). Stunted in its growth by lopsided economic development, the Egyptian middle class later could not take up the burden of leading Egypt and her industrialization in the twentieth century.[12]

There are several reasons why Egypt's middle class is not entrepreneurial. First, because of Egypt's colonial position, the entrepreneurial functions had been taken up by foreigners, and later native Egyptians, having no experience, found it difficult to compete—the existence of foreign entrepreneurs discouraged Egyptians from entering the field. Second, those who wanted to climb up the socio-economic ladder, traditionally favored bureaucratic and administrative positions. Third, the first attempts at industrialization and modernization were promoted by the state—first by Muhammad 'Ali, and then by the Khedive Isma'il (1863—1879).[13]

A further reason why Egypt did not develop independent entrepreneurs and a creative middle class in the European sense is presented by Baer:[14] the characteristic of the Egyptian guild system.

Gibb and Bowen had established that the characteristic feature of the social organization of towns and the core of the medieval Islamic culture was the guild or corporation (taifa).[15] Baer writes:

> ... even if Muhammad Ali's "industrial revolution" or his so-called "complete transformation of the way of production" affected the artisan guilds ... and their members ... it was mainly foreign trade which Muhammad Ali monopolized, and it was mainly the fellahs whom he recruited, not the townspeople. In any case, the establishment of his industries as such did not affect the overwhelming majority of the guild members, who did not even have any contact with the new factory workers.[16]

Muhammad 'Ali, in his efforts to integrate Egypt "as an agricultural unit in the world-wide economic system',[17] despite a shortage of agricultural labor,[18] concentrated on land improvement and on the fellah as a part of his agricultural revolution. He did not, however, destroy the guilds, as Baer conclusively demonstrates. Merchant and transport guilds were not affected by 'Ali's policies; some guild members were even recruited into the army and worked for the government.[19] In fact, Baer argues, Muhammad 'Ali harnessed the guild corporative system for his purposes, and thus many governmental and bureaucratic functions in industry and trade were carried out by guild members:

> Since the government was unable to replace them (the guilds) by a new modern administrative system, it had to keep them intact in order to fulfill a number of important public functions.[20]

The guilds supplied labor; they arbitrated their own disputes; the Shaykhs, as heads of the guilds, were responsible for collecting revenue from the guilds.[21]

The preservation of the guilds served to employ " . . . the whole gainfully occupied town population except the higher bureaucracy, the army, and the ulema".[22] Except for the latter and the guilds, the entire urban population was in government employ enhancing Muhammad 'Ali's modernization program.[23] What Muhammad 'Ali really wanted was to establish his dynasty over Egypt and perhaps over the Ottoman Empire. He realized that he needed to transform Egypt, and this he did. Thus, if he did not encourage the guilds he supported the corporate system which fitted his ambitions and aided him in reaping the fruits of Egypt's modernization for his dynastic purposes. The fact that the guilds have survived into the twentieth century has been offered here with the purpose not only of stating Muhammad 'Ali's attitude toward industrialization but also of explaining why he preferred *this* type of economic development for Egypt.

The government did not intervene in society's urban economic structure—a policy that had crucial consequences for industrialization.

> This period, 1816-1840, saw Mohamed 'Ali, in a great effort to achieve independence and empire, gather into his hands all the productive resources of Egypt and with indomitable will impose

upon the people an almost incredible effort of development. To his ownership of all the land of the country, Mohamed Ali added the ownership of all the agricultural and manufactured products by declaring one after another of them government monopolies. . . [24]

'Ali's industrialization program extended government control over industry. " . . . the existing industries were decreed government monopolies . . . " writes Crouchley. "The system of industry was not changed, the artisans remained in their workshops and kept their machines, but they had to take their raw materials from the government and deliver to the government their finished products at prices imposed by the government."[25] Such a system of modernization was hardly conducive to the growth of independent entrepreneurs and a creative middle class.

In an atmosphere of discrimination against Egyptian capitalists, part of Muhammad 'Ali's factories were liquidated and sold by his successors, Abbas (1849-1854) and Said (1854-1863), and capitalists were discouraged.[26] Baer enumerates "two important factors" deterring investment in industry and responsible for a subsequent decline of Egyptian capitalists. (1) The memory of Muhammad 'Ali's discrimination policies and government control, (2) the great risk of investing in industry for the small Egyptian market. Investment in agricultural land was considered a better risk and a more profitable venture.[27] Thus, Baer concludes that " . . . after the failure of Muhammad 'Ali's industrial experiment, no serious industrial development took place in Egypt for decades".[28] Later, both Baer and Issawi agree, industrialization was further discouraged by the British government's hostile attitude.[29]

Another related factor in the decline of industry during Muhammad 'Ali's regime was that his hopes for immediate returns and great profit in industry were foolish. "In this he was deceived," writes Crouchley. "Far from being a source of profit, the industries were a drain of money and an expense as long as they continued to exist."[30]

Government monopolies in industry and agriculture and the British occupation further discouraged industrialization. Lord Cromer and the British authorities definitely did not favor it. Cromer's land reform, furthermore, created an absentee landlord class which re-emphasized the already conservative nature of the country's ruling class. The middle class of this era was already one of foreigners.

Muhammad 'Ali, a foreigner who conquered Egypt, laid the foundation for bureaucratic modernization in that country. But from the beginning, bureaucracy depended upon Muhammad 'Ali. He established a large bureaucracy to carry out his reformist and empire-building plans. One of his central points of reform was the agricultural system; he emancipated, not because of liberal convictions, but for *raison d'état*, to ensure his own and his dynasty's power. Muhammad 'Ali wanted to raise the fellah to the level of an acceptably efficient producer. In conjunction with these policies, he promulgated a revolution in land tenure, and abolished tax farming. But he also granted large estates to his relatives. The effect of these changes was the improvement of both the fellah's position and that of the large landlord. Muhammad 'Ali's industrialization policy created no bourgeoisie because he did not intend to encourage Egyptian entrepreneurs—regardless of whether they were a potential threat to his power or not.

With Muhammad 'Ali's death Egyptian rulers became dependent upon the bureaucracy he had created. However this bureaucracy was no longer an instrument of the dynasty or subservient to the khedive as it was under Muhammad 'Ali. The change from the tyrant to his lesser heirs did not change the practices of Muhammad 'Ali: domination of the bureaucracy by coercion, intrigue, and espionage. He had used these practices to good political purpose and, under his personal rule, had indeed exploited the bureaucracy for the economic modernization of Egypt. The political management of Egypt had been completely dominated by Muhammad 'Ali. Because his heirs lacked his talent for manipulation, they shared the political management of the country with the bureaucracy.

The resulting absence of industrialization, entrepreneurial initiative, and the concern for the formation of a nationalist bourgeoisie had its social and political implications. If we are to compare Egypt with any of the late-industrialized countries of the world, perhaps Germany and Japan would be most fruitful for abstracting general patterns. David Landes has pointed out that neither Germany nor Japan could have developed and industrialized were it not for the reforming politics of their modernizing elites.[31] The nation, and especially its bureaucracy, was identified as above local, regional, and even class interests. Leadership in both Germany and Japan, furthermore, emerged from conservative and economically backward groups, the Junkers in Prussia, and the Satsuma-Choshu in Japan. In neither case was reform launched by the economically developed and liberal middle classes (of Hanover and Kyoto, respectively), for these middle classes could not begin to rival the power of the agrarian ruling classes of East Prussia and Satsuma-Choshu. In both countries the traditional ruling groups sought new bases of economic and political power. Thus, in Prussia, an "alliance" was formed between the plebes and the junker bureaucracy. Eventually, the junker bureaucracy came to dominate the landed Junkers.[32] In Japan, the samurai, with little loyalty to land and class, found the new Meiji identity of nation desirable. Both groups eventually became aware that the reform slowly eroded their own power, but by then the die had been cast.

By successfully managing economic modernization, and inspired by patriotism, the bureaucracy in Japan and Prussia eventually became public-serving, even if the "public" at times was limited to the Meiji oligarchy or the Prussian junkerdom. Achieving legal autonomy and undergoing rationalization processes (in the Weberian sense), bureaucracy did bring about a widening of the scope of political management. In Egypt, however, bureaucracy was not transformed into an autonomous political structure. Nor were rational procedures, introduced by Muhammad 'Ali, institutionalized.

The growth of an independent and powerful landowner-ship class was a consequence of Muhammad 'Ali's unfinished modernization policies. First, investors, as pointed out earlier, preferred agricultural land over industry. Second, Muhammad 'Ali's successors lacked his genius of controlling conflicting bureaucratic systems, patrimonial and rational. Thus, bureaucracy turned to serve itself rather than the dynasty. Muhammad 'Ali's policy of state monopoly over agricultural land and his tight control over landowners and fellahs was reversed under Tawfiq during the latter part of the nineteenth century. The state released its control over agricultural land, and it gradually came into private ownership. With the development of finance capital[33] Muhammad 'Ali's modernization and state control was completely reversed, with the consequence that bureaucracy no longer served his dynastic aims, as in the early part of the nineteenth century, but instead served the increasing power of absentee rural landlords dominating politics, finance and administration.[34]

The landowning classes swelled as the bureaucrats of Muhammad 'Ali's successors manipulated their "offices" so as to become landowners. If 'Ali used intrigue as a technique to control his bureaucracy, his lesser heirs, while bidding for the power of bureaucrats, rewarded them with land titles. Politics became the arena for securing land and offices from the dynasty. Muhammad 'Ali's personal tyranny was replaced by small tyrannies of office seekers and land owners.

The dynasty-oriented bureaucracy had become a self-serving structure. The driving entrepreneurial and reformist efforts, characteristic of 'Ali's dynasty, were channeled into efforts to divide his land among competing bureaucrats turned landowners. The failure of Muhammad 'Ali's successors to institutionalize an independent bureaucracy turned this institution into an instrument of political and economic patronage for the few and the powerful.

II. THE NMC, THEORY, ASSUMPTIONS, POTENTIALS

Morroe Berger, although aware of the dissimilar development of the European and Middle Eastern middle classes, still seems to believe that economic growth can produce the conditions under which the Egyptian middle class, or the Middle Eastern middle classes, could play a role similar to that played by the Western European middle classes. He writes:

> If economic growth can open up new ... [avenues of social mobility] and if new social groups can acquire a stake in

continued economic advance and in the sharing of political power, the Middle East may well enter a period of greater social and political stability. The middle class can play a limited but important part in such changes, especially by its example; through its flexibility and its familiarity with the new patterns, and its close relationship with those elements of the population that want to cling to the old. If the various types of elite groups in the middle class can develop a spirit of independence and of responsibility to the entire society rather than only to their own narrow and immediate interests, they may be able to provide a good measure of the leadership that may take some parts of the Arab world into a new era of spiritual and political development as well as of economic growth.[35]

The number of "ifs" in the above argument indicates the extent to which Berger is still reasoning on the basis of Western European experience. With the "ifs" met, the middle class, in a sense, can come into its own. Not that Berger argues for a similar capitalistic development; but he does see the middle class as the potential, although limited, consolidator of the state.

Berger divides the Middle Eastern class into two sectors: first, the merchants and small manufacturers "whose income and influence are not great enough to place them among the really powerful men in political and economic life".[36] Second, a mixed group of independent professionals and employed bureaucrats. He does not specify which of the two " . . . has had enormous influence as a vehicle of modernization and introduction of Western elements into the Arab world".[37] One assumes that he means both groups. Halpern, however, assigns this innovative function only to the second group, that is, to the salariat which he identifies as the new middle class.[38]

According to Halpern:

> The new middle class has been able to act as a separate and independent force because: (1) prior to its seizure of power, it is freer than any other class from traditional bonds and preconceptions, and better equipped to manipulate armies and voluntary organizations as revolutionary political instruments; (2) once it controls the machinery of a modernizing state, it possesses a power base superior to that which any other class in the Middle East can muster on the basis of prestige, property, or physical force; (3) it is numerically one of the largest groups within the

modern sector of society; (4) it is, so far, more obviously cohesive, more self-conscious, and better trained than any other class; (5) its political, economic, and social actions, in so far as they come to grips with social change, are decisive in determining the role other classes will play in the future; and (6) it has shown itself capable of marshalling mass support.[39]

The remainder of the present paper will examine the validity of the following correlated principal qualities of the NMC: (1) The NMC is "more obviously cohesive . . . than any other class". (2) The NMC is "better equipped to manipulate armies". The first two assumptions are combined in the discussion to follow because the cohesiveness of the NMC is dependent on the army as one stratum of this new class.

III. THE ARMY AS THE INSTRUMENT OF NMC COHESION

According to Halpern, (1) the military is the most cohesive stratum of the NMC, and the NMC is "at least" represented by the army when the army is "securely anchored in a well-organized movement";[40] and (2) the NMC's success in marshalling mass support depends on the army, as its most powerful instrument.[41] The military plays an extraordinary role as the consolidator of the NMC because "[it has] served as national standard-bearer when others who claimed that role proved irresponsible and ineffective".[42] The army has been propelled into the political arena by its organization and, compared with the rest of the society, was early in modernizing. The consequences are that "the more the army was modernized, the more its composition, [and] organization, spirit, capabilities, and purpose constituted a radical criticism of the existing political system".[43] Halpern himself summarizes his argument:

> Within the army, modern technology was eagerly welcomed and its usefulness and power appreciated. By contrast, the political system showed greater inertia, inefficiency, skepticism, and greed in utilizing the products of modern science. Within the army, merit was often rewarded. In civilian politics, corruption, nepotism, and bribery loomed much larger. Within the army, a sense of national mission transcending parochial, regional, or economic interests, or kinship ties seemed to be much more clearly defined than anywhere else in society.[44]

The acceptance of this new class as potentially cohesive and the coming consolidation of all new middle class strata under the auspices of the army, are not convincing arguments. A much less convincing argument is identifying the NMC as an intelligentsia.[45] "The intelligentsia is the predominant force of this class" because "it originates in the intellectual and social transformation of Middle Eastern society" and therefore its various strata consist of new men who intervene in the process of modernization and hence assume additional roles in modernization.[46] In military-dominated politics, neither the civilian nor the military strata tends to be cohesive. Also, the dynamics of transformation may increase division among NMC strata, rather than consolidating them into one coherent unit. Recent transformation of the Egyptian and Syrian societies, especially, has increased conflicts among the NMC strata and intensified the brutal internal struggle for power and primacy, particularly in Syria. Apparently, Halpern's new class is like Mannheim's "socially unattached intelligentsia" (*freischwebende Intelligenz*).[47] That is, the NMC strata have become a class in Halpern's analysis because they are *potentially* cohesive. Mannheim admits that this intelligentsia is not homogeneous—although it has absorbed a common *Weltanschauung* and a readiness for action. But homogeneity and a common *Weltanschauung* are not sufficient condition for cohesiveness and common action.

The political histories of Egypt since 1952, Syria since 1949, and Iraq since 1958 demonstrate that neither the new middle class nor the army are, even potentially, one social, ideological or political class. Thus, social scientists would therefore do well to concentrate on the complexities and *divisions* within the stratification system of each stratum of the NMC.

It may, indeed, be more relevant to ask what the lines of potential conflict are rather than those of potential cohesion. In fact, Halpern sees the problem of internal conflict but he does not use it as the key to his analysis. He writes:

> The army in politics cannot become an institution above the battle. It intervenes as a partisan, representing a new class with whom the majority in the country does not yet share a common consciousness. It is itself a most sensitive mirror of internal

conflicts within the new middle class. . . . It will be unable to avoid factionalism within the ruling junta unless the whole junta or its dominant faction is securely anchored in a well-organized movement representing at least the new middle class.[48]

Halpern's observation that the military coup in Egypt was without violence,[49] and that a new social class displaced the landed ruling class, indicates the political apathy of the population; at the time of the coup the apathy could be found in the army, certainly in parts of the new middle class. And such apathy was typical of the palatial intrigue politics of a state dominated by feudalism in which Nasser and the Free Officers significantly participated between 1945 and 1952. When the army was finally "securely anchored" in 1954, this did not demonstrate the ideological conviction of a new class, a new intelligentsia. Only in 1961 did Nasser finally opt for a Socialist system. "Ten years after the revolution of 1952, the Egyptian free-enterprise system had been effectively transformed into a centrally-controlled economy."[50] Even now, the Egyptian army has not established "a well-organized movement". The concept of the new middle class runs into all the problems that the former concept of the middle classes encountered.

Neither social stability nor mass political participation, as suggested by Halpern, has in fact been brought about by army rule in the Middle East. In Syria and Iraq the army has been responsible for the regime's political instability; in Egypt, recent political stability is a product of traditional political apathy, political coercion, a dependent bureaucracy, rather than of the consolidation of social and political groups. The newly-acquired prestige of Egypt's officers' class has made the rest of this new class presented by Halpern not more cohesive but merely more dependent.

Middle Eastern officers tend to be the products of modern organizations, more so than the rest of the population. They reflect modern values and orientations and, especially, modern tools and techniques they use and manipulate. But all this says very little about their ability to transfer these characteristics of the military organization to the rest of the society. This requires leadership qualities, and especially leadership qualities of a political kind. Are the military "skills" of honesty, ability, and decisiveness identical with political leadership skills? The divided and fratricidal Syrian and Iraqi armies, for example, cannot utilize these qualities in the political arena precisely because of their division. Sometimes these able men are left to the mercy of civilian and opportunistic groups in their own midst. Lack of political leadership and cohesion among army men tends to reduce the usefulness of these above-mentioned qualities. In fact, when it comes to leadership, the civilian political organizations—FLN, MB, PPS, Ba'th—could serve to teach the army. But these political groups, too, are susceptible to the same conflicts as the new middle class, although these parties themselves may represent only sectors of the class.

Halpern's eulogy of Middle Eastern armies and their capability and potentialities withstands neither the logic of theory nor the burden of facts. The number of "ifs" (the conditions under which the army may become the NMC)[51] is reminiscent of Berger's propositions for Middle Eastern stable and powerful middle classes. The army as "the most powerful stratum of the new middle class" is only demonstrable in Nasser's Egypt, after the military dictatorship between 1952 and 1956 eliminated all political opposition. Halpern is not willing to forecast the next steps in the Arab world or in Egypt. But his concept demands prognosis which, in turn, threatens its basic assumptions. The existence of strong civilian rival members of the same strata in Syria does not demonstrate the so-called resiliency of the latter. The "inner" and "inter" civilian-army rivalries in Syria demonstrate that when either emerges to power, it is not "securely anchored". It shows, in fact, that when the army is in power, it represents not the NMC but its ashes.

The danger for social scientists lies in putting all eggs in one basket. The fall of Nkrumah, Ben Bella, and Soekarno demonstrates how badly needed is a comparative dynamic explanation as a basis for theories in the social sciences. Causal explanations are of value only where based on more durable theories than reasonable "ifs". The weakness of Halpern's concept of the NMC is that it assumes a static explanation. "We speak of a static explanation", writes

Harsanyi, "when a social variable is explained exclusively in terms of variables belonging to *the same time period*."[52] Thus the potentials of the NMC, the intelligentsia, the army, (and all other "New Men") must be explained in terms of a dynamic model which "allow[s] for slow, delayed, or staggering adjustment, and which include the social conditions of earlier periods (and/or the time trends due to the changes going on in society)".[53]

IV. THE MILITARY AND POLITICAL MOBILIZATION

Can we then believe that the revolutionary fervor, expressed in the *Falsafat al Qawmiyyah* (The Philosophy of Nationalism) and *Ikhtarna Lak* (We Have Chosen for You) agitatory political literature, will change Berger's "pliable" and "servile" bureaucrat[54] into an innovative and administrative political leader? Will the military succeed where the political parties have failed in consolidating the new middle classes and leading them to sustained modernization and industrialization? Is it capable of marshalling mass support?

In line with the entire historical trend, Nasser and his followers have created bureaucracies for the modernization of the country. The army officers themselves also emerged from the bureaucracy. They preferred administrative to political solutions as most suitable for modernization and for maintaining their authority, and this preference is in line with Egypt's entire history. This time the dependent bureaucracies are run by the military in alliance with technological elites, and they take the place of parties and independent associations essential for political virtue, a conscientious act, or a mechanism of consensus—it is but an auxiliary of étatist practices. The army and its allies among the new classes and within the salariat ask not for participation but for plebiscitory approval and integration into étatist politics.

Apparently, Nasser's elite seeks a formula for modernization and restricted political mobilization. It seeks to sustain power without facing alienation or cleavages. It is gradually seeking to avoid the penalties of functional differentiation, without fragmenting Egypt's social order, or, for that matter, without encouraging pluralist community and political tendencies.[55]

The economic policies of Nasser clearly demonstrate these tendencies.[56] The collapse of guided capitalism and the demise of the free-enterprise system by 1960 left Nasser and his followers with little choice. Their ideological and political commitments to promote social reform and economic growth put the regime into an ideological strait-jacket. The Socialist solution for Egypt became inevitable. Chapter 6 of the 1962 Charter proclaims "The Socialist solution to the problems of economic and social underdevelopment in Egypt—to achieve progress in a revolutionary way—was never a question of *free choice*. The Socialist solution was a historical inevitability imposed by reality, the broad aspirations of the people and the changing nature of the world in the second part of the 20th century."[57] (Italics mine). The 1962 Charter was a turning point in Egypt's history. After that time the principles of the Charter became a point of no return for the regime, which would find a reversal from socialism politically hazardous. The regime was confined to the kismet of its own doings—commitment to economic growth and to the ideology of social change.

Political and ideological mobilization were harnessed to *accommodate* "inevitable" economic modernization. Thus Nasser's political formula is to confine politics to the carefully selected officials of the Arab Socialist Union, to delegates to the National Assembly, and senior bureaucrats, all *dominated* by a small group of Veteran Free Officers. As yet Nasser's Egypt has not allowed for independent or autonomous political structures and procedures.

Thus, to speak of the NMC (and in this case its foremost stratum) as being "the first class for which the choice between democracy, authoritarianism, and totalitarianism is a *real* and *open* choice"[58] (italics mine) demonstrates the gap between a simplistic prescription invented by some social scientists and the more confining and "inevitable" circumstances which confront those whose "choice" was actually determined by their ideological commitments.

This does not mean that Nasser's bureaucracy promises the success that was achieved by the samurai. But the Egyptian inner circle and its allies are searching for a modified samurai-Junker solution to the country's developmental problems. They want to combine reform and nationalism short of revolution. The modernization model taken up by the military men is pragmatic and couched in ideological parlance. Much of the current modernization resembles the manner in which it was started by Muhammad 'Ali. The difference is the ideological commitment of Nasser and his followers. Particularly the similar attitude toward an independent bureaucracy and the autonomy of political institutions. For whereas the French Revolution posed no threat to Muhammad 'Ali, the contemporary nationalist-communist revolutions do pose a challenge to the military governors of Egypt, for they have been propelled to accept the "inevitability of socialism".

That Nasser's inner circle has moved Egypt to a point of no return, is unquestionable. That they are modernizers is a fact. However, as indicated, their attitude toward mass mobilization and social and structural differentiation is reminiscent of the attitude of the successful samurai and Junker once they had taken power. Both leading groups of Japan and Germany were sustained largely by the formula of political reform.

There are, of course, dangers in comparing Japan and Prussia—the two most successful industrializing polities of the pre-1939 era—with Egypt and its still unsuccessful modernization reform. However, the comparison does illustrate that these successful, modernizing autocratic regimes did design formulas for political and economic reform without revolution; social change, in these cases, was politically restrained.[59] In Egypt, too, the regime is attempting to harness nationalist ideology and communal sentiments to organizational problems. Community is conceived within an organizational model: organization is to create a community by fiat. But it has not done so—at least not so far.

Muhammad 'Ali, modernizing Egypt to fulfill his personal and dynastic ambitions, carried out reforms by ruthless means. He did not seek the consent of the people whose territory he had chosen to exploit. Egyptians were recruited, as were foreigners, only if they could serve dynastic purposes.

Nasser's program of modernization is intended not to aggrandise personal rule but to help Egyptians and Arabs. Thus, his policies must seek certain measures of consensus which were superfluous for 'Ali. The tactics and aims of Nasser's political structures are bound to be different from 'Ali's.

The test of the army-dominated bureaucracies, Egypt's only political structure, does not end with its orientation toward public service. In the absence of other political structures serving the public, Egypt's dominated bureaucracy, its actions, attitudes, and behavior, is the politics of Nasser.

The role of ideology in Egypt has already been discussed elsewhere.[60] The regime, in defining the goals of the Egyptian Revolution, also formulated Nasser's ideology, which is composed of Egyptian identification, Islam and Arabism. Nasser's party, The National Union (1958-1961), designed for political mobilization of the U.A.R. and especially Syria, was no more than a blueprint. Nasser's failure to instill his ideology into this newly formed party turned it into a non-functionary structure dominated by the *Rais* and his Syrian satraps. In contrast to Muhammad 'Ali's dynasty-serving modernization, Nasser identifies the modernization efforts of his bureaucracy as a first layer of nation-building. The burdens of Nasser's only political structure—the bureaucracy—are immense.[61] To expand the role of bureaucracy from the historical bureaucracies in Egypt since Muhammad 'Ali, it must be imbued with a vision if it is not fused with ideology. The vision, as Heaphey clearly demonstrates, is organizational.

> What Nasser does not like is the politics of politics. It clashes with the image of organization, and is alien to a society that admits only the goodness and rationality of man. . . . Political behavior is ugly in the eyes of the organizational vision.[62]

Nasser's bureaucracies deal with politics as an organizational task. Here, then, the "skills" of the officers recommended by Halpern—honesty, ability, and decisiveness—become virtues. But, as Heaphey demonstrates, these virtues are political burdens, for the organizational model is not a substitute for community if not fused with ideology.[63]

If Nasser's bureaucracy could be differentiated from 'Ali's —since it is now public-oriented—the difference would be that Nasser's commitment is ideological and Muhammad 'Ali's to personal aggrandisement. The aim is toward a larger constituency than that of the historical bureaucratic political system—it is toward a nation, people, community. It thus behooves Nasser and his followers to create new political structures for political mobilization, in addition to Egypt's historically powerful structure, the bureaucracy. Delegating new functions to a bureaucracy committed to nation-building does not guarantee differentiations of this structure if it is dominated and manipulated by a small inner circle of veterans of the Free Officers Club. The differentiation that exists between the Socialist Union established in 1961 and the government of the UAR is not competitive or political. It is the difference between overseeing and executing bureaucracies. In fact, in an era less committed to nation-building and paying lip service to political participation, between 1919 and 1952, separate political structures emerged in Egypt, in the form of political parties (the Wafd, the Muslim Brotherhood and others). But soon these, like the bureaucracy, became self-serving. Now, only one tightly controlled structure exists, the bureaucracy, engaged in all the functions of nation-building. This single political structure has the following major duties: It is expected to create a political community by fiat: it serves as a governmental executive; as an administrator of large-scale economic functions; as a political party; as a military bureaucracy; as the inculcator of Egyptian Revolution in Egypt and a chief agent of agitation in the Arab world; as an instrument to combat conservatism and "reactionary" forces in South Arabia; and as a military machine facing a serious enemy, Israel. All these burdens and others are heaped upon an institution which was discredited, corrupt, and pliable as recently as 1952, and has been oscillating between the duties of a watch dog and an administration. In other words, *all* talent must be drawn into the bureaucracy to fulfill the Egyptian revolution.

The politics of modernization could bring structural and functional differentiation and competition. Arenas for the development of autonomous or semi-autonomous political goals must be offered by the rulers of Egypt. Political activity, to some extent, must be diffused. All this is not yet forthcoming in Egypt.

To reiterate Heaphey, "President Nasser knows in functional terms why he needs a political party—he needs it to legitimate what is going on in the country by providing a more permanent vanguard than now exists in the persons of Nasser and his associates. But he cannot accept a political party in real behavioral terms."[64] No successful process of modernization can be carried out alone by the army-dominated bureaucracy and its technocratic allies, as is being done in Egypt.

In Prussia, "the prime determinants of decision and action were always political".[65] The collaboration of the bureaucracy and the bourgeoisie were crucial to the success of Hardenberg's reform. In Japan, the combined effort of entrepreneurs and government bureaucracy is duly credited to the success of the Meiji reform.[66] This is not to argue that a complete harmony prevailed between the two—on the contrary, diverse social origins of bureaucrats and businessmen were sources of permanent conflict,[67] especially in designating priorities for the execution of reform. Japan was no more fortunate than Germany on this score. But, without the recruitment of the major strata—especially bureaucracy and entrepreneurs—for reform, neither Japan nor Prussia would have become successful industrialized countries.[68] They became successful only because both these strata submitted to the primacy of the political.[69]

Shelving politics, i.e., failing to relate "tensional forces of society" to political order[70] can only curtail the good intentions of the regime. The problem in Egypt, as some authors correctly observe, is not the crisis of political participation. The problem is the suspension of politics as an autonomous goal, i.e., the developing of regulative procedures, mechanisms and organization patterns of communication and the institutionalization of organs for political struggle.[71] As far as the middle classes (in the sense of nineteenth-century Europe) are concerned, they have been stifled in Egypt. The achievement motive and the expectant growth of entrepreneurs so far have had as little chance in Nasser's Egypt as with 'Ali's entrepreneurs, lacking an autonomous, independent, and creative arena, and being strangled in one political structure—the government bureaucracy.

The margin of independent political action and entrepreneur initiative between 'Ali's historical-bureaucratic system and Nasser's nation-building-oriented bureaucracy is meager.[72] The 'new' middle classes of Egypt have lost their chance again.

Government intervention is practiced cautiously, lest the polity be fragmented into class and interest groups. The administrations are to accomplish the task of political integration. Communication is established through the regime-appointed intermediaries of the Socialist Union. National independence and the ideologies of Islam and Arabism, are utilized to consolidate a military-dominated regime rather than to mobilize politically. The state has priority over society. The state is, of course, also the chief author of the organizational and administrative model preferred by the military. The military thus far has failed to marshall mass support in Egypt.[73]

The rural middle class and its urban offshoots are now heavily represented in the bureaucracy. The expectations of this strata, politically and socially, are those of a ruling bureaucracy rather than that of a proletariat or a middle class attempting, as a class, to bring about change. These expectations deny any suggestion that they act as a middle class in the same way as the middle classes of Western Europe.[74] As yet, Egypt does not have a cohesive middle class, old or new. To argue that a "new middle class" or salariat, with cohesion and clear objectives, could emerge and play the role traditionally played by the entrepreneurial middle class of Western Europe is unrealistic. Egypt since 1952 demonstrates the limitations of the NMC and the demise of its political and entrepreneurial potentials. Undoubtedly, the middle classes—first merchants and bankers, then corporate and individual entrepreneurs—enhanced economic and political growth in the West. Middle classes, industrialization, modernization, political emancipation, all have been interdependent in nineteenth- and twentieth-century Europe and the United States. But this has not been true of Egypt's salariat (vividly and accurately described by Berger).[75] No captains of industry have, as yet, emerged in Egypt. Neither did the NMC establish independent political structures and institutions. The bureaucracy is harnessed to étatist requirements.

In fact, it is the military which complains and severely criticizes the bureaucracy in Nasser's Egypt. Muhammad Hasanyan Haykal spares no effort in denouncing bureaucracy's "old practices", especially in the new administrations (Suez, Aswan, Hilwan, etc.).[76]

The political journal *Ruz al-Yusuf* in the last two years has not ceased to criticize and even to denounce bureaucratic "corruption", especially in the administration of land reform.

If the "new middle class" is an analytical category, it offers much less than an explanation of the politics of the modern Middle East. If its political potential is a prescription, hardly any stratum of the NMC fulfills it. If it pretends to describe the struggle for power between the strata, the theoretical assumptions of its potential integration are denied by the fact that a brutal competition of power and mutual annihilation prevail. And if it represents a foregone conclusion, it does not describe Nasser's and his circle's type of domination which consciously restricts political mass participation. And in attempting to explain what one stratum would do once in power, as the army-dominated bureaucracy in Egypt, we must completely abandon such a theory and search instead for other expectations and practices, for the system of authority, and the society and organization preferred by the ruling group.

To turn a well-conceived general theory of the role of the middle class in the system of production (in the West) into a theory explaining which group, other than the "traditional middle class", will modernize (or is modernizing) Egypt, is not simply an abuse of the general theory. It prevents the understanding of the dynamics of Egyptian development, or for that matter, of any other Middle Eastern regime where the rivalry between civilian and military of the same strata has not yet been resolved.

NOTES

1. Manfred Halpern, *The Politics of Social Change in the Middle East and North Africa* (Princeton, 1963), pp. 51-78 (reprinted as Chapter 2 of this work). See especially footnotes 3 and 4 on pp. 54-55, also pp. 56-57, on the qualities of this new class, and on Young's and Johnson's evidence for the emergence of what Johnson prefers to call the "middle sectors" (a designation accepted by Halpern), as a new class, in developing areas.

2. *Ibid.,* p. 258.

3. *Ibid.*

4. *Ibid.,* pp. 274.

5. *Ibid.,* p. 54, footnote 4.

6. John J. Johnson, *Political Change in Latin America: The Emergence of Middle Sectors* (Stanford, 1958), pp. VII-IX.

7. *Op. cit.,* pp. 54-55. "Among these two [Johnson and Young] and the present essay, there are common intellectual lines."

8. George I. Blanksten, "In Quest of the Middle Sectors" in *World Politics,* Vol. 12, no. 2 (January, 1960), p. 326.

9. *Ibid.,* p. 78.

10. Omitted

11. John Harsanyi defines dynamic explanation "when at least some of the explanatory variables used to belong to an *earlier period* than the variables to be explained. More generally, we should speak of the dynamic explanation also if what we directly try to explain, and/or what we offer as explanation, involve not only the *values* of certain social variables at a given time, but also their *time trends* (time derivatives, i.e., the directions and rates of their change)." John C. Harsanyi, "Explanation and Comparative Dynamics in Social Science", *Behavioral Science,* Vol. 5, no. 2 (April, 1960), p. 137.

12. Charles Issawi, "Egypt Since 1800: A Study in Lop-sided Development", *The Journal of Economic History,* Vol. 21, no. 1 (March, 1961), pp. 1-4.

13. On Ismail's ambitious program and its failures see David S. Landes, *Bankers and Pashas: International Finance and Economic Imperialism in Egypt* (Cambridge, Mass., Harvard University Press, 1958), pp. 128-146.

14. Gabriel Baer, *Egyptian Guilds in Modern Times* (= *The Israel Oriental Society,* no. 8) (Jerusalem, 1964).

15. "If religion was the cement of the Islamic structure, the corporations were the bricks of which it was built." H. A. R. Gibb and Harold Bowen, *Islamic Society and the West,* Vol. 1, Part 1 (London, Oxford University Press, 1950), p. 277.

16. Baer, *op. cit.,* p. 132.

17. Issawi, *op. cit.,* pp. 4-5.

18. A.E. Crouchley, *The Economic Development of Modern Egypt* (London, Longmans Green, 1938), p. 50.

19. Baer, *op. cit.*, pp. 130-138.
20. *Ibid.*, p. 133.
21. *Ibid.*, pp. 133-134.
22. *Ibid.*, p. 5.
23. As for the *ulema* 'Ali was aware of its potential danger to his modernization policies. The Mameluk massacre of 1811 served as a warning to the *ulema*. A British traveller, Augustus St. John, described the *ulema's* opposition to 'Ali in visiting mosques, bazaars and schools. See James Augustus St. John, *Egypt and Mohammed Ali: Travels in the Valley of the Nile*, 2 volumes (London, Longman, 1834), Vol. 1, pp. 39-48.
24. A.E. Crouchley, *op. cit.*, p. 41.
25. *Ibid.*, p. 67.
26. Baer, *op. cit.*, pp. 136-137.
27. *Ibid.*, pp. 136-138.
28. *Ibid.*, p. 136. See also A.E. Crouchley, *The Economic Development of Modern Egypt, op. cit.*, pp. 72-76.
29. *Ibid.*, and Issawi, *op. cit.*, p. 12.
30. Crouchley, *op. cit.*, p. 72.
31. David Landes, "Japan and Europe, Contrasts in Industrialization", in William W. Lockwood, ed., *The State and Economic Enterprise in Japan* (Princeton, N.J., Princeton University Press, 1965), pp. 145-153.
32. *Ibid.*, pp. 133-135.
33. Landes, *Bankers and Pashas* ..., pp. 147-172.
34. Crouchley also maintains that the 1838 commercial treaty between England and the Porte was a blow to 'Ali's state monopoly system. The treaty was designed to break 'Ali's powered profit making. Crouchley, *op. cit.*, p. 74.
35. Morroe Berger, "The Middle Class in the Arab World", in Walter Z. Laqueur, *The Middle East in Transition* (New York, Frederick A. Praeger, 1958), p. 71.
36. *Ibid.*, p. 63.
37. *Ibid.*
38. Manfred Halpern, "Middle Eastern Armies and the New Middle Class", in John J. Johnson, *The Role of the Military in the Underdeveloped World* (Princeton, N.J., Princeton University Press, 1962), pp. 177-315.
39. Halpern, *The Politics* ..., p. 59.
40. *Ibid.*, p. 274.
41. *Ibid.*, p. 258.
42. *Ibid.*, p. 259.
43. *Ibid.*, p. 258.
44. *Ibid.*
45. *Ibid.*, pp. 56-57.
46. *Ibid.*, p. 58.
47. This term Mannheim has borrowed from Alfred Weber but made wider use of it. See Mannheim, *Ideology and Utopia* (New York, Harcourt, Brace, 1953). Mannheim elaborated and modified this concept in his "The Problem of the Intelligentsia", *Essays on the*

Sociology of Culture (London, Routledge & Kegan Paul, 1956), pp. 91-170.

48. Halpern, *The Politics* ..., p. 274.

49. *Ibid.*, pp. 76-77.

50. Patrick O'Brien, *The Revolution in Egypt's Economic System* (London, Oxford, 1966).

51. *Ibid.*, pp. 278-280.

52. *Op. cit.*

53. *Ibid.*

54. Morroe Berger, *Bureaucracy and Society in Modern Egypt* (Princeton, Princeton University Press, 1957).

55. On the crisis of political participation in Egypt see Leonard Binder. "Political Recruitment and Participation in Egypt", in Joseph La Palombara and Myron Weiner, eds., *Political Parties and Political Development* (Princeton, N.J., Princeton University Press, 1966), pp. 217-240.

56. See P.K. O'Brien: *The Revolution in Egypt's Economic System* (O.U.P., 1966). The Arab Socialist Union formed in 1961 was restricted to meet the demands of economic modernization, while restricting political mobilization. See also author's book, *Egypt: the Praetorian State* (1968).

57. *United Arab Republic: The Charter* (Cairo, UAR, Information Department).

58. Omitted.

59. These dangers are clearly demonstrated in Bendix's illuminating comparison of Japan and Germany. See Reinhard Bendix, *Nation-Building and Citizenship* (New York, John Wiley and Sons, 1964), Part II, Chapter 6, pp. 177-214, especially p. 208-213.

60. Leonard Binder, *The Ideological Revolution in the Middle East* (New York, John Wiley and Sons, 1964), pp. 49-74.

61. The Arab Socialist Union is another governmental bureaucracy designed among other things to inculcate the ideologized Arab Socialism into the bureaucracy.

62. James Heaphey, "The organization of Egypt: Inadequacies of a Non-Political Model for Nation Building", *World Politics*, Vol. 28 (January, 1966), p. 191.

63. See Franz Schurmann, *Ideology and Organization in Communist China* (Berkeley, University of California Press, 19(6), pp. 18-23.

64. Heaphey, *op. cit.*, p. 191.

65 Landes, "Japan and Europe", *op. cit.*, p. 150.

66. *Ibid.*, pp. 150-151.

67. *Ibid.*, pp. 151-152, Also Eisenstadt. *The Political System* ..., pp. 156-175.

68. On the role of entrepreneurs in Meiji Japan see Johannes Hirschmeier, *The Origins of Entrepreneurship in Meiji Japan* (Cambridge, Mass., Harvard University Press, 1964).

69. Again we caution with Bendix against the "fallacy of retrospective determinism" (Bendix, *Nation Building, op. cit.*, p. 208), in comparing such different states, social structures, and political practices. Egypt under Muhammad 'Ali suffered from *total* lack of local political

autonomy. In Japan and Prussia local government was fairly well established and acted as an intermediary between the national government and the people. Once harnessed to national authority, local authorities acted to diffuse political and economic policies and were thus instrumental in reform. Comparing political management with the emergence of autonomous political structures and practices in Japan and Prussia and its absence in Egypt only demonstrates the extraordinary burdens which have been relegated to the NMC. On the rise of central power in Japan see John Whitney Hall's seminal *Government and Local Power in Japan 500 to 1700* (Princeton, 1966); on Prussian bureaucracy see Hans Rosenberg's excellent treatise *Bureaucracy, Aristocracy and Autocracy: The Prussian Experience 1660-1815* (Harvard, 1966).

70. This is borrowed from Sheldon Wolin, *Politics and Vision* (New York, Little, Brown, 1960), p. 7.

71. See S.N. Eisenstadt, *The Political Systems of Empires* (New York, The Free Press, 1963), pp. 94-112.

72. On the collapse of entrepreneurial and capitalist institutions in Egypt between 1952 and 1960 see O'Brien, *op. cit.*, pp. 68-103.

73. Binder, "Political Recruitment ..." in La Palombara and Weiner (eds.), *Political Parties and Political Development,* pp. 217-240.

74. On the predominance of the rural middle class and its urban offshoots in the Egyptian military see Eliezer Beeri, "Social Class and Family Background of the Egyptian Army Officer Class" in *Asian and African Studies,* Vol. 2. *Annual of the Israel Oriental Society* (Jerusalem, The Hebrew University, 1966), pp. 1-40.

75. Berger, *Bureaucracy ..., loc. cit.*

76. See vehement criticism of Egypt's new bureacracy by Haykal in *Al Ahram* (Cairo), March 6, 1964, pp. 2-3.

CHAPTER 4

Reaffirmations and New Explorations

By Manfred Halpern

Amos Perlmutter's essay attacks the myth of a new middle class seen potentially or now as a cohesive group embodied by the army and capable of modernizing Egypt and the Middle East. He describes me as the principal creator of this myth. In the form and substance in which he presents it, the myth is his, not mine. Those who have already read *The Politics of Social Change in the Middle East and North Africa* (Princeton, 1963) in which I first published some hypotheses on the relationship between social classes and modernization, or who missed Perlmutter's false image of it, need not read Part I of this response. Those neither bemused nor amused by distortions and their resolutions may wish to skip to Part II. There I try to add a few suggestions to my 1963 work by responding to the main question which Perlmutter raises but has done little to answer: why has the salaried new middle class not done well so far in modernizing the Middle East?

I. THE SALARIED NEW MIDDLE CLASS REVISITED

Perlmutter and I begin in agreement. He "does support" my contention that the salaried new middle class (NMC, to follow Perlmutter's abbreviation) "has become the chief locus of political and economic power and social prestige". He adds that this is "easily demonstrable". Wish it were so! The

97

number of official colleagues who shared this view in the U.S.
Department of State slowly grew after such an analysis was first
drafted almost a year before Nasser gained power, but its
perspective never came to be accepted by any Secretary of
State. American policy in the Middle East and North Africa
has generally persisted in holding the rise and fall of personalities as historically more strategic than the emergence and
decline of social classes. The U.S. Government, like the Soviet
Government, has given higher priority to the balance of
international power than to the foundations of any kind of
enduring power—namely the creation of new capacity to give
just and coherent structure to rapid historical change.

When I elaborated this analysis for a scholarly audience in
1963, a few doubts had already been expressed about the once
prevalent thesis of a two-class structure in the Middle East:
on top, in antagonistic collaboration as for a thousand years,
landlords, military officers, bureaucrats, most of the rich
traders and some of the intelligentsia; at the bottom, highly
segmented agglomerations of peasants, workers, and most of
the intelligentsia.[1] Still, there was room then for the first book
that would focus on the rise of a salaried and would-be
salaried new middle class and seek to explain the ideological,
institutional, social and political direction of the Middle East
and North Africa in terms of issues and choices confronting
that class. I would certainly hope that the many readers of
The Politics of Social Change in the Middle East and North Africa
have found this core analysis of my book "easily demonstrable". Though Perlmutter thinks so too, he did not, I fear,
understand it.

He misses the basic fact that this book offers a departure
into a new theory on the relationship of social classes to
system-transforming change in the modern age. Instead, he
blames me for "an abuse" of "a well-conceived general theory
of the role of the middle class in the system of production [in
the West]" because he is under the impression that I am
turning that inheritance "into a theory explaining which
group . . . will modernize" Egypt and the Middle East. I
began my original discussion by rejecting all

    classical economic divisions of classes. . . . Where a modern economy is still to be created, and where control over the state and the forces of social change is more potent than ownership of property, property relations alone cannot serve to define class relations. . . . Separate individuals . . . form a class only in so far as they play a common role in relation to social change, and have to carry on a common battle against another class or seek collaboration with it. Otherwise, they may be on hostile terms with each other as competitors. . . . That means taking account of all who either already perform the roles of a member of the salaried middle class or who are bent by revolutionary action, if necessary, to gain a chance to perform this role [in relation to social change] and no other.[2]

An entire chapter spelled out how the evolving interests, opportunities, and behavior of the salaried new middle class in relation to the transformation of modern society differ from those of all other social classes. There is no need to repeat that exposition here, except to summarize for the reader entirely unfamiliar with it. In the 1963 volume, I did not define this class by the occupational or administrative fact that they drew salaries. Many Middle Easterners drawing salaries today are traditionalists left over from an earlier era, narrow careerists, or efficient or status-conscious techno-crats unconcerned about history or society. The new middle class is defined by its interest in ideas, actions, and careers relevant to modernization. In contemporary Middle Eastern society, almost all positions that give scope to that kind of consciousness, creativity, institutionalized power, and sense of social justice are salaried. That is why I speak of a new "salaried" and would-be "salaried" middle class. Perlmutter did not notice the radical difference bet-ween a new theory of class and conventional liberal, Marx-ist, or academic theories. Thus he deprived himself on an opportunity to place his own discussion inn the context of comparisons in class theories. Since he misunderstands and rejects my class theory but offers no other, I see no theoretical grounds on which anyone could accept his "support" of my hypothesis that a new class has become the chief locus of political and economic power and social prestige.

Next he mistakes what I mean by salaried middle class. He

says that "middle sectors" is "a designation accepted by Halpern" for the salaried new middle class, and then takes me to task for not even mentioning George I. Blanksten's "severe criticism of [John J.] Johnson's vague 'middle sectors' concept". I do not mention Blanksten's well-taken criticism because I use the term 'middle sectors' only once in 420 pages, and then in a footnote in order myself to reject Johnson's concept as "too broad", because Johnson includes within it the "poorly paid white-collar employee in government" as well as the "wealthy proprietors of commercial and industrial enterprises". With "sectors" as a concept, I went on to say one cannot do class analysis, "relating changes in social structure to changes in political power".[3] "Sectors" is probably an appropriate term for Johnson's broad spectrum of society. In our original State Department analysis of *Political Instability in the Near East*, this term had been a compromise born of quadruple cross-pressures during the process of official clearance. Against the proposal of "class", some found unacceptable a new usage not sanctioned by academic tradition; some believed that nothing fundamental ever changes in the Middle East, and hence yielded reluctantly to recognize a change in "sectors" if not in "classes"; some thought it imprudent to mention "classes" in relation to social change in the midst of intense McCarthyism; some were skeptical that our official readers cared much for any theory, and struggled for clarity and solidity of facts and conclusions amid pressures for compromise. After the "middle sectors" of the Middle East regained in the 1963 volume their most revealing name, I am especially loath to see it, shrouded again in this, and several additional ways, by Perlmutter.

Perlmutter finds it even "a much less convincing argument" that I should be "identifying the NMC as an intelligentsia". That indeed would have been unconvincing. That is why I began my entire discussion by rejecting the notion that nothing more had come into existence than a rootless intelligentsia. That is not an adequate portrayal of change in the social structure of the Middle East. Instead, I argued that this view would "overlook the emergence of a new social class in the Middle East as the principal

—and potentially stabilizing—force".[4] I also recognized that "the intelligentsia, that is, those with knowledge or awareness to see that a social and political revolution is in progress, form the largest and politically most active component of the new middle class". In the very next sentence I added: "But they are not the only component of this class. Some members of this new class are already middle class in their pattern of consumption but still searching for ideas (hence new in a society once sure of its truths). Others are interested only in ideas about means and not, like the intelligentsia, also about ends, and the concern for truth of the intellectuals does not interest them".[5]

Perlmutter's most disastrous error in restructuring my analysis so that it becomes his own myth lies in his attempt in the "remainder" (i.e. the second half) of his paper to "examine the validity of the following correlated principal qualities of the NMC: (1) the NMC is 'more obviously cohesive . . . than any other class', (2) the NMC is 'better equipped to manipulate armies' ". Since Perlmutter acknowledges that his attack on the first and major point regarding NMC regimes in power depends on the second, let us look at the second point first.

He quotes me as saying that the NMC is "better equipped to manipulate armies". In my original text, that phrase is much longer and also very different in meaning. Originally it read exactly as Perlmutter copied it out in an earlier paragraph of his: "*prior to its seizure of power, it is* freer than any other class from traditional bonds and preconceptions and *better equipped to manipulate armies* and voluntary organizations as *revolutionary instruments*". I have now italicized additional parts of the proposition, not merely the portion Perlmutter tore out of context. This passage refers explicitly to the period prior to the seizure of power, and not afterwards, as Perlmutter supposes. It is not enough for a critic to copy a quotation in full. He must also read and remember that quotation until he writes his own paragraph. Had he read carefully for another two pages in my text, he could have found as well what I think happens *after* the new middle class comes into power:

What, then, determines . . . choices on the part of the new middle class? The factors that readily come to mind—the burden of the past, available skills and resources and the awareness and opportunities to utilize them, differences in individual character and temperament, the force of ideas and the exigencies of particular local power constellations—are all relevant and important. An elite in power, whatever the social class from which it springs, faces problems and temptations in the very business of maintaining itself in power which will often distinguish it from those who have the same hopes and interests but not the same responsibilities. Membership in a particular social class is by no means the sole determinant of policy decisions. Differences in political choices among members of the new middle class, however, also reflect differences among the strata of that class and the variant character of its class consciousness. Such differences are real enough, but they usually become politically important only after the new middle class has achieved power. Earlier, all its members normally concentrate on the battle for power, mobility, and status in order to open up the controlling positions in society and administration. Soon after the triumph of the new middle class, however, it becomes apparent that there is simply not room for all of them—that some will be "in" and most will be "out". It also becomes clear that, although they are agreed on the need for the transformation of their society, they are not of the same mind as to what to do with their historical opportunity.[6]

When Perlmutter states that "in other words, in the absence of a cohesive new middle class, its most powerful instrument—the army—becomes the New Middle Class", these are, in truth, other words and they are exclusively Perlmutter's. The Perlmutter sentence just quoted, moreover, bears a footnote in Perlmutter's text referring to page 274 of my book. Where was Perlmutter when he read that page? Towards the top, he must have seen the statement that "the army's monopoly of force also is no longer as efficacious as it was in the Islamic past when, subject only to the challenge of superior arms, it could dominate a stable social system. Force today cannot, by itself, hope to remold the relationships of individuals and social classes, once thought natural and God-given, into a new balance capable of motion". Next follows a sub-heading which reads "The Army as a Partisan in Conflicts Within the New Middle Class and with Other Classes". Then I said:

Among all the limitations of army regimes, there is one that is far-reaching and that cannot be transcended. The army in politics cannot become an institution above the battle.... It is itself a most sensitive mirror of internal conflicts within the new middle class, reflecting the fissures of partisanship and ideology that differences in age group, education, and opportunity can create. It will be unable to avoid factionalism within the ruling junta unless the whole junta, or its dominant faction, is securely anchored in a well-organized movement representing at least the new middle class.... Forceful efficiency alone can produce only a temporary stability which is soon destroyed by the continuing pressures of uncontrolled social change. By itself, military rule can be no substitute for the art of politics.

It is thus the reverse of truth that, "according to Halpern, ... the NMC's success in marshalling mass support depends on the army as its most powerful instrument". (Page 258, which Perlmutter cites in the instance, does not contain a single word directly or indirectly dealing with "marshalling mass support".) However, had he turned to pages 281-4, he would have read what it may take to marshall mass support:

There is no substitute yet devised for political parties as agents of modernization—i.e., in creating and maintaining a new political culture....[7] Only a party can be in daily contact with the constituency, teach, propagandize, or put pressure upon that constituency to adopt new ideas and patterns of action. Only a party can stimulate involvement in campaigns for literacy and higher production no less than particular political issues, and gather new talents and thus regularize recruitment into the new elite.... A political party offers an opportunity for binding together four forces which can ... create a viable political culture: charisma, ideology, organization, and accountability to an increasingly larger constituency.

Regarding Egypt in particular, I add on page 312 that "Nasser's repeated efforts [to overcome his failures to create a political party] thus amply demonstrate that a charismatic leader committed to rapid modernization cannot avoid trying to solve the problems of political organization, ideology, and accountability".

I must finally return to Perlmutter's principal attack—namely on my hypothesis that the new middle class is "more

obviously cohesive . . . than any other class". I actually think
so. But it is a relative statement. It must be read as
Perlmutter quoted it, rather than as he used it: it must be
read as Point 4 of a total of six reasons why the new middle
class "has been able to act as a separate and independent
force", namely fourth, because "it is, so far, more obviously
cohesive, more self-conscious, and better trained than any
other class. . . ." This statement is introduced by a passage
which recalls important conclusions derived from three other
chapters entitled respectively "Kings, Landlords and the
Traditional Bourgeoisie: The Declining Elite", "Peasants:
The Silent Majority at the Threshold of Politics", and
"Workers: The Growing Tide of the Unskilled and Unemployed". This introductory passage on the new middle class
reads: "Unlike the traditional elite of landowners and trading
bourgeoisie or the tradition-bound artisans or peasants, it is thus
the first class in the Middle East that is wholly the product of
the transition to the modern age. Unlike the emergent new
generation of peasants and urban workers, it is already powerful
and self-conscious enough to undertake the task of remolding
society".[8] In context of comparison with other classes, I continue
to hold that the new middle class is more obviously cohesive,
more self-conscious and better trained than any other Middle
Eastern class. And even Perlmutter admits "that they are
modernizers is a fact", and that among them, "Nasser's
program of modernization is intended not to aggrandise
personal rule [in contrast to Muhammad 'Ali's 'modernization'] but to help Egyptians and Arabs".

However, Perlmutter would like to call attention above all
to growing incoherence within the new middle class, and he is
right to do so. "In fact", Perlmutter writes, "Halpern sees the
problem of internal conflict but he does not use it as the key
to his analysis". Here Perlmutter forgets the key argument of
the book, for when he writes of it, he represents it in its
opposite form. He says that "the weakness of Halpern's
concept of the NMC is that it assumes a static explanation",
i.e., in terms of variables belonging to the same time period,
and just as statically, "Halpern is not willing to forecast the
next steps in the Arab world or in Egypt". Perlmutter has
missed the main purpose and content of the book.

The Politics of Social Change in the Middle East and North Africa begins by announcing that "from incomplete knowledge of present forces and trends, it projects probable estimates of the future". Thereafter, it focuses on conflict and disintegration. Thus most pages of the chapter on the new middle class are devoted to its inner conflicts and likely transformations. The six chapters on ideology are devoted to the different ideologies different segments of the salaried middle class may choose. Hence my conclusion that "if time passes without sufficient help, the non-totalitarian leaders in the Middle East are almost certain to find their task beyond their strength".[9]

II. NEW EXPLANATIONS FOR
INADEQUATE HISTORICAL PERFORMANCE

Perlmutter has in the present instance disappointed us three times over: By not reading my book well, he destroyed a myth he needlessly invented. By reading other books closely, he presented us with a picture of Egypt's past that was not new. That, at least, might have proved a useful introduction to a new interpretation of the travail of the present salaried middle class in modernizing the Middle East. But Perlmutter had no such plans.

It would be a pity to let matters rest here. May I outline a few suggestions for going beyond my analysis of 1963 for explaining why the new middle class has performed inadequately so far in modernizing the Middle East?

Perlmutter's review of the relationship between Egyptian bureaucracy and government between 1805 and 1919 still carries a contemporary ring. Has nothing changed? How can we make useful comparisons between different forms of collaboration and conflict that affect continuity and change in relationships? How can we compare the costs and benefits of intended and unintended transformation from one such form of conflict and collaboration to another? In a work now moving toward completion, *The Dialectics of Modernization in National and International Society*, I speak of the encounter of individuals and groups in conflict and collaboration as polarities. A polarity is a relationship among concrete individuals and groups so conceptualized that any interaction may be analysed simultaneously in terms of how the *type* of *conflict-and-collaboration* manifested is likely to affect the *continuity* of that type of dialectical encounter. Eight types of polarities would appear to be sufficient to analyse at this level of abstraction and for the sake of the italicized and connected set of problems all dialectical encounters among individuals and groups in all history and any society, and thus set the stage for systematizing contrasts and comparisons.

For the present discussion, I need only mention a few of these polarities, and in simplified form. Let us begin by conceptualizing in this manner the fact that relationships among many Arab bureaucrats today still reflect a mode visible a century, indeed a millennium ago, i.e., a mode characteristic of the Polarity of Direct Bargaining. Each individual occupying a pole in this type of dialectical encounter in Islamic society persistently demands submission of the other but, since both cannot achieve submission and one is likely to be unequal in power to the other, a bargain is struck over the terms of this submission. This bargain is subject to change at any moment—as soon as the balance of power changes or can be made to change. It is a style of collaboration and conflict that encourages unstable assertiveness no less than unstable dependence, and the impulsive quest for high, short-term gain. Consonant with this type of behavior, bureaucrats cannot afford to consult each other freely, change their minds openly in the presence of colleagues, or place urgent problems above status. Planning today thus turns into casuistically fixed formulas rather than a problem-solving process. Vulnerability to demands for submission, or at least diminished rewards for submission, remains the dominant threat in all encounters.

No enduring collaboration among citizens for a common public purpose can be built upon this type of relationship. No army fielded by a society based predominantly upon traditional manifestations of the polarity of Direct Bargaining is likely to win against a modern foe. Regardless of spurts in economic growth or feats of political power, the elite drawn from the salaried new middle class has not yet overcome its greatest burden—human relations throughout Arab society, including portions of its own class, based upon this polarity. Until this polarity has also been transformed, the salaried middle class will not be able to persist in modernizing any other aspects of society.

Is the new salaried middle class at all different as a class in terms of its polarities? Especially in Tunisia, also in Egypt, and occasionally in Iraq, a portion of the salaried new middle class has moved a fundamental step beyond the unconscious acceptance of the Polarity of Direct Bargaining. It has consciously and deliberately utilized this type of relationship for the sake of beginning the transformation of society. The new elite has continued to make demands for submission, but now for actions novel in substance: in return for accepting the discipline of our new political party, you will get priority in jobs. Such demands are accepted as long as they retain the familiar mode of this polarity—i.e., if they are specific and not total, focus on behavior and not spirit, and are subject to concrete and flexible bargaining. The dangers in this instrumental use of the Polarity of Direct Bargaining are obvious. The initial ease of producing change may lead to the illusion that modifying behavior is enough and that it is not necessary to transform the very modes which have hitherto governed Muslim capacity to deal with continuity and change, collaboration and conflict. Yet stopping short of such transformation threatens the very gains already achieved. For as long as the intrinsically unstable relationships of the Polarity of Direct Bargaining persists, *both* sides remain free to change or resist changes in the balance of power[10]

In the face of such behavior, Perlmutter suggests that "the politics of modernization needs both structural and functional differentiation and competition". In terms of the theoretical framework I have sketched here, I submit that this proposal, though supported by the mainstream of Western social science, is in large part a culture-bound answer. It confuses "Westernization" with "modernization". The dominant polarity of the modern West so far has been the Polarity of Boundary-Management, in which the occupant of each pole has been able to claim an autonomous zone of jurisdiction, based upon grounds of revelation, morality, law, politics, or competence. Conflict is limited to struggles designed to shift the boundary of jurisdiction between two poles. Occupants of polar positions must not try to affect each other's behavior directly (in contrast to the Polarity of Direct Bargaining), but only indirectly through pressure on boundaries.[11]

Modern Western bureaucracies, both civil and military, and in both private and public institutions, plainly exemplify this type of relationship. It need hardly be demonstrated by now that such relationships are characterized by unusual kinds of rationality, freedom, efficiency, legality, uniformity, and productivity. The extraordinary achievements of the modern West in peace and war thanks to the capacity inherent in this type of relationship have led many in the West and beyond, politicians and scholars alike, to believe that differentiation and co-ordination are the main secrets of social and political modernization. However, the changes of Europe in the modern age have often been marked by violent politics at home and abroad because the autonomy and stability characteristic of the rational and legal manifestations of the Polarity of Boundary-Management can only be achieved if polar occupants are in fact prepared to defend boundaries. Hence the advantages of the modern West have often been paid for by strongly articulated institutionalization designed and armed to oppose at least initially any shift in boundaries, and bar any new group from gaining autonomous possession of a polar position. Since the organization of violence, like all other public activities, tends to be far better co-ordinated under the Polarity of Boundary-Management than under any other polarity, the costs of living with such forms of violence also tend to lead frequently to crises producing expansive aggressiveness against another growing or weakening group, or repression based on rationalized inflexibility or intolerance or the kind of co-ordinated differentiation that allowed the Nazis to be efficiently evil.

Surely we have already begun to recognize that conscious, deliberate, and persistent transformation has no place within the Polarity of Boundary-Management.[12] In the West and elsewhere, that type of creativity has been generated and sustained through quite a different type of relationship, i.e., the Polarity of Transformation. Most of *The Dialectics of*

Modernization in National and International Society is devoted to an analysis of the capacity required in that type of relationship. Perhaps it suffices to say here that this capacity is reflected, for example, in sustained efforts to transform peasants bound to family, faction, landlord, and habit into farmers fully participating in society's modernization. That capacity may also be reflected in party leaders prepared to persist in transforming ideologies (viewed here as explicit political frameworks of means and ends capable of inspiring action) as social theory and social reality change.

It is much to the credit of the salaried new middle class that already, in parts of the Middle East, it has been able to transform part of its bureaucratic apparatus from relationships manifesting the unstable Polarity of Direct Bargaining into relationships manifesting the more stable and productive Polarity of Boundary-Management. That type of polarity had never been manifested in traditional Islam. No previous class in Middle Eastern history perceived such a transformation to be in its interests. As several writers quoted by Perlmutter have pointed out, however, Egypt has in fact already gone too far. It has in many areas of life substituted administration (in the style of Boundary-Management) for politics, reserving by far the largest claims of jurisdiction to the pole occupied by the government. But I do not think that the answer lies where Perlmutter suggests—in "diffused" and "competitive" politics. Under present circumstances, that can only mean initially a return to the still dominant Polarity of Direct Bargaining. Since action in that mode, as we have seen, cannot cope with the kind of changes set in motion in the modern age, such a return would soon lead to incoherence, i.e., the absence of polarity on any ground, and hence the absence of capacity to deal with continuity or change. Yet this kind of anarchy is a likely outcome, since men who differ fundamentally on whether or how to modernize cannot persist in the Polarity of Direct Bargaining or any other form of tension-management, for they will not even be able to agree on how to disagree. Since I hold that modernization requires an enduring capacity to generate and absorb persistent transformation, I conclude that political relations relevant to modernization must manifest this same capacity.[13]

Perhaps proportionately as many members of the salaried middle class in the Middle East have recognized the need for such a new capacity as have members of the same class in the United States, the U.S.S.R., or Germany—i.e., rather few. No country in the world is any longer exempt from attaining this new capacity, or else of reaping the consequences of unintended and incoherent change. In the Middle East, the leaders of the new salaried middle class have done far more for their people than their predecessors. They have ended some forms of misery and exploitation. They have begun deliberately and creatively to transform a few relationships —and succeeded in fashioning new kinds of polarity between a few men and women, between a few fathers and sons, between a few teachers and students, a few officials and other officials, a few leaders and followers, a few citizens and others—but not yet between most men. Incoherent change, therefore, remains more powerful in shaping the history of the Middle East than deliberate generation and absorption of change.

Once again I have ended my analysis on a somber, and perhaps even pessimistic, note. But if one truly relates analytical categories to changes in history and society, it is not enough to observe the seeming survival of traditional authority, the limits of charisma, or the virtues of rational-legal authority. I would propose categories of tension-management or polarities, in which the costs and benefits of such relationships change as the problems of tradition yield to the problems of modernization or else modern incoherence. Thus the question does not merely become "interest-aggregation" but aggregation or else transformation of interests for the sake of tension-management in society relevant to fundamental problems of historical change. Perhaps this brief sketch suggests the potential of a new framework for linking the historical actions of social classes to all human relationships involving continuity and change, collaboration and conflict, and justice.

NOTES

1. The conservative scholarly position, however, was also being reiterated during this period. First in a series of lectures as Visiting Professor of Sociology of the Middle East at the University of California at Los Angeles in 1961-62, and subsequently in a book published in 1965, Professor C.A.O. van Nieuwenhuijze challenged the various newer interpretations presented by Morroe Berger and H. al-Sa'aty as "premature". "Clearly important changes are taking place. But as yet, they do not add up to a development in the sense that one could already distinguish [the makings of] a middle class as part of an encompassing stratification pattern in a fundamentally integrative rather than composite society." Instead van Nieuwenhuijze believes that each of the various "effendi" categories, among them officials, officers, educators, and engineers, will "for quite some time to come" be rated somewhere in the middle brackets of a vague, flexible, variable social scale that eludes description insofar as its overall consistency would be concerned. . . . It may thus be wise to count with the possibility that, notwithstanding some important changes in sectors of society that would reflect in the rating of categories, the traditional structure of ruling elite plus broad masses, enriched with some in-between entities of secondary nature, would persist." (C.A.O. van Nieuwenhuijze, *Social Stratification and the Middle East*, Leiden, E.J. Brill, 1965, pp. 27, 25, and 78.)

2. *The Politics of Social Change in the Middle East and North Africa*, pp. 62-3; 66-7, note 21; p. 54, note 4.

3. *Ibid.*, p. 55, note 4.

4. *Ibid.*, p. 51.

5. *Ibid.*, p. 56; see also p. 59, note 10.

6. *Ibid.*, pp. 61-2.

7. I have more recently turned to a different and I think better conception of "modernization" which is explored in the second part of this essay. In terms of creating a modernizing political culture, however, the original statement remains adequate.

8. *Op. cit.*, p. 59. Developments in Turkey and Iran since 1963 suggest that the propertied middle class is growing in economic, social and political importance more so than elsewhere in the Islamic Middle East but without utilizing its power deliberately to overcome the growing incoherences in these societies.

9. *Ibid.*, p. 364.

10. In *The Dialectics of Modernization in National and International Society*, I also speak of the advantages and disadvantages of utilizing several other polarities once unconsciously employed in Islam as instruments for the genesis of modernization. For example, in the Polarity of Emanation (to simplify the point), one individual relates to the other as an

extension of the other's personality. In the pre-modern era, the Polarity of Emanation was manifested frequently in crises which, if endemic, were also discontinuous and familiar, and required the transformation of a few and not the persistent transformation of the many. Now Emanation is intended to embody and produce both unity in permanent crisis and also the new and changing model of modernizing man. To persist in the deliberate transformation of men now in the throes of varying and largely unintended forces of change through covert manipulation, and emergent or routinized charisma has proved a much harder task. Though Muslims are still tempted to rely upon particular leading persons, modernization is a transformation of society that requires the sustained commitment of at least one social class.

11. The Polarity of Boundary-Management is also manifested by behavior in several pre-modern and non-Western societies, for example, among peasants in Thailand. While I confine the present discussion to specific manifestations of that polarity in the modern West, my argument that these are insufficient for modernization may be generalized to apply to any behavioral manifestation of the Polarity of Boundary-Management anywhere and at any time.

12. For a brilliant and detailed demonstration of the contrasts between styles of relationship abstracted in the present paper as Boundary-Management and Transformation, see Michel Crozier, *The Bureaucratic Phenomenon*, Chicago, 1964.

13. In *The Dialectics of Modernization*, I have attempted to clarify the crucial components of freedom and participation required for persistent transformation. Here I mean to clarify only the unintended results of applying conventional ideals of 'competition' to the contemporary Middle East.

CHAPTER 5

The Myth of the Myth

By Amos Perlmutter

In his rejoinder to my essay, "Egypt and the Myth of the New Middle Class", Professor Halpern clings to a limited and dysfunctional concept. The concept of NMC was of limited use in 1963 when he wrote *The Politics of Social Change in the Middle East and North Africa;* since then, it has proved to be a misleading tool for explaining the politics of change in the Middle East, yet he persists in reaffirming it. For seven years, Professor Halpern has been arguing the same tautologies. On the one hand he proposes a theory of a new middle class; on the other, he explains why the NMC still has not evolved. The NMC concept is so fundamental to his book that I, for one, have examined it closely—and have found its validity and usefulness limited. Halpern writes of the need for a new theory of the relationship between social classes and system-transforming change in the modern age, but he offers no good descriptive and analytical data to support his thesis. In fact, as we shall demonstrate later, his thesis is shaken by a confrontation with rigorous empirical and correlative analyses. A cursory review of recent literature shows us many recantations by authors who once applied Grand Theories to Comparative Politics.[1] In the spirit of the era post-Committee for Comparative Politics-neo-scholasticism, I have consented to write a rejoinder. Let me state at the beginning that I will refrain from comments on Halpern's new vintage, "The

Dialectics of Modernization in National and International Society", although in his rejoinder he insists that the NMC has been reaffirmed and reappraised in his "Dialectics". This would require more than a rejoinder. In order to review or refute Halpern's new work, I would need to write a new article, and scarcity of time does not allow me this luxury.

Also, I would like to avoid a rejoinder *ad hominem* for my differences with Halpern are methodologically, conceptually, and intellectually profound.

Halpern's *The Politics* attempts to prove that the new middle class is a new and revolutionary approach to analysis of the politics of social change in the Middle East and North Africa. While I agree that the better part of the book is the part which is not affected by the New Middle Class concept, Halpern holds that the NMC is of critical importance. Therefore, I have chosen not to challenge the non-theoretical part of *The Politics*. I believe that the new middle class does not offer a revolutionary approach, and, if this is true, then the rest of the book is of considerable importance. In Halpern's own words, he first demonstrates the "ifs" of the new middle class and then talks about its expectations, political and otherwise. Finally he proclaims but does not demonstrate why this new middle class may not be forthcoming. I hope to demonstrate why this new middle class *could* not be forthcoming, and if supposedly it was, certainly it would not fulfill the role assigned by some social scientists.

I

The major challenge to Professor Halpern's fundamental assumptions and expectations is precisely the potentiality of the New Middle Class. Professor Halpern develops what he considers to be a revolutionary hypothesis. Hence he must explain why and how these classes are potentially more successful than other classes.

The major dispute between Professor Halpern and myself is whether the concept of the new middle class is a feasible *focus* for explaining the creation of political order and stability in the Middle East and North Africa. Professor Halpern wonders why I do not offer a class theory of my own or a concept which is tantamount to the New Middle Class concept. He, himself, does not offer a class theory. In a 420-page book and in a chapter of some 30 pages on the New Middle Class, Halpern defines "class" in only one footnote (*The Politics*, pp. 54-5). While he elaborates on the differences between middle sectors and the new middle class, etc., and tells us why he thinks that traditional and economic theories of class are not useful, all that he actually says about classes is this (*The Politics*, p. 55, footnote 4):

> Once the term "class" is freed from its ideological strait jackets and defined dynamically in terms of the evolving interest, opportunities, and behavior of a class in the midst of the transformation of a *society*, and not merely of its *economy*, "class" may well continue to serve us as the most useful category for relating changes in social structure to changes in political power [author's italics].

Halpern defines the New Middle Class *only* in contrast to the so-called "old middle class". He tells us that the difference between the new middle class and the old middle class is that the former does not defend property and order but creates them and that the former has a revolutionary task while the latter does not consider it so (*The Politics*, p. 52). Halpern is telling us not which class but *which* group in the middle class will bring about *orderly* social change in the Middle East and North Africa. This is not a theory on class but an arbitrary deduction that some segments of the middle class are new. The new middle class are extracted from the "old" middle class to serve as expected pillars of stability and progress. I have offered ample examples to demonstrate that not only is the New Middle Class not the creator of order but it is itself unstable and capable of causing more disorder. When the New Middle Class is equated with the military, the chances for praetorianism and political decay are only enhanced by the rise of the NMC.[2] According to Professor Berger, who must have inspired Halpern's New Middle Class concept (no guilt by implication) (*The Politics*, p. 54, footnote 3), the middle class of the Arab world is composed of two groups:[3] (1) those merchants and small, self-employed manufacturers whose income and influence are not great enough to place them among the really powerful men in political and economic circles; (2) a more mixed group, including independent professionals such as doctors and lawyers, employed managers, technicians, and administrative workers such as clerks, bureau chiefs, and civil servants.

Berger's second group, especially the latter occupations, are Halpern's "new middle class". In other words, the NMC includes *certain* occupational groups within Berger's broad but adequate definition of the middle class in the Arab East (*The Politics*, p. 54, footnote 3).

This brings us back to the fundamental problem of defining class. Class obviously is related to social stratification. What is a stratification system? How can we relate the new middle class to such a concept? After all, what we challenge are the uses and abuses of class theory. We cannot escape a categorical definition of class as a value stratum holding a common position along some continuum in the economy. In other words the scale of stratification goes along the continuum of a system of stratification which *essentially* is an expression of the value system of that society. Any stratification system gives names to classes which fall into this relatively uniform pattern. Are the different strata of the New Middle Class uniform, relational, and continuous? One could say that the "old" and the "new" middle classes are interested in status, order, security, prosperity, and property. In the case of the NMC are the values of its strata uniform and continuous? The scale of stratification must follow the continuum of order in both the old and the new middle class. Halpern's concern with the New Middle Class if not identified with economics (or occupations) must identify with something else. Thus what is "new" about this class is its capacity to create political order. This is the crux of the concept of the New Middle Class. Nowhere has Halpern convinced us that the New Middle Class has created a new order. In fact, the new middle class has only succeeded, so far, in undermining the old one—or, really, not even in undermining it, but in toppling the old order in the last stages of its decay. It has established no alternative, stable, *existing*, visible, or even hypothetical new order in Egypt, elsewhere in the Middle East, and North Africa.

The fundamental question is which strata belong to the new middle class and which are excluded. If we argue again that one cannot escape a definition of class as the holding of common positions along an economic continuum or along another continuum, such as modernization, change or new order, it becomes rather difficult to decide which strata belong to the new middle class or, for that matter, to any other "new" class. For here we do not have the uniform and relational continuity between the strata which marks a class. If we pursue a classical definition of class, for instance Marx's economic definition or Weber's status one, we must still *cluster* the strata along a certain continuum. If the continuum is as amorphous as "expectations for modernization", and strata are defined as belonging by virtue of their common ideas, actions, and careers, one would suggest that Johnson's middle sectors, or Berger's middle class, however unfortunate, fit the new middle class better than does Halpern's own definition. After all, a class must operate as a class, however uncohesive and weak its composite strata may be, as long as its major strata lead. The difference between mechanical stratification and class is the latter's uniformity along a clearly defined continuum. The different strata must collaborate, co-operate with one another in *certain* actions. If you take modernization as a continuum, then you are using an amorphous concept which has not yet been clearly defined anywhere in the literature—even in the diffuse and widely disparate literature on modernization.

We must ask the following questions: What is the style of the new middle class collaboration? And how do we measure collaboration and cohesion, especially along such a vague continuum as modernization? It seems likely that if common ideas or careers are important criteria of belonging to the new middle class, then a differential such as the distribution of prestige should precede class action. Then could we test the status increment of "belonging to modernization"? If a characteristic of the New Middle Class is its adherence to modernization and order, what guarantees the NMC's cohesiveness more than "belonging to the modernization class"? In fact, adherence to modernization and order (as we shall demonstrate later) is the *chief* obstacle to the development of the NMC, which has been freed from the "old middle class" and its institutions, as a revolutionary group.

The relationship between the new middle class strata is only another *type* of elite circulation within the old middle class, not a *new* class. Halpern chose to focus on some strata of the middle class as potential elements to shoulder the burden of change and stability. The fact is that they have not fulfilled either proposition.

What Halpern is talking about is no more than a typology of elite circulation, a concept which is not capable of predicting which elite will rule now and which one will rule later. Could the theory of the new middle class explain, for instance, what type of palatial, governmental, and institutional combinations Nasser will prefer after his disastrous defeat of 1967 (or explain the type of combination that existed previously)? Will Nasser make an alliance with the army against the Arab Socialist Union? Will he make an alliance with the Arab Socialists against the army? Will he make an alliance with the army, the Arab Socialist Union functionaries, and the students? Will he encourage rivalry among all these groups to enhance his power? Will he encourage the kind of palatial intrigue and counter-intrigue on which the Egyptian regime has thrived from 1952 to 1968? Or will he choose a new type of social revolution which will involve the masses and will no longer depend upon the so-called "representatives" of workers and peasants, who are only the functionaries of the Arab Socialist Union? Does Nasser, the most prominent representative of the NMC, differ politically from the old middle class in his views of the peasants, the unskilled workers, the bureaucracy, and the intellectuals?

The new middle class is not new in the literature. Professors Lederer and Marschak [4] developed the new middle class, or the *Neuer Mittelstand*, in 1926 and stirred social scientists to a formidable debate. According to Lederer-Marschak *Neuer Mittelstand*, Professor Dahrendorf finds that the new middle class is an *occupational salad* of salaried employees, from post office clerks to senior executives. He concludes that the new middle class has stubbornly resisted all attempts to define its upper and lower limits.[5] The NMC is not an independent class, its strata are part of the middle class. The broad definitions of Berger and Johnson are most suitable for explaining the political behavior of the middle class. Why create an *artificial* class from several disparate strata of the middle class? If the middle classes in the Middle East were broad and variegated—i.e., if over 20 per cent of the male labor force were employed in commerce, banking, finance, technical, administrative, and clerical work—then it would be meaningful for us to stratify it into other than occupational groups. The confusion grows when we ask if the NMC is a ruling class or a working class.

After all, if we cannot define the upper and lower limits of the new middle class, then how do we know what group we are talking about? Are we talking about a ruling class? Then we could describe it in terms of salary, status, and position *vis-à-vis* modernization, in the expectation that a new order would legitimize this class in power. Or are we talking about a group which we could call a working class, a group whose concern and interest is purely economic?[6] Obviously, without an economic continuum of class, the New Middle Class is a mishmash. In fact the only way to identify this class, if it exists at all, is on an economic-status basis.

It is true that, in terms of prestige and income, many salaried employees occupy a position somewhere between the very wealthy and the very poor, somewhere in the middle of the scale of social stratification. But in a situation of conflict—whether conflict is defined in Marxian or other terms—this kind of intermediate position does not exist, or at least, exists only as a non-participatory one. Professor Dahrendorf quotes Michel Crozier:[7]

> The situation of the salaried employee is one that makes possible an identification with the world of the ruling class and promises considerable rewards if this succeeds. But at the same time it is a working-class situation and therefore suffers from most of those limitations to which all other workers are subjected—limited income as well as lack of autonomy and a position of subordination.

The members of Halpern's new middle class (supposedly defined by its ideas, actions, and careers *vis-à-vis* modernization) are really Lederer-Marschak-Crozier and Dahrendorf's middle echelon bureaucrats. Halpern dismisses an economic definition of class in favor of one based on class as order-maker. If we can discern and *demonstrate* the *fulfillment* of New Middle Class *expectations*, then we may have a criterion to distinguish "old" from "new" middle classes. But Halpern's argument fails on precisely this point, and it is here that we have challenged his assumptions and argued that the new class is useless as an explanation of the politics of change in the Middle East or elsewhere. Those strata which belong to the new middle class are nothing but new elites clustered around modernization and probably created by modernization. *They have not cut themselves off from their middle-class origins or expectations.*

Thus, the theory of the new middle class does not explain social change. At best, it can only explain patterns of conflict over *political power* within the strata of the middle class.

The most feasible way to use information on improvements in power status is to analyse the effects of these improvements on economic and occupational positions and political orientations. In other words, role *relationships* are the fundamental criteria by which one assigns a particular stratum to a particular class (if one forges an economic explanation of class). The concept of role could be more useful in explaining change in developing countries than a rather vague concept of a new middle class.

Dahrendorf writes:[8]

> The decomposition of labor and capital has been the result of social developments that have occurred since Marx, but the "new middle class" was born *decomposed* [italics mine]. It neither has been nor is it ever likely to be a class in any sense of this term. But while there is no "new middle class", there are, of course, white collar workers and bureaucrats, and the growth of these groups is one of the striking features of historical development in the past century. What is their effect on class structure and class conflict, if it is not that of adding a new class to the older ones Marx described? It follows from our analysis that the emergence of salaried employees means in the first place an extension of the older classes of bourgeoisie and proletariat. The bureaucrats add to the bourgeoisie, as the white collar workers add to the proletariat.

If we accept Professor Dahrendorf's description, then, of

course, we find Halpern's book useful. For after all, Halpern has explained throughout his book that salaried employees emerged as an extension of the older classes of bourgeoisie and skilled proletariats. And if one accepts an explanation of class which is neither Marxist, economic, or sociological, one might choose Dahrendorf's explanation. For all intents and purposes, the salariat is not a new breed of the old bourgeoisie but another extension of this class; probably it suffers from the weaknesses of its predecessor.

II

Again we challenge Halpern's two basic propositions on the military and the NMC: (1) the military is the most cohesive stratum of the NMC, and the NMC is "at least" represented by the army when the army is "securely anchored in a well-organized movement", and (2) the NMC's success in marshalling mass support depends on the army, as its most powerful instrument. The military plays an extraordinary role as the consolidator of the NMC because "[it has] served as national standard-bearer when others who claimed that role proved irresponsible and ineffective".

Halpern's expectations of the order-making capacity of the army could not have been higher. Is the army not an instrument above battle? Halpern says that the army intervenes as a partisan group, representing a new class, with whom the majority in the country does not yet share a common consciousness (*The Politics,* p. 274). "As the army officers corps came to represent the interests and views of the new middle class, it became the most powerful instrument of that class" (*ibid.,* p. 258). This is a categorical statement. Indeed, is it not possible (as we shall demonstrate later) that the army will be unable to serve as an "organized movement", that the army is divided and incohesive? Examples are abundant. Where, except in the Kemalist revolution, has the army acted as "an organized movement"? Where else in the Middle East have they *responded* to the political demands so clearly enunciated in their *pronunciamientos?*

In an unpublished paper, "Governmental Structures and

Responsiveness to Popular Aspirations: Some Notes, Hypotheses and Cross-National Data" (C.F.I.A., Harvard University, January 1969), Professor Eric Nordlinger tests his hypotheses (one is on the military responsiveness to modernization) with data on governmental performance: "Performance viewed as government's level of accomplishments, its ability to fulfil its desired and desirable requirements" (Nordlinger, p. 2).

In his analysis of Cross-National Data, Nordlinger has provided us with most persuasive results demonstrating that the officers' middle-class identities *detract* from their governmental responsiveness: "Thus by birth and achievement they have learned to place a high value on the preservation and development of the economic and political requisites of their class; they are far less responsive to the aspirations of lower classes and quite unresponsive to peasant and working-class aspirations" (*ibid.*, pp. 56-7). On the surface, this hypothesis would seem to apply only to Latin America where there are fairly large middle classes.

Next, Nordlinger correlates political strength and military and economic output with the size of the middle class. He has chosen to correlate Adelman-Morris' indicator (*Society, Politics and Economic Development*, Johns Hopkins, 1967) "the importance of the indigenous middle class" with the indicator "the political strength of the military". To establish the first indicator, Adelman-Morris grouped 74 countries according to the proportion of active male population in commerce, banking, insurance or in technical, professional, managerial or administrative and clerical employment (Adelman, p. 31). At the same time they stratified those countries in which at least 20 per cent of the active male population was employed in these areas, those in which 10-19 per cent were so employed, and those where less than 10 per cent were so employed (*ibid.*, p. 95). The second indicator, "the political strength of the military", according to Adelman-Morris, is stratified in the following way: countries in which the military was in direct political control during some part of the period 1957-62; those in which the military was in direct control during the entire period; and those in which the military controlled the government during only one to two years of the period.

Next Nordlinger set himself to "control" the first indicator by stratifying the size of the indigenous middle class. He then discovered that there was *no* significant relation between the political strength of the military and economic outputs and in some cases the relationship was even negative; this is the case when the middle class is relatively large and/or middle size (see Table 1).

When the politically influential military is correlated with economic outputs in these different socio-economic contexts we find that the military are not likely to provide for economic outputs when there is a sizable or even a medium-sized middle class. Apparently once such a middle class (between 10 and 19 per cent of the active male population)

TABLE 1*

The Political Strength of the Military and Economic Outputs
According to Size of the Middle Class

	Rate GNP	*Change industrialization*	*Change agricultural productivity*	*Expansion education*
Relatively large middle class (N = 12)	–.17	.5	–.12	.12
Medium-sized middle class (N = 26)	–.06	.17	.04	–.18
Minuscule middle class (N = 36)	.34	.44	.17	.34
	Tax level	*Change tax level*	*Investment level*	*Change finance*
Relatively large middle class	–.15	.01	.19	–.18
Medium-sized middle class	–.25	–.07	–.48	.23
Minuscule middle class	.35	.09	.07	.35
	Change infrastructure	*Leader's commitment*		
Relatively large middle class	.22	.17		
Medium-sized middle class	.12	–.02		
Minuscule middle class	.02	–.04		

* Nordlinger, p. 96.

emerges, the officers in mufti are likely to conserve its perquisites against present and future challenges and aspirations from below. *Only when the middle class is practically negligible do the military in politics provide some measure of fulfillment for economic aspirations.* Among these countries the military's political strength is significantly correlated with growth in GNP (.34), with industrialization (.44), and with expansion of education (.34).

> At this stage of the process of economic development there is a confluence of interests between the middle class officers and both middle class and lower class citizens. But even here the officers are not committed to economic development in any sustained manner given the correlation of $-.04$ between the military in politics and leadership commitment to economic development. Which would imply that what economic change does take place here is largely due to the officers' provision of a suitable political context for it to take place rather than their engaging in strenuous developmental efforts themselves (*ibid.*, p. 57).

Based on Nordlinger's hypothesis that the military act in accordance with their class interests we can demonstrate that *military interference in politics hinders governmental responsiveness.*

Thus we can tentatively conclude from the Adelman-Morris and Nordlinger cross-national aggregate data analyses and correlations that only among countries with the lowest level of demands and the smallest middle class does the military contribute to economic change (*ibid.*, p. 99).

The claim that "In the Middle East, the salaried new middle class . . . uses its power not to defend order and property but to create them . . ." (*The Politics*, p. 52) is supported by *no* empirical evidence, no analytical or statistical data; it has no social, political, or intellectual basis. In view of imposing empirical and analytical data, a "hard-headed" social scientist becomes a minority of one defending NMC as "the first class for which the choice between democracy, authoritarianism, and totalitarianism is a real and *open* choice" (*ibid.*, p.67, italics mine).

Much has been made, written, and speculated in the burgeoning literature on the relationships between the military and the middle class. For instance, Professor Johnson considers the middle class in Latin America a buffer to praetorianism. José Nun argues the opposite, that the military coups and interventions are middle-class organized and inspired. Halpern considers the military in the Middle East a salariat, a new middle class, while Eliezer Beeri argues that they are representatives of the rural middle classes, or at best urban offshoots of the rural middle class. Nordlinger's correlations support Nun's theses.

I. L. Horowitz, following after Nun and Lisa North, agrees that "The military [in Latin America] simply failed to act as an autonomous or unified group. Oftentimes they act as agents of other social classes or powerful government alignments."[9] However, our researches into the Middle Eastern armies conclusively demonstrate the opposite. The military in Egypt, Syria, and Iraq since 1952 intervened as an *autonomous* political organization, representing the "nation" against "corruption". The officers were indifferent to class interests even if their origins were from the rural or urban middle classes.

The 1952 Nasser coup was planned, organized and executed by the army, in the army, for the army with little or *no* support from movements or classes, even if the officers were inspired by a variety of nationalist, religious fundamentalist, fascist and anti-foreign cliques, coteries, groups, parties and movements. The 1958 Qassem coup in Iraq was conceived, planned, organized and executed *exclusively* by the military with no outside support. The military coup makers were supported by the United National Front (the bloc of anti-Hashemite parties) but the latter's help was not crucial, essential, or even necessary for the success of the military coup.[10] In Syria we know of no coup that was conceived, organized and executed by *any* class or with its help. The three successful coups in 1949 were planned by the army's high command as was Adib Shishakly's coup (he was supported by civil servants and merchants but these were not crucial to his success or failure in 1954). The 1961 anti-U.A.R. coup was conceived, planned and executed in and by the army as were the 1963, 1966, and most recent 1969 coups. In none of these countries did the military represent the *interests* of the middle class old or "new" and it was no surrogate for the middle or any other class. (This may be true in a few Latin American countries,

Argentina, Chile, and Peru.) Military rule represents the military without executive or political responsibilities. In the Middle East it demonstrates the chaos of social structure and the decadence of politics, the most distinguished characteristics of praetorianism.

What I find quite enlightening here is Halpern's description of the original State Department analysis of political instability in the Near East, particularly the controversy between various authors on the Near East. Now I have always doubted the uses and abuses of social theories when they are explained and adopted by policy-makers. But it seems that, despite the rather vague compromise which resulted in *inventing* middle sectors in the Middle East, the State Department has chosen the *army* as the most important stratum to be supported in the Middle East. It also seems that policy-makers at the State Department, oblivious to social science, might have rejected Professor Halpern's class theory and accepted instead Professor Johnson's rather vague middle sectors. What is most significant about all this is that *one* stratum among these middle sectors—the army—was chosen as the instrument of future American policy in the Middle East. Whoever reads Professor Halpern's chapter on the role of the army among the new middle class will learn that, as a policy-maker, he should put all his eggs in that particular basket. If I had been a policy-maker too, I would have been baffled and would not have been able to choose any more "reliable" stratum of the NMC than the military.

The difficulty of communication between social theorists and policy-makers is a well-established fact. Some consultants to the Rand Corporation and the State Department have committed the social scientist's typical error. They have given advice without being able to follow up and modify their advice in the light of new events. Again, on carefully reading Halpern's *The Politics*, as a policy-maker I would have chosen the new middle class as my best bet and the army as the segment on which I must rely. In retrospect, a decade after the Halpern-Johnson paper, what could be a greater disaster than having followed their advice—relying on either the Syrian army, the Yemeni army, or the Egyptian army (the Argentinian or the Brazilian army), as the source of stability or "revolution" in the Middle East (and Latin America). At best, in the past fifteen years, these were elite circulations in an asymmetrical and non-synchronized way, interested in power and in modernization to buttress it. In Syria, Iraq, Yemen, and the Sudan military palace intrigues fomented upheavals, not stability.

This again is not *ad hominem*. We challenge several social scientists as policy-makers. Were their "theories", "constructs", "mobilization-reconciliation systems", "crises in political participation", "integrative revolutions", and "scientific efforts" schemes adapted to *Zeitgeist*? What is the relation between good theory and good policy?

These questions disturb us all. Reviewing the vintage of the period 1953-66, from Almond's *pronunciamiento* (1956) to the last volume of the SSRC Committee on Comparative Politics (1966), one asks: are we dealing with pioneer efforts of social science or with a new neo-scholasticism? Should we ask our students to read this literature in a serious quest for knowledge, to deal with the literature as a threshold, or should we remove the literature from the shelves to the cellars? Maybe there, after all, it will not turn to vinegar.

III

Professor Halpern inquires why my review of the relationship between Egyptian bureaucracy and government between 1805 and 1919 "carries a contemporary ring". In an attempt to expose the myth of the new middle class, I did not find it necessary to discuss the period 1919-52. This period, and especially the years since 1952, only further supports my refutation. The so-called expectations of the NMC become even more awry when we analyse events since 1919. I could not offer a supplementary essay, although I do that in my book on Egypt on the periods between 1919 to 1952 and 1952 to 1967. In particular, I argue that the relationships between Egyptian political structures and bureaucracy since 1919 only demonstrate more vividly the dilemma of the middle class. Actually, between 1805 and the time Halpern wrote his book, the middle class ("old" or "new") has not been given much of a chance. In a paper delivered at Harvard in March 1966,

Professor Safran analyses the period 1919-52 and demonstrates the thesis I have established elsewhere on the relationship between bureaucracy and the middle class in Egypt. It compounds my own pessimism and my suspicions of Professor Halpern's faith in the new middle class. In fact, Morroe Berger's book on Egyptian bureaucracy demonstrates quite clearly what I have demonstrated for the period 1805-1919 —that the burdens upon the middle class and its different strata and upon its theorists is heavy. The fact is that since 1919 the Egyptian bureaucracy and government have acted in the way Berger, Safran, and I have described it: true to its historical form, servile, pliable, and scheming. The hope that this polarity will be transformed so that the NMC can triumph is as utopian as an optimistic view of the "collaboration" (or better, fratricidity) demonstrated in a decade and a half in Egypt, Syria, and Iraq.

In short, Professor Halpern's persistent faith that the new middle class will be elevated when the polarity of direct opposition is transformed is extremely unfortunate. He only compounds a myth upon a myth, built upon the dialectics of the polarity of opposites and other cabalistic statements and propositions—so mystical that I refuse to deal with them here.

José Nun has written the epitaph of the Middle Class, "new" or "old", in developing polities, its ideology and its dilemma. What are the aspirations of the middle class?

> Economic development *and* monetary stability; state protection *and* non-intervention; better public services *and* tax reduction, increase of rural productivity *and* respect for rural property, freedom of opinion *and* repression of the manifestations of anti-status quo opinions; abolition of privileges and access to aristocratic drawing rooms; etc. All this must be encompassed in a phraseology able to attract the feared masses without alienating the protected oligarchy.[11]

Quo vadis the new middle class?

End of the Halpern—Perlmutter debate.

NOTES

1. See Joseph La Palombara, 'Macrotheories and Microapplications in Comparative Politics: a Widening Chasm' in *Comparative Politics*, Vol. 1, No. 1 (October 1968), 52-78.

2. See my essay 'The Praetorian Army and the Praetorian State: Toward a Taxonomy of Civilian-Military Relations in Developing Polities', *Comparative Politics*, Vol. 1, No. 3 (April 1969).

3. Morroe Berger, 'The Middle Class in the Arab World', in Walter Z. Laqueur, ed., *The Middle East in Transition* (New York: Praeger, 1958), p. 63.

4. Emil Lederer and Jakob Marschak, 'Der Neuer Mittelstand', in *Grundriss der Sozialökonomik*, Section IX, Part 1 (Tübingen, 1926).

5. Ralf Dahrendorf, *Class and Class Conflict in Industrial Society* (Stanford: Stanford University Press, 1959), p. 52.

6. *Ibid.*, pp. 52-3.

7. *Ibid.*, p. 53.

8. *Ibid.*, p. 56.

9. Irving Lewis Horowitz, 'Introduction', in Irving Lewis Horowitz, ed., *Latin American Radicalism* (New York: Random House, 1969), pp. 6-7.

10. Uriel Dann, *Iraq Under Qassem* (Jerusalem: Israel Universities Press, 1969), pp. 19-32.

11. José Nun, 'A Latin American Phenomenon: the Middle Class Military Coup', in *Trends in Social Science Research in Latin American Studies*, Institute of International Studies (Berkeley: University of California, March 1965), p.82.

CHAPTER 6

The Syrian Military and the Ba'th Party

Syria has had no stable civilian rule since 1949, the year of her first army coup; her politics have become a theater for ambitious army men.[1] In the thirty-four years since Syria gained independence from the French, the country has had eight years of parliamentary rule (1945-49 and 1954-58) and five years of semi-parliamentary government (late 1961 to February 1966). Long periods of military intervention have alternated with shorter eras of parliamentary and semi-parliamentary rule, while the government has always stood under the shadow of military domination.

Since March 1949, Syria has experienced some fourteen army coups—nine of them successful. Only three times did the officers who achieved successful coups pass the reins of power to civilians and call for a retreat to the barracks. Since 1963 a pattern has developed in which civilians and the army have alternated in power, but the army has never retreated to the barracks. One instance of this syndrome was the coup of March 1963, when officers, who were members of or sympathetic to the Arab Socialist Ba'th party, overthrew the parliamentary system and handed the government over to the civilian faction of the Ba'th. The army-Ba'th faction acted as king-maker. Between 1963 and 1964 Syria was governed by the Ba'th-army coalition supported by pro-Nasserist Arab unionists. The army increasingly became the dominant group in a Ba'th-dominated government. When unity talks with Egypt failed, Ba'th succumbed to a military dictatorship of General Amin al-Hafiz. This was the end of parliamentary rule in Syria. The army-Ba'th faction which staged the February 1966 coup seemed ready to hand the government over to the civilians but the transfer of power never took place. And, since that time, the Syrian army has never returned to the barracks, never yielded full executive power and political control. The recent coups, as well as the former ones, have not always been engineered independently by the officers: several have been supported, encouraged, and initiated by individual civilian politicians, and by political parties and groups. In fact, some Syrian politicians have even spoken of the coup recently as an election. Since the collapse of the U.A.R. in 1961 there have been at least six "political parties" in the army: the "leftists" and the "mainstream" (moderate) Ba'thists; the champions of civilian and military governments, the Nasserist Unionists, and the anti-Nasser Unionists. Between 1963 and 1966 a six-cornered struggle raged between the two Ba'th factions and the Nasser and anti-Nasser forces, some advocating civilian rule, others military domination. (As we shall see, conflicts which divide Syria go beyond the political-ideological divisions rooted in the traditional ethnic pluralism, in the ancient urban-rural rivalries, and, above all, in the gap between center and periphery.) Since 1966 the army-party rule has sustained two abortive coups, the 1973 war with Israel and the Lebanese civil war between 1975 and 1977. The 'Alawi Ba'th-army rule finally created stability in Syria, but only with the military legitimizing the Ba'th regime.

THE BACKGROUND OF ARMY DOMINATION IN SYRIAN POLITICS[2]

Syria is a product of Franco-British imperialist machinations,[3] specifically of the hasty and thoughtless division of the Turkish Empire after World War I. The diminishment of Syria's territory after the Ottoman reign (1517-1918) brought political instability, economic insecurity and nationalist dreams of grandeur, the vision of Damascus as the center of a rising and progressive Arab Empire. Syria and Lebanon

—and with them Iraq, Palestine, and Jordan, former Arab provinces of the Turkish Empire—emerged in 1918 as semi-independent countries governed, under a League of Nations mandate, by Britain and France. The Syrian Republic, created in 1920 under a French mandate, did not represent an integrated national entity.

Syria's economic power, since the days of the Turks, has lain in two middle-sized cities in its agricultural heartland, Hama and Homs, and their surrounding villages. Another vestige of Ottoman rule is the power concentrated in the hands of the few feudal families who dominate the two cities and the valley between Damascus and Aleppo—the 'Azm family rules Hama, the 'Atasi family rules Homs. These powerful local feudal forces, and religious, ethnic, and cultural differences, were Syria's inheritance when it became independent in 1945. Although the Suni-Moslem population in Syria comprises a majority of 72.2 per cent of the total population, the significance of the ethno-religious division in Syria is political. Ethnic groups form consolidated political-ethnic entities, and the political support these ethnic groups derive from their group identity has since become Syria's most acute political problem. Ethnic identity in an age of Arab nationalism has produced a series of conflicts between a Suni-dominated central government (this before the military 'Alawi takeover in February 1966) and the politically isolated but consolidated ethnic groups, most notably the 'Alawi, Druze, and Isma'ilis. Since 1966, these groups have gone beyond their "traditional" role as protest groups. Under the guise of the military the 'Alawi today dominate Syria's regime.

The mandate power discouraged the mingling of Syria's diverse ethnic groups, Islamic sects, and schisms—vestiges of Ottoman rule. The heterogeneity of Syrian society, the divisiveness of various religious, ethnic, economic, communal, kinship, and provincial elements have contributed to Syria's political instability. Before independence, Syrian nationalists were represented in the National Bloc (*Kutla al-Wataniya*), a confederation of veterans with various backgrounds and interests who united in the struggle for independence. This loose alliance quickly dissolved after the French left, and independent Syria's first nationalist parties mirrored the prevalent divisions. The National party (*al-Hizb al-Watani*) represented the politics of the Damascus groups; the People's party (*al-Hizb al-Sh'ab*) represented the business interests of the north, especially Aleppo, and the interests of the powerful 'Atasi family. The radical rightist *Parti Populaire Syrien* (PPS) or *Hizb al-Suri al-Qawmi al-Ijtima'i*, led by Antun Sa'adah, also represented northern economic interests, but, because it favored a Syrian-Iraqi union, it was the first party to attract nationwide support. It appealed to the youth and the army because of the pan-Syrian doctrines advocated by Sa'adah.[4] The mounting instability of Syrian parliamentary politics

TABLE 1

Religious Communities in Syria, 1964

Religious Group	Estimated No. of Adherents	Per cent of Group	Per cent of Total
Moslem	4,631,000	100.0*	84.7
Sunnis	3,950,000	85.3	72.2
'Alawites	600,000	13.0	11.0
Isma'ilis	56,000	1.2	1.0
Other Shiites	25,000	.5	.5
Christian	654,000	100.0	12.0
Greek Orthodox	246,000	37.6	4.5
Armenian Orthodox	140,000	21.4	2.5
Greek Catholics†	80,000	12.2	1.5
Syrian Orthodox	72,000	11.0	1.3
Syrian Catholics†	30,000	4.6	.6
Maronites†	25,000	3.8	.5
Armenian Catholics†	24,000	3.7	.4
Nestorians	15,000	2.3	.3
Protestants	12,000	1.8	.2
Roman Catholics	10,000	1.5	.2
Others	184,000	—	3.3
Druzes	170,000	—	3.0
Yazidis	10,000	—	.2
Jews	4,000	—	.1

* Actual sum of percentages is 99.9 because of rounding.
† Affiliated with Roman Catholic Church. Not included in this table are the Chaldeans, a small group historically derived from the Nestorians but affiliated with the Roman Catholics.
SOURCE: *U.S. Army Area Handbook for Syria* (Department of the Army Pamphlet, No. 550-47, July 1965), p. 124.

between 1945 and 1949 increasingly revealed the effects of the Ottoman and French legacy of particularism in society and politics.

The short experiment in constitutional politics (1945-49) set the form of Syria's parliamentarianism.[5] The national executive increasingly lost power and influence, the political parties were reduced to cliques and alliances of ethnic, and local religious and cultural interests. The absence of political, social, and cultural cohesion and the deep antagonism between center and periphery doomed Syrian constitutional politics from the start. Corruption, nepotism, filial piety, kinship practices and related ills became the practice of parliamentary politics. A catalyst was necessary; it came threefold. First, there was an economic crisis and inflation which had been increasing since independence. Second, a parliamentary crisis developed, the result of the "cooking-fat" (*Samnah*) scandal when, during the 1949 Palestine campaign, the army had been supplied poor oil, implicating key political and military figures. The third and real catalyst, however, was the debacle in Palestine itself. This defeat brought an enormous burden to all Arab leaders, civilian, religious, and military. In its wake came the assassination of King Abdullah of Jordan in 1951, and the Egyptian coup of 1952.

The Palestine debacle demonstrated the need for reform in the Arab world and provided the *coup de grace* for reactionary Arabs, ineffective politicians, and corrupt army leaders. Syria was politically one of the most sensitive eastern Arab countries—hence her first coup, led by colonel Husni al-Za'im, the army's first chief of staff, came shortly after the Palestine war, in March 1949.

The Palestine war completely changed the nature of the Arab armies. Its effect added to other events that changed the politics of the army as well as Arab nationalism and politics—the decline of colonialism and the growth of nationalist activity elsewhere in the world, and the emergence of the Afro-Asian bloc in world politics. The Syrian coups indicated a dramatic change in the army's political role: the sudden intensification of army officers' political consciousness and the rapid transformation of the Syrian army officers' corps into a political group.[6]

The French policy had been to encourage non-Arabs or non-Muslims to join the army. The nationalist government after 1949, however, encouraged the majority of Suni Arab Moslems and Syria's rural population to serve in the army and go to the academy. The Homs and Hama academies are open to all, and, since 1954, rural and lower class groups have been encouraged to enter a military career; tuition is paid by the government. Homs' military college has become the home of Syria's new and rising army elite, a proud, nationalist, militant group. Serving in the army has become a national duty and a mobility factor for minority ethnic groups. After the Palestine war, nationalist groups attempted to enlarge the army, and to politicize, Arabize, and radicalize its officer corps.[7]

The first three army coups in 1949 were still led by Ottoman and French trained officers: Za'im, Hinnawi, and Shishakly.[8] The first two coups did not yet represent an emergent new army, but they served notice that the Syrian officer corps was a political force to be dealt with. Although civilian nationalist politicians rejected independent army rule, they favored the army's political activity and encouraged the officers' involvement in politics—not because they considered army rule good government but because they felt that army officers would provide able, honest, decisive, and strong leadership. The fragile constitutional period and the strong tradition of provincial, ethnic, and kinship groups had prevented the emergence of political leaders with a national vision. It was hoped that the army group could produce such men.[9]

THE SHISHAKLY ERA 1949-54

In the period after Shishakly's first coup—from the end of 1949 until November 1951—the army acted as arbitrator between civilian rivals and the officers; at this time the military was expected to return to the barracks. Shishakly's second coup in November 1951 initiated a new role for the politically-minded army officers. Shishakly intended to "use" the army to weaken the traditional and conservative forces in Syria, and he soon interpreted the mandate given to him by the "progressives" as a mandate to establish a military dictatorship.[10] He began with a reform of the army, promoting young officers, most of whom played prominent roles in his over-throw three years later and in the military coups in Syria since.[11] The politicization of the army was combined with an intense program of Arabization of the officer corps and the rise to prominence of the provincial military academies, Hama and Homs. Politicization in the academies went hand in hand with the progressive ideology of the Hawrani-Socialist and Ba'th brand.[12] In 1951, Shishakly established the first open political party in the Middle East that was dominated by the army—the Arab Liberation Movement (ALM) (Nasser's clandestine Free Officer Club preceded it by two years). Like Nasser's Liberation Rally of 1953 (which must have been inspired by Shishakly), the new army-dominated party was to abolish the "corrupt" political system of parties and parliaments in Syria. The ALM preached militant nationalism and "progressive" socio-economic reforms. Although it soon collapsed, its emulators have continued to flourish.

There were five primary reasons why the political party organized by the army under Shishakly collapsed: these are very significant for they set the pattern for subsequent civil-military relations in Syria.

(1)   Lack of cohesion among the politically inclined officers, the division of the army into rival factions, and the personal struggles within the ALM organiza-tion. This fratricidal division between army com-manders was responsible for the demise of Shishakly and of later military regimes.

(2)   The antagonism of civilian progressives toward Shishakly's military dicatatorship. Hawrani and Michel 'Aflaq, the leaders of the newly formed (1953) Arab Socialist Ba'th party, formerly Shishakly's protagonists, opposed his "unexpected" military dic-tatorship and his close relations with the PPS, and ceased to support him.[13]

(3)   The old ills of Syria: its feudal and politico-geographical nature. The role of the politically semi-independent minorities, especially the Druze and 'Alawi, and the deep split between urban and rural groups (predominant among the latter).

(4) The ALM's failure to establish national authority in
     Damascus and to subdue outer and rural centers,
     Hama, Homs, Jabal Druze. In fact, Shishakly
     "played cat and mouse with the People's Party"[14] and
     was supported by Aleppo business groups.
(5) The role of inter-Arab intrigues. The Egyptian-Iraqi
     struggle over Syria. The active Egyptian support of
     Syrian progressives, and especially of the Ba'th party.

In February 1954, an army insurrection dominated by a
Shishakly disciple, Captain (later Colonel) Mustafa Hamdun, and some Druze officers, and inspired by Hawrani,
ended the reign of the military dictatorship and the political
party of the army. But the way was open for future
civil-military relations patterned after Shishakly's model.
"Shishakly's rule made the Syrian army an unashamedly
political instrument."[15]

THE BA'TH PARTY AND THE SYRIAN ARMY 1954-58

The fall of Shishakly's reign in February 1954 restored
constitutional order to Syria. The first free elections since
1947 brought new forces and ideologies to Syria's political
arena. Although the old parties returned to power, the
greatest beneficiary of the 1954 election and of Shishakly's fall
was the newly emergent Arab Socialist Ba'th party. This
party had been formed at the end of 1953 when Akram
Hawrani's small Socialist party (actually Hama's anti-feudal
group) joined the Ba'th (Renaissance) party, a small Damascus coterie of intellectuals and school teachers under Michel
'Aflaq and Salah al-Din Bitar. The latter group had been
established in 1947 but had not participated in elections until
1949, when it secured one seat in parliament. In 1954, the
Ba'th party received 15 per cent of the vote and elected
twenty-two representatives, although it won only a poor third
place in the election.

'Aflaq and Bitar became, next to Hawrani, Syria's key
politicians during the short constitutional period, 1954-58.

'Aflaq, Greek Orthodox and intensely intellectual, had
flirted with communism as a student in Paris but had lost his
communist inclinations. Upon his return to Syria in the

middle 1930's, he began pamphleteering. His collection of essays, *The Road to Renaissance (Fi Sabil al-Ba'th)*, written in 1940-41, remained the chief doctrinal source of the Ba'th party until 1964.[16] He became the chief ideological scribe of radical and socialist nationalists in the Arab East and served as their secretary general between 1953 and 1966. His writings reflect much of the mystical and chiliastic thinking prevalent among nationalist "philosophers" in Beirut and Damascus. The concept of Arabism (*al-'Urubah*) and of humanitarian socialism (*Insaniyyah*), which have currency among many radical and nationalist intellectuals in the Arab East, have influenced 'Aflaq's writings much more than his early infatuation with Marxism.

Salah al-Din Bitar, 'Aflaq's Moslem collaborator, is much less of an intellectual. A Damascus school teacher, he is an able administrator and politician, and has acted alternately as Syria's prime minister and foreign minister between 1954 and 1963.

Most importantly, the Ba'th party added a socialist ideology to Syrian nationalist politics. Another new dimension, after Shishakly's fall, was the rise of Egyptian influence. International and inter-Arab politics had played an important role in Syria since 1949. Za'im, the instigator of Syria's first coup, had seen Syria in a wider Arab context and at first had negotiated with Iraq. However, when Za'im had begun flirting with the Egyptians (the Farouq regime), Hinnawi—with Iraqi support—staged his successful countercoup. When, in 1954, army rule in Egypt was consolidated under Gamel Abdel Nasser, and his group sought friends and influence in the Arab East, their most natural allies were the Syrian Ba'thists, especially in the army. Thus, the Egyptian army coup was forging an alliance of great consequence for Syria and the Ba'th party.

The Ba'th was convinced that neither Arab unity nor security for Syria was possible without eventual union with Egypt. At that time, Soviet support of Syrian and Egyptian radical nationalists enhanced the position of the Ba'th (as well as that of the Kurdish-dominated Syrian Communist party led by Khalid Bakhdash, another resourceful Syrian politician). The rise of the Ba'th and its nationalist and socialist ideology, the projected union with Egypt, and Soviet military aid brought an <u>expectation of unity to Syrian politics</u>.

For a while, army rule and Syria's historic ills of divisiveness and particularism seemed things of the past. The new graduates of Hama-Homs academies and their leaders, veterans of the Palestine campaign, supported, and some even joined the Ba'th. A new group of <u>Suni-Moslem</u> Arab officers emerged, <u>dedicated to Arab nationalism</u> and the aggrandizement of the army. Outstanding among them were Adnan al-Malki (assassinated in an alleged PPS plot in 1955), Mustafa Hamdun, 'Abd al-Hamid al-Sarraj, Amin al-Nafuri, and others. The appeal of Ba'th ideology, the leadership of Hawrani-'Aflaq-Bitar, and the projected Egyptian alliance <u>drew many junior officers into the Ba'th fold and made others strong Ba'th sympathizers</u>. The Ba'th became the first national party since the formation of the PPS, and it cut across Syria's traditional divisions. The pursuit of military alliances, such as the Baghdad Pact and the Dulles-projected Northern Tier, directed against the meager Communist infiltration in the area, actually encouraged the U.S.S.R.'s active intervention in Arab politics, aided the Syrian Communists, and put forward the Dulles military pact as the nationalists' chief villain. This policy eventually influenced the struggle between Iraq and Egypt in the latter's favor. After the Suez affair of 1956, it was clear that the Syrian radicals, the Ba'thists, and their allies in the army would move toward union with Egypt. During the 1954-58 period, parliamentary politics gradually became paralysed, while the forces of "resurrection" were rising. When the Egyptian-Syrian union, the U.A.R., was formed in 1958, politically oriented Ba'thists in the army and their civilian allies believed in a break with the past and that a new political order would begin in Syria. Expectations were high that the Ba'th, pursuing a progressive policy with Egyptian aid, would unite all Syrians.

It will be useful here to pause and evaluate Ba'th-army relations before the U.A.R. period. Since 1954, Syria has depended on the resilience of the Ba'th and the cohesion of her army. The Ba'th has depended on army support and the army on the organization, ideology, and leadership of the Ba'th.

The Syrian army is a mirror of Syrian society. Unlike the Egyptian army elites, the Syrian officers bridge the gap between urban and rural, poor and rich. The Syrian army represents nationalist and egalitarian aspirations in the army as well as in the radical parties. The officer corps is a mixed group: scions of the lower echelons of the kinship groups, the wealthy and influential (Mardams, 'Atasis, and Kuzbaris), and the impoverished (the 'Alawis' Muhammed 'Umran, Jasan 'Alwan, and the Suni Aleppo officer Amin al-Hafiz) have equal opportunities to rise. In fact, since 1963 the chances of the poor have been better. Although officers' groups in the Syrian army are predominantly of Suni-Moslem origin, non-Suni sects such as the 'Alawi, Druze, and Isma'ilis have proportionally greater representation in the officer corps, the army elite, and the high command than among the population. Since 1965, and in the 1966 coups, the 'Alawi have dominated the army high command and the left wing of the Ba'th.[17]

The nationalist awakening and the reform of the Syrian army since the Palestine war made the officers incline toward the Ba'th because its ideology and aspirations fulfilled their nationalist desires. The army officers found in the Ba'th party a supporting political organization, although they sometimes clashed with the personalities of Ba'th leaders and politicians. Over the years, the Syrian Ba'th and the politically inclined army officers fluctuated between co-operation and recrimination, a process detrimental to both the Ba'th's and the army's political power and influence.

In 1949 the Ba'th was only a small coterie of a very few Damascus intellectuals ('Aflaq, Bitar, his cousin Dr. Midhat Bitar, Dr. Mu'nif al-Razaaz, and Dr. 'Ali Jabar from Beirut).[18] At that time, the politically inclined officers were also few. The simultaneous emergence of the Ba'th and the politically-oriented officers at the end of Shishakly's reign precipitated an eventual rivalry. Divisiveness and personalism within either group encouraged the ambitions of individual officers. Without group solidarity neither group could prevail.

In 1949, the infant Ba'th and the Socialist party and its

leaders considered the political officers useful to further their ambitions. The politically minded officers, in turn, saw in the Ba'th their "natural" home and embraced 'Aflaq's ideology indiscriminately (as they had done in the past with PPS ideology only to find to their dismay that the pan-Syrianism of the PPS contradicted their aspirations of pan-Arabism, which they had mistakenly believed was shared by the PPS).[19] Although few officers actually joined the Ba'th or became activists in the Ba'th during the middle 1950's, most pan-Arabist and Syrian nationalist officers embraced the Ba'th ideology.

From the beginning, Ba'th had difficulty attracting the masses and winning elections. Although 'Aflaq had served as Colonel Hinnawi's minister of national education in 1949, this did not increase the party's electoral strength. 'Aflaq resigned after three months and lost his seat in parliament during the November 1949 elections, the only Ba'th seat in parliament. In the October 1954 elections—the first free ones since the reign of Shishakly—the Ba'th received 15 per cent of the popular vote and 22 out of a total of 142 parliamentary seats.[20]

THE BA'TH, THE ARMY, AND THE U.A.R. 1958-61

The Ba'th and the Ba'th-oriented officers were instrumental in forging the Egyptian-Syrian alliance which culminated in the formation of an Arab progressive union, the U.A.R., in 1958. However ambiguous were the circumstances and rationale of the Egyptian-Syrian union, it emanated from a sincere desire on the part of all parties, especially the Ba'th, to advance the cause of Arab nationalism and its progressive wing.

The forces and circumstances which led to the formation of the U.A.R. have been analysed elsewhere.[21] From the evidence available, it was the Syrian Ba'th party rather than Nasser who wanted the union in the form it took. The Ba'th motives for desiring the union and its conception of how it was to be instrumentally effected were different from those of Nasser. The party expected to be strengthened through the union, while Nasser wanted to dismantle the Ba'th, with the

National Union acting as the instrument for the unification of the two countries, achieving Egyptian hegemony over the Arab world.

During the July 1959 elections to the Egyptian-Syrian Union government (1958-61), only 200 members of Ba'th were elected out of 9,445 People's Base candidates[22] (candidates elected through a complicated process by the National Union, the U.A.R.'s single party). The party which engineered the Union was reduced from fifteen per cent to two per cent of the electorate! Between 1954 and 1958 Hawrani and 'Aflaq sought to use the army as an instrument of the Ba'th. But when the Ba'th penetrated the army it favored the politically minded officers who soon became its worst enemies. The rise of Adnan al-Malki (a leader of an abortive coup against Shishakly in 1954) and his colleagues 'Abd al-Hamid Sarraj, Mustafa Hamdun, and 'Abd al Ghani Qanut, signified the first effective alliance between the Ba'th and army officers. In 1955, however, when al-Malki was allegedly assassinated by pro-PPS officers, Ba'th and the army lost a potential leader. Others of the Ba'th-oriented officers, such as al-Sarraj and Hamdun, would soon play an important role in the U.A.R. (1958-61). During the first year of the U.A.R. 'Aflaq-Hawrani sought the aid of Egypt, again viewing Egypt and Nasser as the Ba'th's true and "natural" allies. Unity with Egypt was sought as a cure for all ills: for the fratricide of the officer corps and the impotence of Ba'th at the polls.

The Ba'th was soon disenchanted with the U.A.R. The Egyptians were trying to weaken the party, and the Ba'th was torn asunder over the issue of support of the U.A.R. Instead of consolidating the party, the U.A.R. became a source of division which did not end even after its collapse in 1961.

Some Ba'th members even wanted to "ideologize" and "educate" Nasser in pan-Arabism of the Ba'th kind. Here, the inflexible Ba'th leaders soon clashed with Nasser, as they had clashed in 1949 with the nationalist officers. This brought to an end Ba'th's first ascendancy based on its support of Egypt. A second blow came when, after the bitter experience with Egypt and Nasser, the party's most resourceful politician, Akram Hawrani, resigned, splitting the party. Ba'th was further torn asunder between its pro- and anti-Unionists (with Egypt). Some of the loyal Ba'thists—officers and sympathizers—betrayed the party and offered their services to Nasser. Leading the pro-Nasser faction among the officers was 'Abd al-Hamid Sarraj who became president of the executive council of the Northern U.A.R. region (Syria) on December 31, 1960, after Ba'th ministers and officials resigned from the U.A.R. cabinet and administration, and from senior positions in the Union party—the National Union. Now that the 'Aflaq-Hawrani faction was purged, some leading army Ba'thists joined the Egyptians, hoping to unify the officer corps with Egypt's help.

On the whole, the Suni-Moslem nationalist, and politically inclined, officers supported the U.A.R. The Syrian government during the last year of the U.A.R. (1960-61) was run chiefly by officers—Egyptians and Syrians. But, when the Ba'th clashed with the Egyptians, those Ba'thist officers and sympathizers who remained loyal to Ba'th were gradually removed and others joined the Egyptians. The Egyptians had encouraged, wherever possible, non-political and non-Ba'thist officers. Loyal Nasser followers were elevated. The legacy of U.A.R. rule was not the unification of the officer corps that had been expected. On the contrary, the U.A.R. legacy to the Syrian army was a deepening and newly ideological split between unionists, and anti-unionists and gradualists.

The anti-U.A.R. coup was directed by non-political officers who resented Egyptian and Sarraj's rule over Syria. The coup of September 28, 1961, led by Colonels Kuzbari, Dahaman, and Nahlawi, brought an end to the U.A.R.[23]

1961-1970—YEARS OF ASCENDANCY AND FRATRICIDE

After the U.A.R. debacle, the fact that the Ba'th never succeeded in becoming the most popular party in Syria is crucial to the understanding of its weakness and its search for "outside" help from the army and again from Egypt or, for that matter, from any Arab country willing to help. Even as recently as 1963, ten years after its formation, Ba'th received only one-fourth of the seats in parliament or fifteen per cent of the electorate. It is the party with the greatest potential among the Arabs, its leaders are revered, its ideology is espoused throughout the Arab world. It is the party of the new Arab intelligentsia, the party of the ambitious nationalists in the Syrian army, the only Arab nationalist party to penetrate the rest of the Arab world (having branches in all Arab countries, including secret ones in Egypt), and yet, for reasons that we shall discuss, it has never succeeded in getting a majority of votes and seats in its homeland. This failure left the party at the mercy of the Syrian army.

The period of constitutional government after the dissolution of the U.A.R. did not last long. Again no one party received a decisive majority in the elections to create a lasting coalition government and to end the fighting. The raucous Egyptian-Syrian denunciations only opened the way for a new army intervention. At the end of March 1962, six months after the formation of a civilian government, the army revolted again. This time the rebels were the army leaders Nahlawi and Dahaman, anti-Egyptian officers in Damascus, who had led the anti-U.A.R. coup in 1961. Three days later pro-U.A.R. forces in Aleppo, led by Colonel Jasan 'Alwan, revolted against army pro-U.A.R. factions. Egypt did not come to the support of the Aleppo rebels who were soon subdued by Damascus. The army entered politics again and the supreme commander, General 'Abd al-Krim Zahar al-Din, became minister of defense in a government of civil servants and the army. Throughout the year 1962 coups and countercoups were successfully suppressed by General Zahar al-Din, a non-political Druze officer. But unity did not last long. The fraticidal, divided officers had found a new opportunity to fulfill political and personal ambitions. This opportunity was sparked by the fall of General Qassem's regime in Iraq in February 1963, and the coming to power of the staunch pro-Nasser General 'Abd Salim 'Arif which changed Iraq from an avid anti-Nasser military regime into a close ally. These events were followed immediately (March 8, 1963) in Syria by a coup staged by General Ziad al-Hariri, Hawrani's brother-in-law and a frustrated pro-Ba'thist officer-seeker, in collaboration with Hama Ba'thists. The coup-makers launched a unity propaganda campaign but hardly mentioned Ba'th or socialism. As soon as the army overthrew Zahar al-Din, rival Ba'thist army officers claimed the coup as their own work.[24] The Revolutionary Council was then headed by one of the conspirators, Colonel Luay al-'Atasi, a Ba'th sympathizer.

Out of twelve ministers in the new government seven were officers. General Hariri became chief of staff of the army. Thus, the Ba'th again was supported by the army but this time the army was no longer the Ba'th's instrument as it had been in 1954. The Ba'th cabinet was an uncomfortable coalition of Syrian progressive nationalists, socialists, and Unionists; nevertheless, the Ba'th hoped to be able to govern successfully.

There were three reasons why Ba'th-dominated rule was not sustained: (1) fratricide within the army; (2) the new unity negotiations with Egypt which started as soon as the Ba'th cabinet was formed in March-April 1963; and (3) the drift of the Ba'th leftward after its sixth national convention in October 1963.

The army's personal intrigues and fratricidal divisions soon were reflected in Ba'th-army rule.[25] Hariri, who opposed Ba'th's demands for agrarian reform and Ba'th-inspired army appointments and removals, was dismissed by the Ba'th government while he was away. This could only have been done with the help of Hariri's chief rival, Colonel Amin al-Hafiz, a pro Ba'thist army officer who soon became minister of defense and later was promoted to general. While Ba'th's rivals were defeated and went into opposition, the party itself was still divided and the army officers intended to dominate the Ba'th-army alliance in the government at the expense of coalition partners and the Ba'th. Ba'th rule was further weakened by the collapse of the party in Iraq six months later, in August 1963, and the strikes and revolts against the government in Damascus. General Amin al-Hafiz seized the opportunity to become the ruler of a Ba'th-army-dominated regime in Syria. Al-Hafiz secured a price for his support of Ba'th—the ouster of his rival, 'Alawi General Muhammad 'Umran, a devout Ba'thist himself. With the fall of 'Umran, another 'Alawi officer emerged, Air Force General Salah Jadid. The Ba'th party was left to face the challenge of its officers and followers in the army.[26]

The second reason for the failure of the Ba'th-dominated rule was the unity negotiations with Egypt. The Ba'th's attitude toward Nasser since the collapse of the U.A.R. was ambivalent and cautious. No longer could the Ba'th advocate direct and immediate union. Thus the Ba'th coalition cabinet was threatened. The Unionists demanded a greater readiness on the part of the Ba'th to accept Nasser's conditions for a new merger between Egypt and Syria. They were supported by Unionist officers in the army. The "mainstream" and 'Aflaq-Bitar faction were not eager for immediate union. Without confidence in the Egyptian-dominated Arab union, the negotiations with Egypt were bound to fail. And the collapse of the negotiations in April 1963 left the Ba'th without the support of its civilian partners, the Unionists, and at the mercy of the army. The party soon fell prey to the ambitious al-Hafiz who decided to chart a moderate course in Syrian-Egyptian relations, thus eliminating the influence of the civilians—Unionists as well as Ba'thists—in the cabinet.

In addition to rivalry between senior Ba'thist officers and the failure of unity negotiations with the U.A.R., the most serious internal threat to the party was its drift to the left. The Ba'th was no longer only a Syrian party; it had become an international Arab movement, dominated by leftists and Marxist-oriented students and intellectuals outside Syria. The regional Ba'th party in Syria—the original Ba'th—was dominated by the moderates 'Aflaq and Bitar, but the international Ba'th was controlled by radicals. In fact, the party founders, 'Aflaq and Bitar, were not elected to the command of the international Ba'th. The leftists at the Sixth Ba'th International Conference were members of the Iraqi Ba'thist organization led by radical students and intellectuals (whose general strike in Baghdad, begun on December 17, 1962, triggered the anti-Qassem coup of February 8, 1963). Most prominent among them was 'Ali Salah al-Sa'di (who for a while acted as minister of the interior in 'Abd Salim 'Arif's first government).[27] Sa'di's faction attacked the party leadership for its "reformism" and lack of revolutionary vigor. The end of the convention found the party divided within Syria and abroad. The mother-Ba'th in Syria was now torn between the militant supporters of the left and the party's "mainstream," the moderates.

Beginning in 1963, the top army command in Syria became more and more Ba'thist and the Ba'thist officers became progressive (or at least paid lip service to revolutionary slogans). The Ba'th officers were divided between leftists and moderates with the predominance of 'Alawis among the former. The radicalization of the army was sought through the formation of a national guard, the party's "ideological army" (an idea born at the sixth party convention), which was dominated by leftist Ba'thist officers. Among the left Ba'thists, 'Alawi and Druze officers (the "countryside boys") were predominant.[28] The struggle for power in the party and within the Ba'thists in the army was resolved in favor of Jadid who prevailed over the national guard. Thus, while Hafiz was allied with the moderate (mainstream) faction in the Syrian Ba'th, Jadid and his allies in the army were supported by the Ba'th International Command, the left opposition in the Syrian Ba'th, and the national guard. Finally, Jadid allied himself with Yousuf Zu'ayn, a leftist Ba'thist, and with the Druze officer Salim Hatum, and—backed by 'Alawi leftist officers—staged a successful coup on February 26, 1966.

The rise of the "countryside boys" in the army and in the Ba'th opened up a new era of erratic and radical politics in Syria. Generals Salah Jadid and Ahmed Swaidani, two 'Alawis, the leaders of the left Ba'th and its national guard in Syria, found a new ally in the chairman of Syria's longshoremen's union, 'Abd Karim al-Jundi, known as the leader of the Red National Guard. The Red Guard has not yet challenged the Ba'th-army leftist regime, but al-Jundi's interference intensified army rivalries which led General Salim Hatum, a Druze and a leader of the February 1966 coup, to seek asylum in Jordan in November 1966 (to be executed on his return to Syria after 1967). Al-Jundi, a leftist Ba'thist and a Suni Moslem supported by Isma'ilis and 'Alawis in his Red Guard organization, became powerful because he could challenge an army divided by fratricide and the faction-ridden Ba'th party. After the Syrian debacle in the June 1967 war with Israel, al-Jundi's influence declined considerably, and he was "eliminated" in the 1969 coup.

Avraham Ben-Tzur[29] has given us most revealing information on the nature, organizational structure, and ideology of the Ba'th since 1966. He has in his possession valuable Ba'th documents, which were captured by Israel in Qunaitra, the capital of the Syrian Army for Liberation of Palestine, when she occupied the Golan Heights. On the basis of these captured documents, according to Ben-Tzur, the renewal of Ba'th in Syria (which Ben-Tzur prefers to call the Neo-Ba'th; however, we see no reason to adopt such a name, since all parties change and become "neos") was accompanied by a group of officers organized as the Military Committee in 1963. This renewal "preceded the revival of the civilian body of the party." This Committee was dominated by 'Alawi-Druze officers, led by Salah Jadid ('Alawi) and Hamed Ubayad (Druze). The group sought "quick injection of party ideology into the views of the army." Here the "Regionalists"-Ba'th organizations in provincial towns and "especially in regions with a marked communal character—'Alawi, Isma'ili, or Druze"—aided the disintegration of the "old" Ba'th ('Aflaq-Bitar-Hawrani) by serving the Military Committee with a base. The regionalists were headed by Dr. Yousuf Zu'ayn, whose close connection with the Military Committee was the basis for their entente. The new ideology which replaced 'Aflaq's was that of a former Communist-Marxist ideologue, Yassin al-Hafiz, himself a leftist Ba'thist. In his *The Ba'thist Experiment* (1963) and *A Few Theoretical Propositions* (1964), Hafiz challenges the "romantic" "old" Ba'th and calls for a "scientific socialist Arab way to socialism," where the class struggle becomes predominant, and for an alliance between the working classes and the intelligentsia.[30]

But the tragedy of Ba'th is not yet complete. The doctrines of Yassin al-Hafiz, however "scientific", are no less millenarian than those of 'Aflaq. Al-Hafiz writes about the working classes who are found in Damascus, Aleppo, Latakia, i.e., in the center—while the Syrian revolution, if ever, begins in the countryside. Oblivious to Maoist doctrines and the Castro-Guevara experiences, al-Hafiz, a blind follower of Moscow, is already discredited as an ideologue. Rival ideologies have now, since the 1967 debacle, been imported by Palestinians.

Fanon has replaced 'Aflaq, and Mao-Castro have superseded Marx and Nasser.

Al-Hafiz' abortive ideological attempts were in part reflected by his unregenerate Muscovite attitude toward the party and the army. While the Military Committee welcomed al-Hafiz' attack on Ba'th's parliamentary orientations, it strongly objected to his attitudes concerning the role of the "military bureaucracy". In view of the insistence of the Military Committee, al-Hafiz deleted his references to the "military bureaucracy" from the *Propositions* (1964) and substituted "Arab unity" for the "class struggle".[31] The Military Committee opted for a Castro-like arrangement of army-party relationship rather than the historical and orthodox Bolshevik concept of the supremacy of the party over the army. Thus, to use a Bolshevik slogan, the Bonapartist faction of Ba'th has prevailed.

The net result of the "ideological army"—the left Ba'thist aspiration since 1963—is that now the Ba'thist officers can occupy the high army command and remove their anti-Ba'thist, "mainstream" and Suni, rivals, or for that matter, any other rival in the army. While the army was Ba'thized and radicalized, the Ba'th party was torn asunder between conflicting Ba'th-army officers and Ba'th-civilian factions. But it is interesting to note that while in Syria the army turned leftward, the leftist tendencies of Ba'th alienated the Iraqi army.[32]

Thus, the Ba'th, in its third trial for power, once more—as in 1954 and 1958—became the victim of the "instruments" it chose to "educate" and abate. It fell prey to the strategy of infiltration and access of groups more powerful than itself. The mobilizing ideology of the Ba'th and its espousal of union with Egypt did not eradicate Syria's old ills—feudalism, parochialism, cultural and religious diversity. In fact, the failure of Ba'th created new tensions. The left Ba'thist stance brought more brutal frictions and antagonisms among Syria's new and emancipatory elites. Failing to unify Syria, progressive forces were themselves split between Unionism and anti-Unionism and between moderate and radical Ba'thism.

The leadership of Ba'th still fails to recognize the Machiavellian dictum that, if you join a stronger partner, your chances of being swallowed or used by him are greater than your chances of persuading him to move in your direction. This was true for the Ba'th-sponsored U.A.R. and especially for Ba'th's increasing meddling in army factional rivalries and politics. Nevertheless, with no other means of gaining political power after its electoral failure, the Ba'th had to return to Nasser and the ambitious army officers. The crisis in the party was only made worse by its alliances with more powerful and determined political forces; but the real crisis of the Syrian Ba'th lies in the increasing factionalism which has stemmed from its growing internationalist leftist movement. The problem that has beset the Ba'th since its formation is that it has not secured great electoral support. And a gradual leftist takeover is not improving its electoral chances.

An Islamic and conservative world to which Arab masses still adhere stands to reject the Marxism and leftism of even the most favored nationalist party. Under a dictatorship-type of regime such as Egypt, support of the left is possible (and Nasser's Arab socialism is mild in any case). Egypt has no organized rival civilian parties, but, in Syria, where parliamentarianism is still more than a formal political practice, where parties and interests compete even if most of them have taken cover politically, leftist doctrines can gain only meager electoral support. The persistence of constitutional life between a series of coups, which we saw in 1954-58 and 1961-63, indicates that the electorate are of great importance to the survival of party politics. The Ba'th would have had to win a decisive majority in the elections, in order to be able to rise to power without the help of the army, Nasser, the National Guard, or Asad's Presidential office.

Under free conditions, no Marxist or real leftist party, such as the Syrian Communist party, can win even five per cent of the Syrian electorate. Communist infiltration into a leftist Ba'th (as is the case now) will estrange the party from the Syrian electorate who view communism with no less fear and contempt than they do Western imperialism and Zionism. A leftist Marxist-oriented party is still regarded by Moslems as a party of "foreigners," such as Kurds, Christians, or Jews. The further Ba'th moves to the left, the more likely will be the party's decline or even suppression by the army or any other coalition of forces in Syria.

THE SYRIAN PRAETORIAN POLITY 1971-1979: PROSPECTS OF BAʿTH

Baʿth's future depends upon its association with non-Moslems or non-Suni Arabs. With Baʿth's top leadership level in the army and in the party organization, these groups—the non-Moslem and Christian Arabs among the Beirut-Damascus pan-Arabist and nationalist intelligentsia—will be able to play a decisive role in the party's appeal to modernist and secular nationalists in the Arab world. Albert Hourani has pointed out in his *Arabic Thought in the Liberal Age 1798-1939* (Oxford, 1962) that, before 1939, Christian Arabs occupied a most conspicuous role among formulators of Arab national philosophy. Most notable were Michel 'Aflaq, the Secretary General and chief Baʿth ideologue, and Constantin Zurayq, a prominent national philosopher.

The Christians of neighboring Lebanon (now Syrian-occupied Lebanon) play a significant role in the heterogeneous environment and pluralism of Syria. In the urban and intellectual centers of Beirut and Damascus, Christian Arabs are conspicuous among the intelligentsia and some of Syria's most prominent Arab nationalist philosophers are of the Christian faith.[33] The next group significant for the future of the Baʿth are its non-Suni Moslems. The founder of this group, the Greek Orthodox Arab Michel 'Aflaq, has attracted a considerable number of members and sympathizers among Druze, Isma'ilite, 'Alawis, and Kurdish groups. There are Baʿth faithfuls, sympathizers, and affiliates in the army high command (predominantly Druze and 'Alawi). The party in Syria will increasingly depend on these groups, especially in the army. Having begun as an avant-garde coterie of Damascus-Beirut Suni and Christian Arab intelligentsia and teachers, it is now led by the rural 'Alawis and Druze in the army.

The split in Baʿth and within the army also reflects a generational change and elite transformation of the last two decades in Syria. The first generation (1919-1939) interwar nationalists, the older Suni-nationalist elite, were replaced in the 1950's by a well-meaning second generation of radicals and militants, who were represented in the PPS,[34] Ba'th parties, and in the army high command. Tenure of the second generation was, however, short-lived. The "old" Ba'th was soon discredited while the Suni-Arab officers in the army were decimated in coups and countercoups, leaving the 'Alawi-Druze officers to dominate the high command, the army, and now the party and the state.[35] This elite, in contradistinction to the former two center-oriented elites, hails from the periphery. Although its orientations and ideologies are universalist, its social and cultural connections are in the countryside. Thus the non-consolidated periphery, a coalition of regional, civilian, and military 'Alawis, have replaced the fratricidal, central, Sunni or "old" Ba'th-PPS elites.

Since 1966, the Ba'th party has undergone serious changes. To begin with it was taken over by the 'Alawi ethnic group and 'Alawi officers. Ba'th has been transformed from a factional radical parliamentary party into a semi-secret organization, a conspiratorial cabal, highly centralized and efficiently organized, infiltrating into Syria's elite structure, the army, and the bureaucracy. The 'Alawi sect and its military cabal are now firmly institutionalized, having weathered the 1973 and Lebanese wars.

The party, an elaborate and complex organization, is probably the Arab world's most efficient party-army organization, from which it derives its stability. It has succeeded in creating the image of the task force of pan-Arabism, the champion of Palestinianism and the party which does not compromise with Israel.

With the emergence of Hafez Asad as President in 1970, the Ba'th began gradually to break its monolithism and allow other political groups a measure of participation. Ba'th has decentralized authority only to increase its influence. "While there is no doubt that the Ba'th Party had by 1978 developed into the major political organ in Syria, its power and authority were constrained":[36] secularism versus Islam, Syria and pan-Arabism and, above all, its relationships with sister Iraqi Ba'th.

The Syrian military prefer a praetorian-patrimonial rule[37] to parliamentary domination. Thus a consolidated, newly mobilized rural elite rules by virtue of force, not by the expectation of political-parliamentary consensus. Legitimacy is sought in the doctrines of the permanent revolution, but the Syrian rulers do not have the commitment that this doctrine demands of its authors. Not unlike the second generation nationalists of the 1950's, the new Syrian elite is searching for new symbols of legitimacy for an organizational structure buttressed by a new ideology. But this search is pursued under military rule, if necessary by force. To overcome its fratricidal tendencies, this elite advocates domination by coercion using the military and the party as its chief instruments. The structure of the Ba'th now more than ever follows the Bolshevik model, while Ba'th's ideology is not marxist-leninist but maoist-castrist.

On the inter-Arab plane, the Ba'th-Nasser antagonism has gone beyond Ba'th disappointment in Nasser's dictatorship. Egyptian and Arab nationalism have not been reconciled intellectually or politically. In the political realm, Egyptian nationalism in its most brutal and pragmatic expression under Nasser could not be reconciled with 'Aflaq's Ba'th, still less with the left Ba'thists who dominate the international and most important section of the Syrian Ba'th. Nor have the intellectual assumptions and postulates which are the foundations of pan-Arabism—as expressed by Ba'th—been reconciled with the assumptions of Nasser's followers. In fact, Syria's new elite is twice removed from Nasser's pan-Arabism. Egyptian hegemony and Ba'th messianism cannot be reconciled unless Arab nationalism charts a new course, liberated from the strait-jacket of Egyptian hegemony, which the army-Ba'th coalition succeeded in creating.

After the Camp David September 1978 Accords the relations between Sadat and Asad were exacerbated. Asad helped organize an anti-Sadat coalition, the Bagdad Summit of October 1978 denouncing Sadat's peace and diplomatic orientations.

Nasserite Egyptian nationalists still assume the hegemony of Egypt in the Arab world. The Syrian Ba'th split on this issue after the collapse of the U.A.R. The Ba'th mainstream has resigned itself to accepting eventual Arab unity under some Egyptian hegemony which, however, is premature. Nasser's personality and Egyptian ambitions were not sufficient to forge this union. This attitude guided Ba'th negotiations during the 1963 unity talks, which ended in a crisis in the Ba'th cabinet.[38] If and when the freedom of political expression is restored in Egypt, the chances are that Egyptian nationalism will be expressed through a new, reformed nationalist party—or any of the historical representatives of Egyptian nationalism. Egyptian nationalist parties could present a more formidable rival to Ba'th than Nasserism did. Thus, those Ba'thists who entertain the hope that the withering away of Sadat's dictatorship or a renewal of political union in Egypt will chart a Ba'th triumph in Egypt are deluding themselves as many have done in other matters since the foundation of Ba'th in the early 1950's. On the whole, this party has made more errors and had more failures than any other contemporary Arab nationalist party in the Middle East and it still survives. Syria is not capable, physically or politically, of sustaining the most messianic Arab nationalist party in modern times. The burden of Ba'th idealogy is too heavy for a country as poor and divided as Syria. The burden of Lebanon, the open war with Israel and Asad's adamant opposition to Sadat's peace moves may some day bring about the demise of party-army rule of the 'Alawis in Syria.

PROSPECTS OF THE ARMY

In almost three turbulent decades, the Syrian army has emerged from the role of a military force to become the political guardian of the country. The continuous civilian interference in army politics, and the politicization and radicalization of the army, has increased the influence of military politicians. The army no longer acts as an arbitrator of nationalist and progressive forces. It has been persuaded of its unique historical destiny and special political role as the "savior" of society from the "corrupt" politician. It has assumed the role of "hero" and considers itself the key and the only hope for honest politics, stability, order, and progress. These expectations and aspirations, now claimed exclusively by the army, have been supported in the last three decades by the civilian politicians, by the progressive forces, by the intellectuals, and the modernizers. Because most of these groups have discredited themselves by one means or another, the Syrian army has remained the only political organization above the battle. But, interestingly enough, the army has not been consolidated since its political emergence. Nor did the officer corps become cohesive under the intense process of politicization. The politicization of the army encouraged independent army officers and cliques to espouse a variety of rival political ideologies which only divided the officer corps. If civilian political groups had acted as the army now does, they would have been discredited. Yet the army still increases its influence, and now actually dominates Syrian society despite its apparent fratricidal tendencies, the machinations of ambitious officers, and the espousal of rival political ideologies by different army officers. It still retains the image of a new modernizing elite; of the honest rescuers of society; of the heroes and knights (Fursan) of Arabhood and of Syria.

The emergence of the office of the Presidency after the 1970 coup was another constraint on the party. Asad's popularity after the 1973 October war and the revised Syrian constitution of 1973 augmented the power of the Presidency, i.e. Asad. Asad's ascendency coincided with executive power that stems both from Asad's personality and Syrian social forces.[39] Asad's centrality however should not overlook the role of Ba'th. Certainly not the role of the military.

For Syria, a reasonably long reign of constitutional life seems unlikely, if not impossible. The Asad reign since 1970 seems quiescent, at least on the surface. The Asad dictatorship is not challenged by Ba'th. But it certainly curtails Asad's moves, as was the case in November 1977 when the Syrian Ba'th adamantly opposed Sadat's peace mission to Israel. Apparently, the rivalry between the Syrian and Iraqi Ba'th factions has not subsided and the war in Lebanon or a war with Israel seems to keep the army-party hyphen still buckled. The chances are that, whatever the outcome, army groups eventually expect independent and army-dominated rule, and they may establish their own political organization as Shishakly, Nasser and Asad did. Asad, serving as a link between the Party and the military, enhanced his role at the

expense of the military, which was not the case before 1970.
The 1970 Salah Jadid abortive coup weakened the military as
an interventionist instrument, but strengthened the Asad-
Tlas military coalition. Asad-Tlas dual power was still
dependent on the military. The military influence on policy
during the reign of Asad is not high. Yet the potential of
military intervention is there as it always was. A shrewd
observer of Syrian politics recently wrote, "The military's
influence in decision-making process, particularly *vis a vis* the
Presidency, must not, however, be exaggerated".[40] This is in
view of the fact that Asad rules the Presidency. Under
another praetorian the institution of the Presidency could
and might collapse. Executive power in Syria is not guaranteed by the Ba'th Party, the people or the praetorian on duty,
but on the praetorian institution of Syria—the military.

NOTES

1. Patrick Seale, *The Struggle for Syria: A Study of Post-War Arab Politics
    1945-1958* (London: O.U.P., 1965), and Stephen H. Longrigg, *Syria and
    Lebanon Under French Mandate* (London: O.U.P., 1958).

2. For background on Syria to 1945, see Albert K. Hourani, *Syria and
    Lebanon: A Political Essay* (London: O.U.P., 1958).

3. For an excellent presentation of the above, see Jukka Nevakivi, *Britain,
    France and the Arab Middle East* (London: University of London, The
    Athlone Press, 1969).

4. See Lebib Zuwiyya Yamak, *The Syrian Social Nationalist Party: An
    Ideological Analysis* (Cambridge: Center for Middle Eastern Affairs,
    Harvard University, Harvard Middle Eastern Monographs, XIV,
    1966).

5. Majid Khadduri, "Constitutional Development in Syria," *Middle East
    Journal,* 5 (Spring 1951), 137-60.

6. Early in this century, most Arab-Syrian officers in the Ottoman army
    had fought with the Triple Entente to the end, but quickly joined the
    cause of the Hashamite King Faysal, Syria's ruler in 1918-20. Many
    former Arab officers in the Ottoman army had joined, and some even
    founded, nationalist groups and clandestine societies; they were to
    play key roles in the politics of Arab nationalism and independence.
    (The first Iraqi cabinet was composed of former nationalist Arab
    officers serving in the Ottoman army.) In French-mandated territories
    a newly formed *Troupes Spéciales du Levant* was established as a
    gendarmerie to protect French interests in Syria and Lebanon.
    Because the French discouraged the Moslem population from joining

the army, and because many Arab-Moslem families considered the military college a second-rate school, the Syrian officers' corps under the French mandate consisted, in addition to former Syrian Ottoman officers, mainly of members of minority and ethnic groups. Thus, the senior officers of the *Troupes Spéciales* were principally French. Most Syrian officers were in the middle and junior ranks. The army was small—less than 10,000—and it remained so to the end of 1945. (During the Palestine campaign, about 12,000 men were in the Syrian army, another 4,000 were in the police force.) The Syrian officers, fewer than 300, formed a professional group with little education: only a few had high school degrees. In Syria the military academy was actually the only avenue for mobility of children of the lower class. (In contrast, the Egyptian academy was not opened to children of the middle and lower classes until 1936.) The army was therefore an important mobility vehicle for sons of the periphery and of the non-Suni ethnic groups as well as for the children of lower middle-class peasants, artisans and periphery politicians.

7. It must be remembered that the academies were still dominated by peasant and poor boys. This also accounts for the predominance of minority groups among the cadets, especially 'Alawi and Druze. Despite the growing national prestige of the officers and the army, members of urban Suni-Moslem middle classes seldom join the military schools which they consider socially and intellectually inferior.

8. Alford Carleton, "The Syrian Coups d'Etat of 1949," *Middle East Journal,* 4 (January 1950), 1-11, and Seale, *op. cit.,* chapters 4-10, pp. 24-99.

    In Arabic see Bashir al-'Auf, *al-Inqilab as-Suri* [The Syrian Coup d'Etat] (Damascus: Maktabat Husain an-Nuri, May 1949); Ahmad 'Isa l-Fil, *Suriya l-jadida fi l-Inqilab al-Awwal wa'thani* [New Syria in the First and Second Coups d'Etat] (Damascus: Matba'at ibn Zaitun, 1949); Jurj Farah, *al-Inqilab as-Suri* [The Syrian Coup d'Etat] (Aleppo: Dar an-Nashr as-Siya-siya, 1949); Na'im Zaila', *Mat az-Za'im 'ash az-Za'im* [Le roi est mort, vive le roi] (Beirut, 1949); 'Abdallah Naufal, *Suriya baina l-Inqilabain* [Syria between the Two Coups] (Beirut, 1949); Salim Taha t-Takriti, *Asrar al-Inqilab al-'Askari l-Akhir fi Suriya* [What's Behind the Last Coup in Syria] (Bagdad: Manshurat al-Basri, 1950).

    In Hebrew see Yaacov Shimoni, "Suriyah Bein Ha-Hafichot" (Syria Between Revolutions), in *Hamizrah Hehadash* [The New East] (Tel Aviv), Vol. 1, No. 1 (October 1949), pp. 7-21.

9. On the Syrian army before 1949, See Hourani, *op. cit.:* Gordon H. Torrey, "The Role of the Military in Society and Government in Syria and the Formation of the UAR," in Sydney N. Fisher (ed.), *The Military in the Middle East* (Columbus: Ohio State U. Press, 1963), 53-70; and Eliezer Beeri, *Ha-Ktzuna veha-Shilton Ba-Olam Ha-Aravi* [The Officer Class in Politics and Society of the Arab East] (Sifriat Poalim Tel-Aviv, Israel, 1966), 48-62.

10. Patrick Seale, *op. cit.,* pp. 116-17.

11. *Ibid.,* p. 119.

12. Yitzhak Oron, "The History and the Ideas of the Arab Socialist Renaissance Party," *Hamizrah Hehadash,* Vol. 9, No. 4 (1959), pp. 245-48, 263; Seale, *op. cit.,* pp. 38-39.

13. Seale, *op. cit.,* p. 127.

14. *Ibid.,* p. 118.

15. *Ibid.*

16. Michel 'Aflaq, *Fi Sabil al-Ba'th* [*The Road to Renaissance*] (Beirut: Dar al-Taliah, 1959). Munif al-Razzaz, *Ma'alim al-Hayat al-Arabiyyah al-Jadidah* [*The Nature of New Arab Life*] (Beirut: Dar al'Ilm li al-Malayin, 1960). Also, see the writings of Abdalah al-Rimawi and Salah al-Din Bitar. See also Seale, *op. cit.,* pp. 153-58, and Kamel Salah Abu Jaber, "The Arab Ba'th Socialist Party's History, Organization and Ideology" (doctoral dissertation, Syracuse University, January 1965), pp. 211-44, which is, unfortunately, poor on Ba'th-army relations.

17. Beeri, *op. cit.,* pp. 114-19, 358-61.

18. Jaber, *op. cit.,* p. 56.

19. Seale, *op. cit.,* pp. 64-68.

20. *Ibid.,* p. 182.

21. For a recent interpretation of the Union, its merger and collapse, see Seale, *op. cit.,* pp. 307-26; Malcolm Kerr, *The Arab Cold War, 1958-1967,* Chatham House Essays, RIIA (2nd ed.; London: O.U.P., 1967); and Jaber, *op cit.,* 106-50.

22. *Middle East Record,* 1960, Vol. 1, compiled by Israel Oriental Society (London: Weidenfeld and Nicolson, 1962), p. 497.

23. Beeri, *op. cit.,* pp. 104-7.

24. Malcolm Kerr even goes so far as to maintain that "it was by accidental circumstance, when the coup came on March 8, the Ba'th was on hand to assist and take credit for it."

25. Beeri, *op. cit.,* pp. 358-61.

26. Hafiz then turned to eliminate his rivals in the army, Ziad Hariri, Luay al-'Atasi, and Muhammad 'Umran. The latter was purged with the help of a fellow 'Alawi, Salah Jadid. To eliminate his army rivals, Hafiz' position with the Ba'th was not sufficient. He needed support of senior army officers, predominantly 'Alawi and Druze. Facts compiled from *MER 1960, The New East* chronology sections for the years 1965-1967; the Beirut paper *al-Khayat;* the Egyptian paper *Al Ahram;* and various Ba'th and Unionists' pamphlets and documents. See also Kerr, *op. cit.,* pp. 39-102, and Jaber, *op. cit.,* pp. 156-59.

27. Jaber, *op. cit.,* pp. 153-56, 180-82, 188-94. For a most comprehensive analysis of the Iraqi Ba'th, see Uriel Dann, *Iraq Under Qassem* (New York: Praeger, and London: Pall Mall, 1969), pp. 145-55.

28. On the rise of the "countryside boys," see Eric Rouleau, "La Syrie Baasiste ou la fuite à gauche: III La revanche des campagnes," *Le Monde,* 10/16-10/17/66, p. 3.

29. Avraham Ben-Tzur, "The Neo-Ba'th Party of Syria," *Journal of Contemporary History,* Vol. 3., No. 3 (1968), pp. 161-82.

30. All these are borrowed from Ben-Tzur, *ibid.,* 164-72.

31. *Ibid.,* pp. 172-73.
32. The formation of an "ideological army" by the Iraqi Ba'thists, who attempted to turn Iraq into a left-Ba'thist fortress and established a 65,000-man national guard in February 1963, alarmed the Iraqi army, which considered this para-military ideological army a threat. This fear triggered the 'Arif counter-Ba'th coup in November 1966, and the political annihilation of Iraqi Ba'th. Since the army coups of 1968-69 the Ba'thist have returned but, as yet, they cannot be said to govern Iraq, except by execution, elimination of rivals, and decimation of the army high command.

The Iraqi army's distaste for a party oriented or dominated by the national guard is not unique to the Arab world. The struggle between the S.A. and the army in Nazi Germany was resolved by Hitler in favor of the army in 1934. Purging the S.A. was one of his shrewdest moves: it first neutralized the army, then gained its support, and finally made it subservient to the Nazi state. The ongoing struggle in China also indicates the army's and especially the professional soldier's distaste for the Red Guard and militias. The controversy over the formation of the Israeli Defense Army in 1948 was resolved by dissolving militias and special army groups, which were supported by leftist and extreme nationalists' political parties, and by creating a professional army subordinated to civilian control. Here, as elsewhere, the leftists supported the concept of militia against a regular "bourgeois" professional army. (On Germany-S.A. army relationships, see J. W. Wheeler-Bennett, *The Nemesis of Power: The German Army in Politics 1918-1945* (London: Macmillan, 1953), Part II and Part III, pp. 157ff.; D. K. Bracher (ed.), *Nationalsozialistische Machtergreifung* (Cologne and Opladen, 1962); Robert O'Neill, *The German Army and the Nazi Party, 1933-1939* (London: Cassell, 1966). On China, see Ellis Joffe, *Party and Army Professionalism and Political Control in the Chinese Officer Corps 1949-1964* (Cambridge: Harvard East Asiatic Monograph Series, 1965). On Israel, see Amos Perlmutter, *Military and Politics in Israel* (New York: Praeger, and London: Cass, 1969). See also Jaber, *op. cit.,* pp. 180-83.
33. See Shimon Shamir, "The Question of a 'National Philosophy' in Contemporary Arab Thought," *Asian and African Studies,* Vol. 1, 1965.
34. On the role of center-periphery conflict in modern praetorianism, see Amos Perlmutter, "The Praetorian State and the Praetorian Army," *Comparative Politics,* 1 (April 1969), pp. 396-418.
35. Beeri, *op. cit.,* pp. 100-110, 358-61.
36. A.I. Dawisha, "Syria under Asad 19780-78: The Centers of Power", *Government and the Opposition,* Vol. 13, no. 3, Summer 1978, p. 344.
37. See the analysis of the Sultanist-praetorian-patrimonial role of Arab military elites, in Perlmutter, *op. cit.*
38. Kerr, *op. cit.,* pp. 75-85.
39. A. I. Dawisha, *op. cit.,* pp. 347-8.
40. *Ibid.,* p. 353.

CHAPTER 7

The Arab Military Elite *

The field of modern civil-military relations is not a totally fresh one, still unexplored. Kurt Lang's 1969 bibliography on military sociology lists over one thousand items—books, articles, and unpublished material—and this catalogue includes only the material available in English. His section on civil-military relations lists some 250 items,[1] an impressive accumulation in a supposedly new field.

Nevertheless, students of civil-military relations, particularly those concerned with developing polities, still assert that they possess meager data. Some still contrive sloppy conceptualizations and offer inelegant explanations for the relations that exist among the military, politics, and society. Students

* I am grateful to Professor Samuel P. Huntington, Government Department, Harvard University, for his valuable criticism of this paper, and to Jane Kumin and Gary Orren for their assistance. However, no one but the author is responsible for the point of view expressed in the article. The books under discussion are: Jacob C. Hurewitz, *Middle East Politics: The Military Dimension*, Frederick A. Praeger, New York, 1969. Uriel Dann, *Iraq Under Qassem: A Political History 1958-1963*, Israel Universities Press and Praeger, Jerusalem and New York, 1969. Eliezer Beeri, *Army Officers in Arab Politics and Society*, Israel Universities Press and Praeger, Jerusalem and New York, 1969.

160

of contemporary politics assume that little or not enough has been done in the area of civil-military relations, that it is still a "new" field. In fact, even students of civil-military relations could probably list fewer than ten scholars who have contributed at least one significant, *pioneering*, and *influential* study in the field. These would be Samuel P. Huntington, Samuel E. Finer, Morris M. Janowitz, Stanislav Andreski, and possibly certain earlier scholars such as Samuel Stouffer, Hans Speier, Edward M. Earle, and Harold D. Lasswell. What we have is an enormous imbalance between the quantity of literature on civil-military relations and its significance—except for the work of a few very talented scholars and some of the books under review here demonstrate the reasons for this imbalance. It is clearly related to the dynamic but asymmetrical state of the contemporary social sciences, the lack of general acceptance of value orientations and research procedures, and the absence of governing standards and procedures concerning definition, conceptualization, frames of reference, theories, and taxonomies. These deficiencies prevent the systematic analysis of civil-military relations and the development of a general theory concerning them. At the same time, concepts of the military, society, and politics are heavily saturated with ideological orientations that are inherently controversial and even explosive. In the absence of an accepted general theory of conflict, the demarcation lines between order and instability, among politics, society, and the military depend upon such vague or all-inclusive concepts as total war, revolution, dynamic change, and the universal ethic of modernization.

A historical examination of contemporary politics and the study of civil-military relations demonstrates our second contention: the value-orientations and ideological inclinations of social scientists have both impelled and hindered the development of an all-inclusive and useful general theory of civil-military relations.

Going over the literature, and especially the contributions of the influential authors mentioned earlier, we find strong ties between their conceptual and analytical positions and the political and ideological climate of the times. In fact, in a period of over forty years, four different analytical models at least have been designed, all closely related to the politico-ideological *Weltanschauung* of the authors.

During the 1930's, democratic and liberal political scientists in America reacted against the rise of three totalitarian systems in Europe. From this background emerged Lasswell's construct of the Garrison State, a concept that focused on the rise of the technician of violence. Thus our first model—the Garrison Officer. Lasswell mistakenly identified this figure as the high priest of totalitarianism. Later events have shown us that the grand inquisitors and villains of the garrison state were actually the civilian ideologues and demagogues, the romantic primitivists of Japan and Germany. Nevertheless, Lasswell's theory was an important one. When, in January 1941, the *American Journal of Sociology* devoted an entire issue to the rise of militarism, the lead article was Lasswell's "The Garrison State." In the other articles, war and the military were examined from different angles—anthropological, sociological, and historical. This was the first attempt at a taxonomy; it was hindered, of course, by the liberal fear of the emergence of the military Frankenstein's monster.

Now, in a later period, the monumental research of Samuel Stouffer and others on the American soldier has yielded enough material for a new generation of American scholars to re-examine the analytical truisms of the pre-war generation. Curiously enough, the war gave us a better understanding of the military and its role. Stouffer's study signified a transition from Lasswell's interpretation to modern, less ideologically colored ones. Since its publication two young and perceptive scholars have emerged—S.P. Huntington[2] and M. Janowitz[3], the latter strongly influenced by Stouffer. These two have removed the problem of civil-military relations from the ideological orientation of anti-totalitarianism and proclaimed an open analysis of the modern military, this time the American military.

The totalitarian-oriented Garrison Soldier model has been replaced by the liberal and civilian-oriented Professional Soldier. Thus our second model.

Huntington's *The Soldier and the State* is one of the first and best attempts to set up a theoretical system of civil-military relations. He argues persuasively that the military professional (in contradistinction to Lasswell's totalitarian technician of violence) is a new social breed. Guided by his professional ethic and corporate orientations, he is not Lasswell's ideologue but a responsible, intelligent, and civilian-oriented professional, loyal to his master, the civilian-dominated, democratic state.

Huntington draws his theory of the civil-military from analyses of the United States,[4] and his concept of the professional soldier emerges from his study of the strains between a professional military and a liberal society.[5] Huntington also analyses and explains the deviant cases of professionalism in Germany and Japan. His general theory focuses on the relative power of the civil and the military in controlling the state: "What is essential [in civil-military relations] is the relation between the power of military groups and the power of the civilian governmental leadership."[6] Huntington distinguishes between two models of civil-military relations: the objective control model, where the military is small, exclusive, highly professional, indifferent to ideologies, and subject to civilian governmental control; and the subjective control model, which is characterized by the absence of clear lines between civilian and military groups and values. In the latter model, the military is integrated into society and supports dominant political ideologies and social values.[7]

While Lasswell's Garrison Soldier (the technician of violence and an independent variable) served to explain the totalitarian state, Huntington concentrated on the Professional Soldier as a dependent variable. He attempted to explain the nature of the modern military profession, oriented toward the taming of the officer within the state.

Janowitz approaches the military from a different direction—through the sociology of organizations. He demonstrates that the *Holzkopf*, the ritual-oriented, rigid barracks officer, is no longer the representative American officer; the model is rather the technologically-scientifically oriented modern officer, whose organizational concept of authority is manipulation. "The future of the military profession rests on a balance between organizational stability and adaptation to rapid technological and political change."[8] First, the revolution in military technology is changing the patterns of organizational authority in the army. Second, as a consequence of this change and of the new strategic realities of international politics and the technological revolution, the constabulary-force concept is emerging. Janowitz calls for a sustained and realistic interest in military institutions, which professional sociologists have avoided in the past, and challenges the fashionable view that the military is not "researchable". He himself does not deny the implications of his analysis of the military organization, nor does he relegate his study to the field of industrial or organizational sociology. The organizational transformation of the military also transforms its analyst. The military is politically relevant, and the sociologist who studies it becomes an ideologist of the role of modern military power in the industrial state. In this role, Janowitz suggests a new framework for the operation of the military in modern times—the military as a constabulary force. "The constabulary force concept encompasses the entire range of military power and organization. At the upper end are the weapons of mass destruction; those of flexible and specialized capacity are at the lower end, including the specialists in military aid programs, in para-military operations, in guerrilla and counter-guerrilla warfare."[9]

The works of Huntington and Janowitz rejuvenated the study of the military and of civil-military relations. They gave the social scientist new tools of analysis and a conceptual framework for explanation. The study of the military in politics was further enhanced by the rise of the modern comparative politics, and the field of civil-military relations led to new analyses and, of course, to new ideological stances on the military and society. This new spurt of research focused on the developing polities.

Among the first attempts at a comparative study of the military in developing states is a work edited by John J. Johnson.[10] This book presents a collection of independent monographs of which the theme—the role of the military in underdeveloped countries—is quite common, but it also offers comparative, theoretical analyses by several authors. Edward Shils, a pioneer in comparative theoretical studies, has written the introductory essay, "The Military in the Political Development of the New States"[11] (drawn from his short essay, *Political Development in the New States*), which sets the theoretical framework of the Johnson book.

The growing role of the military in the politics of new states is explained in this book by the military's commitment to modernization and political development. When these aspirations become operational, they bring about structural and functional differentiation. The military is considered a highly effective instrument of modernization by most authors in Johnson's volume.

According to this school, political development and modernization both determine and explain changes in new states. Among the alternative courses of political development is the modernizing military oligarchy.[12] This has become the most prominent model not only for the role of the military in developing states but for political development and modernization as well. Following Shils, Lucian Pye, in his essay "Armies in the Process of Political Modernization", argues that the military, as the only organized institution in a transitional society, is its most modern and rational organization. The military organization, Pye writes, plays a prominent role in the newly emerging nations because it is a modernizing agent.[13]

Two other authors who explain the emergence of the military in developing states as a product of modernization are John J. Johnson and Manfred Halpern. Both give the military a high position—as the leading stratum of the new middle class. Halpern's expectations for the military in political development surpass any suggested by Shils and Pye. Halpern advances the concept of the New Middle Classes (NMC) to explain politics of change and the pivotal role assigned to the army. He divides the middle class in the Middle East into two sectors—one is the small merchants and the bureaucrats—assigning to the second, the salariat, the role of modernizer and identifying it as the New Middle Class. The NMC's most powerful and cohesive stratum, according to Halpern, is the army, and the NMC is represented by the army, which is its "most powerful instrument", when the army is "securely anchored in well-organized movement".[14] Thus the army will help the NMC to marshal mass support. Here was born our third model—the Progressive Modernizing Soldier.

In assessing modern organization, we might refer to the variables of the Weberian rational bureaucracy scale—efficiency, honesty, skill, and rational orientation. It is undoubtedly true that the military in some developing polities score high on the Weberian scale, and hence may be regarded as representative models of "modern organization". However, several "modern" military establishments in developing nations have contributed much less than we might have expected toward expansion of the political system and widening the political participation of their respective polities. Not one military establishment in the Arab Middle East has so far succeeded in sustaining modern political institutions and structures; political parties remain weak, fragmented, or virtually non-existent, and efficient modern bureaucracies have not yet developed. In fact, interventionist actions of the the military have served only to foster fragile, infant political systems and have increased the numbers but not the efficiency of the bureaucracy.

These pioneer efforts were soon superseded by more penetrating explorations and efforts to reconcile fact to theory, for few or none of the military "progressive" regimes have fulfilled the social scientists' expectations. What has been found to be most significant about the modern soldier in developing polities is that his profession has become more political. Under unstable political conditions, few officers are willing to trade their profession for politics, but those few who do are critical to an explanation of the role of the military in developing polities. Therefore, the focus of students of the military since the 1960's has been on military political interventionism, rather than on prophesying the "goodness" that military rule will bestow on modernizing polities. Scholars have turned to the study of the *political causes* of military intervention and the role of the military as a dominant group in charge of modernization.

Military interventions can no longer be considered isolated or independent events. They are connected with what Huntington broadly defined as the phenomenon of praetorianism. "For the sake of brevity," writes Huntington, "the phrase 'praetorian society' is used to refer to such a politicized society with the understanding that this refers to the participation not only of the military but of other social forces as well."[15] In this review we deal with military "praetorianism" exclusively, as an *aspect* of the general problem of contemporary political participation and political order in developing polities. For now elites who have not been politically interventionist in the past (this of course is not exclusively true of the military), or who were limited in their interventionism, have dared to assume the heavy burden of political responsibility.

In view of the general trend toward modernization, it may be said that various types of praetorianism probably represent certain stages of development. At present, praetorianism often appears in states that are in the early and middle stages of modernization and political mobilization. In developing polities, the army is propelled into political action when civilian groups fail to legitimize themselves. The army's presence in civilian affairs indicates that the government is corrupt and is not expected to improve soon; that material improvements do not match ideological perspectives; that traditional institutions are unable to bring about material improvement; and that modernized elites are incapable of establishing political institutions and structures that will sustain the momentum of social mobilization and modernization.[16] Thus our fourth model—the Praetorian Officer.

The salient characteristic of modern military elites in developing polities is their *aspiration* toward military professionalism—i.e., the control over the military organization. The professionalism and institutionalization of the military entails the establishment of military colleges, specialized training, the formation of a unified professional group and of a national army. Praetorian conditions are connected with professional military establishments and structures, some of which are institutionalized before concomitant political and socioeconomic structures—political parties, parliaments, a centralized administrative bureaucracy, national authority, middle classes, and a nationalist ideology. Thus, corporate professionalism is not a guarantee against military praetorianism. In fact, in praetorian polities the military interventionists are the professional soldiers, the graduates of the military academies.

Praetorianism, and particularly military praetorianism as conceived by Huntington, can be explained by a multitude of preconditions such as: rapid mobilization of men, groups, and resources; low degree of social cohesion, high social polarity and potential for class fratricide, low level of political institutionalization, asymmetrical relationship between center and periphery, ineffective support for sustained political structures and procedures.[17]

Military praetorianism may also arise from special conditions in the military establishment itself, such as frequent military coups and interventions, fratricide within the officer corps, poor tradition of military professionalism, and, of course, the long reign of the "praetorian society", all of which become political. What we must explain is the *connections* among these variables. *How* and *when* do they lead to a military praetorian polity? *Why* is it that the "praetorian society" is permanently subject to the potential domination of the military rather than, for example, of the students, the unions, the clergy, or other "non-professional" political politicized elites? What Huntington has established is that a single explanation no longer covers the phenomenon of military praetorianism. "Military explanations do not explain military interventions. The reason for this is simply that military interventions are only one specific manifestation of a broader phenomenon in underdeveloped societies: the general politicization of social forces and institutions."[18]

The books under review do not resemble one another in conception, argument, focus, or explanation, but all would agree with Huntington that "In such societies, [praetorian] politics lacks autonomy, complexity, coherence, and adaptability." We shall begin with J. C. Hurewitz' *Middle East Politics: The Military Dimension*. Hurewitz, Professor of Middle Eastern International Politics at Columbia, is an established authority on the diplomatic history of the Middle East and author of the excellent *The Struggle for Palestine*. His book is an attempt to capture the politics of military modernization in the Middle East as it relates to the international politics of the area. It is a blow-by-blow factual account of the history of military modernization and details the proliferation of military establishments and weapons in the modern Middle

East since the rise of Muhammad 'Ali who reigned over Egypt 1805-49. The country-by-country catalogue of events and facts illustrating the "militarization" of the modern Middle East is supported by "explanations" pointing to historical sources and cultural-religious legacies as contributing factors. Here Hurewitz recruits the Islamic legacy as well as Ottoman practices, and the colonial heritage as indicators of why militarization became a "natural" element in the Middle East. In addition, cold-war machinations, inter-Arab rivalries, and the Arab-Israeli conflict dictated the rapidity of military proliferation and its political justification as necessary and "inevitable" forms of security. They also enhanced the emergence of a nationalist zealot officer class (although this point is left implicit by Hurewitz), who, in the absence of any other legitimacy, have legitimated their rule on the basis of the military imperatives of security. In short, the Islamic-Ottoman-Imperial legacies contrived to establish military institutions that since 1945 have proliferated to match the growth of Arab nationalism.

The book ignores the recent social-science orientation of political science and is completely oblivious to its literature. It could be argued that, in view of the author's intention, this point is totally irrelevant; if so, *mea culpa*. However, because of the scarcity of talent, resources, and daring in the study of the modern Middle East, I feel that, as social scientists, we cannot concur with the author's approach.

If the author had restricted himself to one of his stated ambitions in writing this book, if he had produced a general "inductive" study of the "military" establishment, the "states," and the "region" of the Middle East, it would have been a most valuable "inductive", if digest-like book. And that, essentially, is what it really is—another addition to the meager monographic output on Middle Eastern "states" and "militarists". But Hurewitz' *pronunciamento* that "The book was conceived as an inquiry into the causes and consequences of military intervention in the postwar politics of the Middle East" (p.viii) leaves the author at the mercy of his own statement, on the analytical and theoretical firing range. This is especially true since the author writes that the "military dimension" is to be explained by the progress of "military modernization since Muhammad 'Ali (1805-1849)".

Hurewitz' further claim that "The inquiry thus grew into a comparative analysis of political systems in the Middle East" is a most flagrant *reductio ad absurdum* of what the book is about. Neither its title, chapters, content, analyses, explanations, or queries are directed or related to what we know today as "comparative analysis" of "political systems", of "modernization," or of "political development". The "comparative method" employed in this book is reminiscent of the state of comparative political science in the 1920's: the studies of the Great Powers, the Major Foreign Powers, the Great Military States—all under one cover entitled a "Comparative Study". The book is in the tradition of "hard facts", formal-legal studies so adequately exposed elsewhere by Harry Eckstein:[19] at best this is not a comparative study; at worst it is an anachronistic caricature of dated comparative political science. A book that pretends to be an "inquiry" that "grew into a comparative analysis" whose "focus [is] on civil-military relations" (p. viii) has not even one sentence defining "comparative", or "civil-military relations", except in the most literal sense. Most remarkable is that in a book of this size some twenty pages are devoted to "Armies as Agencies of Social Change", of course in a "comparative" way.

It is hard to describe this book's theoretical and analytical impoverishment in a few sentences. Hurewitz "explains" the relationships between army and social change in the Middle East by contrasting Ataturk to Nasser. Here we have a representative example of his "comparative methods": "Both men came from the lower middle class. . . . Mustafa Kemal's father was a governmental clerk and his mother a peasant. 'Abd al-Nasir's father was a deputy postmaster. The two leaders early in life became ardent foes of the privileged classes." "Once the two men reached the top, they clutched their political leadership tightly" (p. 420). "Neither man could claim primary authorship of his modernization program" (p. 421), and so on. These premature echoes of "on the one hand" and "on the other" reach a crescendo in Hurewitz' description of the "differences" between Kemal and Nasser. They differ in their conception of their roles as "instruments of social change"; (p. 422) whereas Kemal restricted his nationalist leadership to Turkey and abandoned Ottoman hegemonial claim to a Caliphate, Nasser is an empire builder who, rather than concentrating on Egypt, has turned his attention to a pan-Arab Egyptian hegemony (p. 424). Modernization is never examined as a concept or even as a state of mind. It is simply modernity, and Hurewitz probably refers to industrialization. Ataturk's modernization, we are told, was "indirect", which means that he "made a rigorous point of civilianizing his regime . . . " whereas " 'Abd al-Nasir and his fellow Free Officers manifestly preferred direct domination of the government . . . " (p. 426). What the author wishes to convey is that Ataturk's industrialization was more successful than Nasser's. Thus Hurewitz "dismisses" a most crucial chapter on armies and social change. We find the idea for comparing Ataturk and Nasser, and some of its subsequent arguments, reminiscent of what Beeri wrote in the Hebrew version of his book in 1966, three years before the publication of Hurewitz' book (compare Beeri's Hebrew edition, pp. 337-340 and Hurewitz, pp. 420-426); we still find this comparison of little value. Kemal is not analytically a useful model for comparison with Nasser. In fact, comparing Nasser with Kemal is as fruitful as comparing Scharnhorst with General Gordon of Khartoum. We shall return to this point.

The two chapters that survey Islamic modernization of military legacies are trite factual recitations of what has been written in the literature several times over. Here Hurewitz does not give us a sophisticated, sociological, Janowitzian explanation of the capacity of the military for intervention, its internal proliferation and differentiation. His account is analytically irrelevant, no more than a statement of the fact that the military in the Middle East has been *modernized* (i.e., more units, more complex command, better equipment) since the early nineteenth century—and has proliferated.

Hurewitz has taught us that the military establishment is large, expensive, modern, and more efficient—this despite three Arab disasters with Israel, the Yemeni-Egyptian fiasco, and several Iraqi defeats by the Kurds. Yet by far the most modern, powerful, expansive, efficient, and capable military establishment is that of Israel. Why do we find military praetorianism in seven Arab countries (and may well in Jordan after Hussein falls, if he does) and none in Israel? Hurewitz is aware that Israel is the "most vigorous democracy in the Middle East" and that it is a "garrison democracy" and not "a militaristic state" (p. 6). But why is this true? Because Israel is democratic, modern, Jewish? Do these variables explain why Israel is non-praetorian and Egypt, which is authoritarian, early modern, and Arab-Moslem, is praetorian? What Hurewitz fails to perceive, and what he could explain, is that military interventionism is not necessarily related to the size and strength of the military establishment. Why has the military in Yemen, the most backward of Arab states with (before 1962) a meager military establishment, produced successive military coups, and why does the fragile military still rule Yemèn? Why is the most modern Arab country, Egypt, plagued by military praetorianism? Why did Kemal succeed in establishing a sustaining and effective civilian establishment and Nasser fail, in four efforts in close to two decades, to form political parties and sustaining political structures? Why is it that restrictive, elitist political participation or domination have been effective in Socialist Egypt, as it is in Saudi Arabia, Kuwait, and Jordan? Why has political participation failed in the homeland of Arab socialism?

Hurewitz does not ask these questions; it seems that they do not even occur to him. He writes that "military politics in the Middle East in the first two postwar decades is usually assessed on the basis of contemporary evidence, which is not always clear or convincing" (p. 15). We must assess the phenomena in "the longer perspective of history" (p.15). Hurewitz is aware that the "study of military politics . . . necessitates a consideration of regional influences" (p. 7) and he does deal with the evolution of the military establishment as it emerged from its Islamic tradition, transformed by the Ottoman center, by Egypt in the nineteenth century; and by foreign military instructors who left a strong mark on the academies (Chapters 2-3, pp. 15-65). However, he fails to perceive analytically the similarities between Ottoman and pan-Arab military concepts of society, polity, and the military.

As for a comparative perspective, we could contrast patrimonialism (the Ottoman system) with Arab military praetorianism. The types of praetorianism, military establishments, recruitment, and structural arrangements that existed in some of the historical empires are *functionally* equivalent to those of some developing praetorian polities. We find a valuable analogy in Max Weber's analysis of patrimonialism and praetorianism.[20] According to Weber, patrimonialism, or domination by *honoratiores,* was a type of authority oriented toward membership in the manorial ("servile") or the patrimonial group, which was manifested in the decentralization of the patriarchal household and the extension of land-holding, empire-building, and "extrapatrimonial" recruitment. In this pre-bureaucratic political system, staff was recruited only to insure subordination to patriarchal rule, extended in "extrapatriarchal" recruitment to relations based on feudal, bureaucratic-contracted, or merely personal rulership.

In the patrimonial state, the chief obligation of the citizen was the material maintenance of the ruler, and the military became a *permanent establishment* as the process of financial rationalization developed. Relations between patrimony and conscripts were based on two models: clientèleship and slavery. The combinations varied with patrimonial rulers and states. Janissaries were recruited among aliens and pariah castes; at other times a "citizen" army of peasants was recruited for the same purpose. The feudal armies, an outgrowth of increased economic rationalism, developed a group of privileged *honoratiores,* using peasants and military technology. Military training became crucial, the relationship between patrimonial authority and the military was altered. Here we see the beginning of military professionalism. Now the military establishment could be used against the political subjects of the patrimonial authority.

But, as Weber points out, a ruler whose sole political authority rests on threats—on military power—ultimately cannot maintain his rule. Here the professional army could play a key role. Weber calls the disintegration of the patrimonial system Sultanism.[21] In our view the functional equivalent of Sultanism is contemporary Arab praetorianism. Praetorianism is connected with the institutionalization of military that becomes an autonomous group if it is not successfully subdued. The emergence of military professionalism increases the political importance of the military. When legitimate authority falters, the military "fills" the gap; it fulfills its historical role—i.e., praetorianism. Thus, in the Ottoman Empire, the ruling institution became identical with the army during and after the reign of Suleiman the Magnificent. "The Ottoman government had been an army before it was anything else." The Janissaries, the praetorian guard of the Ottoman Empire, were the chief instruments of the sultan from the sixteenth century until the nineteenth century (1826). The military became a formidable bureaucracy, proliferating and growing more complex when firearms and cavalry were introduced. As a bureaucracy (in pre-bureaucratic and bureaucratic societies) the military was an active participant in politics, and, in several of the historical bureaucratic empires, engaged in an independent political struggle.

Modern praetorianism differs significantly from the patrimonial mode in one respect: on the whole, the patrimonial military represented legitimacy; the modern military praetorians have generally challenged legitimacy.

Hurewitz has totally failed to explain what Eliezer Beeri analyzed successfully in *Army Officers in Arab Politics and Society*. Beeri used the Ottoman legacy as a model for the political subculture of the military and demonstrated the links between the modern Arab officer and his Ottoman predecessors.

The modern Ottoman army was established in 1826, with the end of Janissary and Bektasi rule. Under the aegis of Sultan Abdul Majid (1839-1861), Captain von Moltke and other German advisors began large-scale reform of the military and the civil service, and opened the army to all subjects of the empire. The new Ottoman army also became a haven for social déclassés and parvenus. Captain von Moltke reports on the Ottoman officer class to two friends on the Berlin General Staff: "The weakest side of the army . . . were the officers. Two Generals in the Army stem from Muhammad Hasai's Harem, a third one was only a porter ten years ago, and the fourth was . . . recruited from the prisoners working on a vessel" (p. 199).

The middle—and even some of the highest—echelons of the Ottoman army were recruited from lower classes. Taken when young from family and village, these recruits lost class and social identity; they found these in their rank and profession in the army, and the Prussian officers encouraged this dedication. Thus the Ottoman army obliterated the potential radicalism or social consciousness of the children of the déclassé, and so it was that Arab officers of this army (especially Iraqis) could participate in suppressing the Syrian revolt of 1919. This legacy was crucial in the formation of the Syrian and Iraqi armies—all with former Ottoman officers. The Arab type, according to Beeri, is heir to the Ottoman officer.

Unlike the Arab armies, the Egyptian army was modernized and reformed as early as the reign of Muhammad 'Ali (1818-1848). But Muhammad 'Ali had no desire to make his army Egyptian. In fact, he planned a mercenary army of black Africans (particularly Negro slaves) led by foreign officers, hoping to exploit the Egyptian *fellah* as a farmer rather than a soldier. Most of the students at the officer training schools were Turks, Circassians, and Georgians.

By the 1830's, however, Muhammad 'Ali's policy had failed, and the army was largely Egyptian although most of the Arab officers (again few in actual number) held positions no higher than Captain. These reforms did give the army a sense of national consciousness. Khedive Isma'il (1863-1879) enhanced this spirit, for his ambitious plans for Egypt's aggrandisement included a large-scale army, again to be dominated by foreigners—this time American officers (pp. 206-210). In 1882, however, British occupation under Lord Cromer put an end to Isma'il's military: the grand Egyptian army was now a small native force. Reduced to a branch of the civil service, the army was not a base for nationalists, revolutionaries, or modernizers from Cromer's time until the mid-1930's.[22]

The Empire was the patron and client of the Ottoman-officer. Although he often emerged from among the poor peasantry of the déclassé, he was conservatively and corporately oriented. This orientation is no longer true of Arab officers. After the breakdown of Ottoman legitimacy, their place was filled by the nationalists, all seeking a new legitimacy under modifying doctrines: socialism, pan-Arabism, Ba'thism, Nasserism, etc. But their dedication to the military organization still persists. Beeri points out that the only non-political army in the Arab East (next to Lebanon) is the Jordanian Legion, which has also been the least revolutionary. Before 1967, the Bedouin officer in Jordan served the dynastic Hashemite kingdom. No other native army in the Middle East, except in Egypt, has supported its monarchs. Bedouins, who constitute over half the Legion's officer class, have a minor role in Arab nationalist politics; the fact that their sole interest is the military organization, their content with the system (at least until 1967), their homogeneity, and their rural conservatism, have saved Hussein on two occasions. But the Jordanian army is being radicalized by Fatah and the militant Palestinians. In Syria, the peasant has been recruited from the agricultural heartland by the "progressive" politicians and officers; thus these officers are clients of a "progressive" state. Their mobility is the product of the army's independent political action and extreme nationalism. This is true of the Iraqi officers and now of the Sudanese, but not of the Egyptians.

All this and a multitude of other points we have learned from Beeri, an autodidact left-wing member of Kibbutz *Hazore'a (Hashomer Hatzair)* who lectures in the Kibbutz academy at Givat Haviva. As a former member of Israeli military intelligence, he has an intimate and detailed knowledge of contemporary Arab military elites. Beeri's investigation of the Arab military and the politically inclined officer is an accumulation of more than two decades of rigorous and painstaking efforts, including personal interviews with Arab officers. This is an original source book of unrivaled factual content. Most of this content is illuminating; some of it straightforwardly challenges several hypotheses offered by scholars who have made general statements without first-hand data. Not a social scientist, but a neo-Marxist, Beeri possesses critical faculties and a strong sensitivity to social structures. His book is well planned, but, like several Marxists or neo-Marxists or, for that matter some sociologists, he fails to be equally perceptive when he links social structural to political analysis. We shall return to this point later.

Beeri sets his empirical investigation against the prevailing model of the Progressive Officer. In his view, what emerges from the Arab world in the midst of a deep crisis of transition and change is "The Doctrine of Inevitability," i.e.: (1) inevitably, no group other than the military can assume the responsibility for change, transition, and the modernization crisis; (2) the officer-politicians can accomplish these goals, which are thus "inevitable." Beeri now sets himself to upset his doctrine and the Progressive Officer model. His data demonstrate clearly that most of the officers who say they belong to the new middle class are scions and offshoots of the rural middle class, sons of 'umadah and respectable middle classes in rural Egypt. Thus by nature, tradition, inclination, they are conservatively oriented. Thus, if the officers have been "inevitably destined" to bring about change, their conservatism (Chapter 6)—particularly in Egypt—demonstrates their inclination toward restricted political participation. Beeri concludes that the officer-politicians are not destined, able, or even willing to become the reformers, the role-expanders of their societies, as the Inevitability Doctrine unrealistically prescribed.

In his view the radical Islamic and Arab nationalist legacies are the foundation of military praetorianism. Modernization of the military establishment does not inevitably lead to political participation. Thus Beeri concludes (see pp. 287-304) that the military elite is *not responsive* to the populism it proclaims (pp. 305-312); that the Islamic legacy, and not socialism or modernization, "plays a key role in the rise of the officer class to political power in the Middle East" (p. 321); that Arab nationalism has been the aim of the officers wherever they have played key roles since the dissolution of the Ottoman Empire; and that the impact of the Young Turks and the Kemalist revolutions must have been decisive for contemporary officer-politicians in the Middle East (pp. 323-326) who chose the Kemalist revolution as their model but failed to follow it. Beeri argues that the "inevitable" stage of military progressivism in the Middle East leads to a political cul-de-sac and to precisely the results that were *not* expected of these "new" classes. Progressive, military-dominated rule, according to Beeri, is no more than a series of oligarchic, restrictive, power-driven military juntas; the military dictatorship has been formed to advance not social change but the political career of the desperadoes. Beeri's greatest pitfall is his simple but somewhat unregenerate neo-Marxist orientations. His oversimplification of political behavior, class relations, and class ideology and his over-emphasis on the social origins of the officers to explain military praetorianism distort his better perception that military praetorianism is an overtone of something more than a "social" or "organizational" factor. Beeri's analysis of the ideology of the Arab military praetorian as a false consciousness, a *camera obscura*, reiterates the Marxist usage of the concept of ideology. When he compares Nasser and the Iraqi al-Sabbagh as "military intellectuals" he fails to perceive that al-Sabbagh, Nasser, and the Ba'th officers of Syria-Iraq are essentially of the Ottoman-Sultanist type—anti-intellectual, socially detached from the center, and power-oriented. They respond to corporatism and are not class-oriented.

The fact is, as Nasser admitted in his recent interview with C. L. Sulzberger of *The New York Times* (March, 1969), that his model—and in our view the model for *all* Arab officers since 1919—was General 'Aziz 'Ali al-Misri, not Ataturk. Both al-Sabbagh and Nasser have patterned themselves after al-Misri, sometimes uncannily identifying with him, seeing him as a fraternal and intellectual great brother. Beeri relates "briefly" (pp. 39-43) that in a military career spanning over half a century, al-Misri served a multitude of causes and patrons: Ottomanism, pan-Arabism, pan-Islamism, and Egyptian hegemonial claims as well as the Caliphate, Sherrif Hussain, the Shah of Iran, Hadj Amin al-Husayni, King Farouq, 'ali Mahir and Gamal Abdul Nasser. This illustrious officer changed his loyalties as others their gloves. Contrary to what his career reveals, he perceived better the workings of personal loyalty than those of ideology, for whose comprehension he was not notorious.

"To many an Arab nationalist 'Aziz 'Ali stands as the 'father' of the Arab Nationalist movement and the revolutionary leader *par excellence* who championed the Arab cause against Turkish domination."[23] Professor Khadduri's statement could not be more perceptive. 'Aziz 'Ali al-Misri is the model for Arab officers: heroic, quarrelsome, arrogant, a desperado and political acrobat, contantly plotting, never loyal to men, regimes, or ideologies, but rather to the advancement of his personal career, the military, and primitive slogans of militarism and of course of romantic nationalism. Al-Misri is the precursor of contemporary Arab military praetorians, a representative of the Arab military nationalist mind, character, expectations, and behavior. Beeri's sections on Nasser, Sabbagh, and the Syrian Ba'th officers describe what a section on 'Aziz 'Ali should have: fervent and often misguided idealism, millenarianism, primitive conceptions of society and politics, Sultanist expectations, authoritarianism, and expertise in palace intrigue, coups, and machinations, rather than dedication to the advancement of social causes and political institutions.

Another type of Arab military praetorian, a variation on the tradition of Misri-Sabbagh-Nasser, was Brigadier 'Abd al-Karim Qassem, who ruled Iraq betwen 1958 and 1963. Uriel Dann's *Iraq Under Qassem* has given us what is most essential to students of military and politics and of "praetorian societies"—an excellent, elaborate, sometimes overdetailed, but captivating narrative of a military man in a military era in a single country. The man, Qassem, was somewhat exceptional when compared to the Misri-Ba'th desperado Arab type; less ambitious than Nasser, he bore a somewhat greater resemblance to Kemal (at least in his attitude to foreign policy) than to his countryman al-Sabbagh. Qassem was a schemer, but he was not as ruthless as his successors (after his assassination in 1963), whose taste for executions was rivaled only by their taste for intrigue and power. Qassem, in his desire to be a reformer, governed by military and dictatorial power, and therefore failed to institute the great reforms that he so badly wanted to realize. Like Misri and his successors, Qassem failed to establish a working relationship with the multitude of capable and willing politicians and other talented civilians. (In this respect Ataturk was superb, and this is what is missing in the Arab Sultanist type.) In the end, he alienated all elites, the army, the nationalists, the Communists, the Kurds, even some of his own underlings. "Qassem had become unpopular with every class, community, or grouping of the population capable of influencing the balance of forces within the country" (p. 356).

As was the case with the Egyptian rule in Syria (1958-1961), which ended in a debacle for the UAR, all the alienated elites converged to reduce Qassem's power, and, when his momentum began to decline, they moved in and brutally assassinated him (1963). The alternative his successors have offered is the present regime, a disorganized government with an ineffective army, prone to executions, fratricidal and vindictive, and still challenged by the alienated Kurds.

Iraq has become the most representative case of the decay that follows the regime of the military praetorians. The Misri-type has prevailed in Iraq without his charm, adventurism, or resilience. And, if Dann's prognostication proves correct, "that in the foreseeable future the army leadership alone can ensure for Iraq a modicum of stability and ordered progress . . ." (p. 328), then the plight of Iraq is more serious still.

Dann's account, like Beeri's, is rigorous, accurate to the point of pedantry (in a terrain that is notoriously slippery). It illuminates several of the problems, hypotheses, and theories that we introduced earlier and provides us for the first time with a reasonably solid and rich source from which old generalizations on military intervention can be challenged and new ones suggested. Take, for instance, the suggestive statement that:

> A study of the Free Officers' social background does not help to shed much light on the character of the movement. The officers belonged to the same classes as their non-aligned equals in rank; the majority were from middle-class, or even lower middle-class, urban families in the professions or trade. Well-known names, such as the Rawi, Tabaqchali and Shawwaf families, were also represented. At least one Free Officer was related to companions of King Faysal from his Syrian days—Maj. Khalid Maki al-Hashimi, a nephew of two former generals and prime ministers, Yasin and Taha al-Hashimi. The lower middle-class element may have been stronger among the Free Officers than among

their equivalents in rank in the army in general, but the difference was not striking (p. 21).

By explaining the political expectations and behavior of the Arab officers, Dann demonstrates that Beeri's Marxist generalizations on their rural middle class origin are not tenable except for Egypt. Beeri failed to see what Dann does —that the *interventionist* officers hail from *all groups and "classes"* and that the common denomination is their praetorian and Sultanic orientations. The burden of proof is on Beeri, for, if he *identifies* the social origins of the officers, he must explain their politics and establish a *link* between social origin and political intervention. In fact, if the Egyptian officers are a rural ruling class, they may be interventionist because they are an alienated rural elite, and if this is so Beeri should demonstrate that recruitment to political power in Egypt is largely from this class and above all that once they are "integrated" they should cease becoming interventionists. As Rustow wrote recently, "The student of political elites typically seeks to establish a correlation between political power and social status. He therefore must do three things: identify each of the two correlates and demonstrate a connection between them."[24]

Beeri has failed to demonstrate a connection. We must keep his excellent analysis of the officers' social origins and wait for another author to establish a correlation between social origin and political power, if indeed one does exist. Neither of our authors has successfully explained the political behavior of the military praetorians by correlating political power and social status. In our view, such a correlation is at best a partial explanation of the nature and dynamics of military interventionism.

We can argue that both a non-rigid class structure (as obtains in Iraq-Syria) and a rigid one (Egypt) produce interventionists. Do social origins other than "poor," "rural", "middle" explain why there would be *no* military intervention? Nasser and Qassem are products of the same background; the circumstances and social-ethnic-religious differences between their respective politics did not produce a *difference* between interventionism and non-interventionism.

We find Beeri's differentiation insufficient for typological-analytical purposes; in the end, it does not explain the *difference* (and if there were differences) between Nasser's military praetorianism and Qassem's. (Dann makes the point more explicit: the political rivalry between the two over hegemony influenced the destiny of both Qassem's Iraq and the short and unfortunate experiment of the UAR that took place simultaneously, in competition with Qassem's rule.) Here the model of imperious al-Misri is most useful to compare Nasser and Qassem. In the last analysis, Beeri's insistence on a distinction between the rural middle-class officer group and Halpern's new middle-class salariat does not explain the nature of military political interventionism.

Dann's study demonstrates another fundamental fact about the behavior of modern Arab military praetorians:

> On examination, two significant features can clearly be distinguished: The rising was military in conception, planning, organization, and execution; the military character of the conspiracy was preserved, though contacts had been made with certain civilian circles opposing the monarchy, and a minimum number of politicians was informed of the date of the coup a day or two in advance.
>
> Secondly, a "central committee of Free Officers" had existed before the coup, but this organization cannot be compared to the closely knit junta led by Gamal Abdel Nasser in the bid for power in Egypt in 1952. Even in its preparatory stages, the revolution in Iraq had become a one-man job, effected by Qassem with Col. 'Abd al-Salam Aref acting as his trusted personal aide. At the same time Qassem's leadership was by no means accepted without reservation by the community of conspirators as that of Abdel Nasser had been accepted in his own circle (p. 19).

Since Beeri's and Dann's works are saturated with carefully researched facts, which are not as yet found elsewhere in the literature on the military in the Middle East, I have designed a table (Table I) based on Beeri's tables and several revealing facts in Dann (as well as some based on my researches), which gives a graphic profile of these two authors' contributions to our comparative theoretical studies. New facts challenge the old as well as casting light on them, in some instances for the first time; they suggest new hypotheses

TABLE I
COUPS IN THE MIDDLE EAST
(7 Countries   41 Coups)
1936-1969

Category		Count	Sum Total
I — Military Intervention	Initiated, Organized, Executed by Military	40	41
	Initiated, Organized, Executed by Non-military	1	
II — Support of Organized Civilian and Political Groups	Support	14	41
	Opposition	27	
III — Mass Support	Support	4	41
	No Opposition	31	
	Opposition	6	
IV — Types of Coups by Orientation	Nationalist	33	41
	Fascist	3	
	Leftist	5	
	Religious-Fundamentalist	0	
V — Rank of Intervening Officers	Senior	29	41
	Middle & Junior	12	
VI — Types of Regime Legitimation	Personal	25	41
	Structural	9	
	Ideological	7	
VII — Outcome of Coup	Successful	23	41
	Unsuccessful	18	Sum Total

and concepts as well as reaffirming a number of older ones. The table is based on an analysis of 41 successful and unsuccessful military interventions in seven Middle Eastern Arab states over a period of three decades (1936-1969). We accept here Beeri's statement that military intervention covers all the attempts, successful and unsuccessful, on the part of Arab officers which were intended to capture the government by a coup or to enforce upon the government a specific political scheme. This narrow definition of military intervention excludes all other forms of violence and revolution not connected with or initiated by the military; civilian governments headed by the military and appointed by civilians without pressure from the military; clandestine activities of officers not connected with the immediate takeover of the government (p. 170).

We have arranged our table by the variables we felt could aid in explaining the type of military intervention most prevalent in the Middle East. (These dynamic variables also *suggest* [and I emphasize *suggest*] methods by which we could seek to explain the type of role and political behavior of the military praetorians.)

I. *The organization of the intervention*
   1. The number of interventions conceived, organized, and executed exclusively by the military.
   2. The number of interventions that, although conceived by the military, were supported by organized civilians and political groups.
   3. Mass support for the intervention.
II. *The type of political orientation and ideology of the coupmakers*
III. *A typology of intervention*
   The legitimization of the intervention: Personal, structural, ideological.

   David Easton[25] writes on legitimacy: "Support mobilized on behalf of the authorities and regimes may derive from several different sources: from underlying ideological principles, from attachment to the structure and norms of the regime as such, or from devotion to the actual authorities themselves because of their personal qualities." We find three types of legitimization of a regime: personal ("overflow from belief in the validity of the incumbents of authority roles to the authority roles"), structural ("independent belief in the validity of the structure and norms"), and ideological ("moral convictions about validity of regimes").[26]

IV. *The military rank from which the intervention was initiated: senior or middle and junior officers*

The detailed studies of Beeri and Dann as well as those of several other theorists on military interventions and coups suggest that we can begin to examine the nature of military-political intervention *in itself* and as an independent analytical unit. We hope that this will give us insights into some of its root causes and eventual consequences.[27] Others have already correlated military intervention with social and economic factors.[28] Thus, a cross-tabular analysis of the different variables listed in the table in bivariate combinations yields several tentative conclusions and poses some interesting questions for further study: (1) almost 80 per cent of the "nationalist" coups resulted in a personal type of legitimation; (2) over 50 per cent of all coups were *both* nationalist and personal; (3) 80 per cent of the civilian-supported coups were successful. However, half as many (40 per cent) of the *non*-civilian-supported coups were *also* successful. None that had mass public support were *un*successful; (4) by controlling the variable of "successful coup" by the variables of "mass support" and "civilian support", we find that the first is not dependent on the second and third; (5) fascist and leftist coups have tended to be more successful than nationalist coups; (6) coups by middle and junior officers were 25 per cent more successful than those organized by senior officers, while it should be noted that 70 per cent of the coups studied are not necessarily organized by junior officers, as has so often been postulated by some writers in the military. Moreover, we have found no correlation between leftist, fascist, and radical coups and the rank of the intervening officers. (7) It should also be recognized that out of 41 coups, 30 have occurred in Syria and Iraq (Syria, 13, and Iraq, 17). Since these two nations are pluralist societies, we might wonder whether there exists a specific relationship between military intervention and the failure of political integration in *pluralistic* societies.

Analyses of Beeri's, and more especially Dann's, material lead us toward the following preliminary hypotheses: (1) that the military's rule in the Middle East is oriented toward a military dictatorship exclusively dominated by one man, and that challenges to military authority by mutinous, disgruntled, or rival officers have the same end in view; (2) that military coups, countercoups, and interventions are planned, organized, and executed by the army, for the army, with little or *no* support from movements and classes, even if the officers had been inspired by a variety of nationalist, religious, fundamentalist, fascist, or anti-foreign cliques, coteries, groups, parties, or movements; (3) that relationships between class and politics are of little or no value in explaining the type of authority, regime, and ideology espoused by the military praetorians.

First, the orientation of the military toward clandestine operations and military dictatorship: like most Middle Eastern coups since 1936 (see Table I), Qassem's, we find, was secretly contrived within the military barracks, with some "awareness" by "outside" groups (sympathetic civilians and generally radical nationalists without parliamentary support). What is most important is that this support was *not* crucial to the military. In fact, in Qassem's case, civilian support was even rejected; this was also true of Nasser's coup in 1952 (Beeri, pp. 63-96). After the coup, the pattern is that the military establishes an autonomous executive arm, the Revolutionary Command Council, as an instrument of authority in quest of legitimacy (Nasser in 1952, Shishakly in 1952, Qassem in 1958), which eventually takes over all sources of power and, in the end, becomes an instrument dedicated more to suppressing the opposition and expropriating the "old" regime than to progress. The issue of legitimacy is crucial, but (in the cases of Qassem, Nasser, and the Syrian officers) the military dictatorship has never been made legitimate without the use of force, or the secret police, or the powers of patrimonialism (the extended family or ethnic group), or foreign powers' support. Qassem failed, as Dann argues, chiefly because he was unusually merciful (sparing the life of his future assassin 'Abd al-Salim 'Arif), tolerant, forgiving (pp. 62-69), and, unlike his rival on the Nile, did not devote much of his time to intrigues. This further supports the proposition that Nasser's resilience stems from his capacity to manipulate palace coups, the military, and the masses (see the case of the "suicide" of Marshal 'Amer in 1967) (Beeri, pp. 287-312).

Nasser, and particularly Qassem (Dann, pp. 1-92, 356-378), could not survive without the support of the military and the threat of force or the manipulation of the mob. This does not mean that in either period of rule civilian groups or organizations were unable to play a significant role. This was true in the case of the Iraqi Communists in 1959-1960—and the Arab Socialist Union in the early 1960's in Egypt. But these "civilian" *interregna* are short, abrupt, and bring with them more violence and brutality when the officers re-establish military dictatorship. Military dictatorship or domination prevails mainly because the leader conceives of no alternative to his *personal* rule or military rule, even if to legitimize his rule he turns to secure structural and ideological sources—by force and the suppression of opposition both within and outside of the military.

It is equally true, as Dann has so adequately demonstrated, that in the era of military-civilian co-operation in Iraq, the Iraqi Communist Party supported the militia that it infiltrated and dominated (1959-1961). But this power did not last long—the Iraqi Communist Party soon collapsed, leaving the military dictator to the mercy of his own failures and the ICP's. Why did the Iraqi Communist Party collapse? In its heyday it was supported by Qassem, and its membership swelled, its organization prospered, it dominated the militia (PRF), took advantage of army fratricidal tendencies, and, during the Shawaaf army mutiny (1959), helped by the powerful and well organized Kurdish minority, it restored Qassem's rule. The ICP also brought about Iraq's withdrawal from the Baghdad Pact and presented the most powerful political front at home—with the exception, of course, of Qassem's (pp. 108-135). Yet "it was caught in a situation [the Kirkuk massacre, 1959] which it could not master by assault; . . ." The same was true of the Egyptian Muslim Brotherhood, who captured the imagination of Egyptian nationalists for three decades, and who, if Mitchell[29] is correct, claimed over half a million members in their ranks. To all intents and purposes the Muslim Brotherhood ran a para-welfare state, infiltrating unions, universities, and the intelligentsia, and maintaining close contact with and even dominating various Free Officers[30] (Beeri, pp. 64-65). Providing a doctrine and an explanation of the plight of Egypt under colonial rule, the Muslim Brotherhood sought personal, psychological, and political redemption for Egypt. Its influence on the Free Officers was considerable. In short, it was the mass movement *par excellence* of the modern Middle East, and yet, like the Iraqi Communist Party (or for that matter the Syrian PPS and Ba'th parties), it disintegrated and was finally overrun by a simple, little known, politically inarticulate, but ruthless military dictator.

An explanation of the failure of the Muslim Brotherhood, the PPS, Ba'th, Iraqi Communist Party, Wafd, and others must be sought not only in the nature of the "praetorian society" but in the type of relationship that exists between ideology and organization in nationalist movements, when organization is not buttressed by ideology and ideology disintegrates.[31] The organizational and political ideology of the praetorian buttresses the military dictatorship. It creates a relatively stable order that approaches political mobilization while remaining unresponsive to political change. It does not evolve beyond a clandestine coterie, for it is barricaded by its own volition. While the non-military political groups are in permanent quest of a constituency, an all-inclusive ideology, and some type of electoral machinery, the military is self-contained and derives the capacity to govern from the barracks. The military dictatorship is sustained by the power of a single manipulator (or, as in Syria, rival manipulators), as Hurewitz writes (p. 426). Thus the most "effective" governments in the Middle East were and still are those of the military dictator; "effectiveness" is related not to organizational infrastructure or ideology in this case, but to the dictator's personal capacity for governing.

Syria has produced two successful military dictators, Shishakly and Asad, who have governed by means similar to those used by Qassem and Nasser, i.e., force, machinations, intrigue, and permanent elimination of political opposition.

In the end, Shishakly's fall was not unlike Qassem's after he had succeeded in alienating all elites, particularly the army (Beeri, pp. 97-119, 224-229, 358-361). From a comparative point of view, we should expect this bitterly divided polity—Syria—to produce a different type of military praetorianism. But it did not. Syria is divided by historical antagonisms: ethnicity and religion; deep urban rivalry between center and periphery; rural antagonisms; disagreements between "Southern-oriented" (Egypt, Saudi Arabia) Damascus and "Northern-oriented" (Iraq) Aleppo; and "contemporary" antagonisms: Ba'th versus Nasserites, union with Egypt versus independence; radical versus conservative; and on top of all this, struggle between generations. And yet, however fratricidal it may be, the military is still the dominant political group in Syria and has been since 1949.[32] The military dictatorship was short-lived, yet no political group in Syria, with the exception of the military, has had since 1949 more than veto power. The military, and not the Ba'th party, has emerged as an armed political congress whose leadership constantly changes, over the "old" ills and now over new divisions: Nasserism, Ba'thism, and the neo-Ba'th.

Structurally, because of its ethnic, pluralistic nature, Syria is not "open" to a military dictatorship, and yet, behaviorally, the military is the highest and most authoritative political group. Despite (or because of?) its heterogeneity and the polarization of social and political forces, the orientation of the Syrian military is toward an exclusive military dictatorship. Politically, the military establishment in Syria resembles the Egyptian type, even if structurally Syria is clearly different from Egypt and even from Iraq. We can safely conclude that the universality of military praetorianism in the Middle East stems from the regime's espousal of the military dictatorship. There is nothing to substantiate Hurewitz' statement—and there is much more evidence to contradict it—that: "In plural societies, therefore, officers by and large are not in fact social revolutionaries, even where they have seized political power" (p. 428). What about the Ba'thist officers, Asad and Qassem?

Millenarian revolutionary commitment to ideology is

better as a medicine for enthusiasm than as a prescription for reform. There is no necessary correlation between a pledge to reform and the modernity (or rationality) of the military establishment that makes the claim. Syrian Suni Arab officers who champion progressive Arab nationalism act slowly on concrete measures of reform.

A study of 320 Egyptian officers in Israeli captivity after the 1967 Arab-Israeli War, as well as a comparable 1956 study of prisoners of war, to which Beeri and I had access, illustrates a similar phenomenon in Egypt. Under Nasser's Arab Socialist regime, the Egyptian officer class clearly exhibits traditional bureaucratic attitudes toward the "lower" classes—the troops, peasants, unskilled workers, and the under-educated. Furthermore, the Egyptian army, on the whole, has failed to institute successfully the land and tax reforms that it has promised to carry out. Yet, incongruous as it may seem, the Egyptian military establishment and its Syrian counterpart (to a lesser extent) are probably the most modern military establishments in the Arab Middle East.

The "heterogeneous", "pluralistic", "ethnic" explanations for the type of military interventions that have occurred in Syria are no more valid than the "social origin" explanation we analysed earlier. At best these are partial explanations for military interventionism. But they should be examined. What the officers demand is not participation but power, not subordination but command. Here, modern organization is their advantage over other political groups. These ends can be achieved in praetorian polity only under a military dictatorship. Social and ethnic "explanations" are related to the praetorian society; they do not explain interventionism.

The second hypothesis was that military coups are militarily organized, inspired, and executed. Dann demonstrates this conclusively. Recently two important studies, one by P. J. Vatikiotis *(Nasser and his Generation)*, the other by Raymond Baker *(Egypt's Uncertain Revolution under Nasser and Sadat)* confirm this hypothesis. On the basis of the literature available in Arabic, and of secondary material in foreign languages, on Nasser's consolidation of power, we must conclude that it was analogous to Qassem's—a gradual but consistent attrition and annihilation of political and civilian rivals. This is corroborated by Beeri's careful and detailed analysis of the rise of the Free Officers and their consolidation of power from the "prehistoric" 1930's through 1956 (Beeri, pp. 63-96). In view of the comprehensiveness of Beeri's survey of the rise of the Free Officers and Nasser's consolidation of the military dictatorship, the case seems to be analytically analogous to Qassem's.

The third and most controversial hypothesis, that the military does not represent a class, even functionally, finds support in Dann's study, but the issue is not yet decided. Various authors, including this reviewer, hold various explanations acceptable, choose different variables, and offer differing interpretations of the military and politics in developing polities.

Class consciousness has always provided only a meager identity for Middle Eastern officers. The military conceive of themselves not as an economic group but as a corporate group. Since the collapse of Ottoman rule (in which the army played a large part), the military have awaited the formation of a new, sustaining and powerful "state" on the European model that would sustain the military establishment. The military in the Middle East do not represent or dominate classes, nor are they dominated by them. The middle-class sector is sharply divided in outlook. This chronic interventionist tradition is nurtured by splits and schisms in Arab nationalist and progressive camps: neither progressives nor moderates could, by political victory, impose their conception of progressivism. Thus the military organization imposes on society the moral of order, not the ideology of class. This of course is buttressed by the organizational weapon at the disposal of a modern military establishment. A modern military establishment can sometimes be detrimental to successful and large-scale socio-economic reform. The military establishment in the Middle East represents the sum total of their professional, corporate, and personal experiences, which is modern, on the whole, but not necessarily reformist.

The first Syrian coups of 1949, in the wake of the Palestinian debacle, were not ideologically or class-oriented. The concern of the reformers was to strengthen the machinery of the Syrian state so that the Palestinian debacle would not recur. The armed forces of Syria were doubled. The military had little sustaining interest in economic change. They had not considered the problem of reform in any other context than that of general "corruption" of "order". Nasser's rise to power stemmed from the concern of the Free Officers over the Egyptian military defeat in Palestine, which illustrated the corruption of the regime to the young officers. Nasser opposed the corrupt regime in general terms—no class label except "corrupt" was attached to the regime until 1956, when the Wafd and the Faruq regimes became "bourgeois-capitalist" and "feudalist monsters". The greatest trauma to the officers was the corruption of their own military establishment while fighting in Palestine.

In the name of becoming strong and of ridding state and army of corruption, one praetorian regime was replaced by another in the Middle East. The military reforms do not reflect the class origin or interests of the military establishment. (See the relatively mild purge and punishment of the Egyptian army after the 1967 debacle.) Military reforms succeed and fail in the Middle East not because they are middle-class or revolutionary, but because of praetorian conditions of low institutionalization, socio-fratricidal tendencies and the decay of the polity and of the military political establishment itself. The concepts of politics, society, and authority among Middle Eastern officers are couched in simplistic, xenophobic, radical nationalist slogans and doctrines.

In the light of the Beeri, Dann, Vatikiotis and Baker studies, there is obviously no contradiction between a commitment to nationalism and a commitment to reform. But commitments to either or both are not sufficient indicators that the motivations of the nationalist are reformist. What seems conclusive at least in our Middle Eastern case is that the correlations between middle class (however "new") and reform are negative.[33] Nor can we establish a positive correlation between peasant origins, mobility, and reform (say in the case of Syria). Military interventionism is explained better by the caprice of the praetorian, his taste for political intrigue and manipulation, his concern for the army, than by his social origins and class commitments. Why invent for Middle Eastern officers "classes" and "consciousness" they do not share, contemplate, or espouse? The army acts as a ruling class and not as an economic group or a surrogate for one. Ataturk conceived of the military in their historical praetorian cohort role: as the protector of the Imperial system, the Senate, and the Republic against the legions. Thus he advocated the separation of the military from politics with the proviso that the army should protect the Constitution from the barracks. Abdul Nasser assigned to the army the role of patrolling Egypt and believed that only the military could successfully reform, govern, and strengthen Egypt.[34] Ataturk believed that European republicanism and civilian control over the military were the magic secret of European strength. Nasser, mistrustful of foreign, and especially European imperialists, and convinced of the futility of parliamentary rule in Egypt, opted first for state capitalism and then, after 1960, for Arab socialism, hoping that this new course would restore the Egyptian state. The Ba'th officers in Syria believed in a variety of leftist and neo-Bolshevik remedies that, unfortunately, have not helped toward strengthening Syria. The major reform that military rule was to bestow on Arab societies has not succeeded very well, but officers come and go making a variety of *pronunciamentos,* and, in the absence of effective rivals, believe they can do better. When rivals emerge, persuasion is not a favorite military tactic. Rulers retaliate by suppression and physical elimination. What the officers want is to reform their "government" and protect their corporate entity and profession; they have conspired to do this by coups and force.

These convictions are not the result of a particular class origin or class consciousness. The major aim was to make the state strong and effective: the pre-1939 generation in the Arab world believed in the remedies of parliamentarianism and republicanism as sources of political strength and mastery. The post-1939 fundamentalists, radicals, and xenophobes put their eggs in a variety of baskets: fascism, state capitalism, Arab socialism, left nationalism, and even communism, and clothed their personal and fratricidal ambitions with colorful mumbo-jumbo "ideologies". As a ruling class, they advocate the restoration of power, especially of military power, not the fulfillment of class ideologies and interests. In the Middle East military rule means a modern regime of the military without executive responsiveness to political participation and the chaos of social structure, the decadence of politics, and military praetorianism—the most obvious characteristics of the modern praetorian society.

NOTES

1. Kurt Lang, *The Sociology of the Military: A Selected and Annotated Bibliography* (Chicago 1969).
2. Samuel P. Huntington, *The Soldier and the State* (Cambridge, Mass. 1957).
3. Morris Janowitz, *The Professional Soldier* (Glencoe 1960).
4. Huntington, vii.
5. *Ibid.*, 143-62.
6. Samuel P. Huntington, "Civilian Control of the Military: A Theoretical Statement," in Eulau and others, eds., *Political Behavior* (Glencoe 1956), 380.
7. Huntington, *The Soldier*, 96-97.
8. Janowitz, *The Professional Soldier* (Glencoe 1960), 417.
9. Morris Janowitz, "Armed Forces and Society: A World Perspective", unpubl. paper no. 54 (Chicago 1966), 5.
10. John J. Johnson, ed., *The Role of the Military in Underdeveloped Countries* (Princeton 1962).
11. Edward Shils, "The Military in the Political Development of the New States", in Johnson, 7-68.
12. *Ibid.*, 52-60.
13. Lucian Pye, "Armies in the Process of Political Modernization", in Johnson, 69-89.
14. Manfred Halpern, "Middle Eastern Armies and the New Middle Class", in Johnson, 286.
15. Samuel P. Huntington, *Political Order in Changing Societies* (New Haven 1968), 195.
16. For elaborate analysis of praetorianism, see Huntington in *Political Order, 193-263*.
17. Amos Perlmutter, *"The Praetorian State and the Praetorian Army", Comparative Politics*, 1 (April 1964), 382-404.
18. Huntington, *Political Order*, 194.
19. Harry Eckstein, "A Perspective on Comparative Politics, Past and Present", in H. Eckstein and D. Apter, eds., *Comparative Politics* (Glencoe 1963), 16-35.
20. We must distinguish between Weber's definition of praetorianism and Huntington's. To Huntington it is an analytic concept, while to Weber it indicates a type of domination.

21. Max Weber, *Economy and Society,* Vol. 3 (New York 1968), 1013-31.
22. For an excellent description of the Egyptian army, see Morroe Berger, *Military Elite and Social Changes: Egypt Since Napoleon* (Princeton 1960).
23. For a sympathetic portrait of 'Aziz al-Misri, see Majid Khadduri, " 'Aziz 'Ali al Misri and the Arab Nationalist Movement", in Albert Hourani, ed., *Middle Eastern Affairs,* No. 4 (Oxford 1965), 140-63. For additional information on Misri and the Free Officers, in addition to Beeri see G. and S. Lacouture, *Egypt in Transition* (New York 1959). For a short but most perceptive analysis of the Arab officers and Misri in the early days of the nationalist movement following World War I, see Elie Kedourie, *England and the Middle East* (London 1956), 46-48.
24. Dankwart A. Rustow, "The Study of Elites", *World Politics,* xviii (July 1966), 201.
25. David Easton, *A System Analysis of Political Life* (New York 1965).
26. *Ibid.,* 287.
27. See the pioneer volume, Henri Bienen, ed., *The Military Intervenes* (New York 1968); Eric Nordlinger, "Soldiers in Mufti", unpub. paper, C.F.I.A., Harvard University (February 1969); and Perlmutter, "The Praetorian State".
28. See Martin Needler, *Political Development in Latin America: Instability, Violence, and Evolutionary Change* (New York 1968); Robert Putnam, "Toward Explaining Military Intervention in Latin American Politics", *World Politics,* xx (October 1967), 83-110.
29. Richard P. Mitchell, "The Society of Muslim Brothers", unpub. diss. (Princeton 1960), 72-150.
30. Mitchell reminds us of the close connection between Sheik Hasan al-Banna, the head of the Brotherhood, and General al-Misri, as with Anwar al-Sadat, later to become a member of Nasser's Free Officers. *Ibid.,* 46-49.
31. The literature on the relation between ideology and organization is growing. See Franz Schurmann, *Ideology and Organization in Communist China* (Berkeley 1967); Philip Selznick, *Leadership in Administration* (New York 1954); and Amos Perlmutter, "Ideology and Organization: The Socialist-Zionist Parties in Israel 1896-1959," doctoral diss., University of California (Berkeley 1957).
32. See Chapter 6 of this work.
33. Nordlinger, 22-25.
34. Gamel Abdul Nasser, *The Philosophy of the Revolution* (Washington 1955), 17.

CHAPTER 8

Experiments in Praetorianism

The major characteristic of a praetorian state is its low level of political institutionalization and support. Professor Huntington and I agree[1] that stable political parties with a wide scope of support and a high level of institutionalization are *necessary* conditions for a non-praetorian system. Thus it becomes crucial to examine the efforts of Nasser and his successor in forming political parties. The stabilization and institutionalization of political parties are the major indicators of both the persistence (if it fails) and the disappearance (if it succeeds) of praetorianism.

Nasser governed Egypt from April 1954 until his death in November 1970. He came to power without institutionalized political legitimacy, but with experience and a profound political understanding of Egypt. He was not a political philosopher, but as a pragmatist he made a considerable contribution to the new style of politics that has become prevalent in the Arab and sub-Saharan African worlds.

Before examining the dynamics of Nasser's political parties, let us turn first to a discussion of the evolution of praetorian regimes in the Middle East in general, and then to the specific evolution of Nasser's single party system.

THE STRUCTURAL EVOLUTION OF MILITARY PRAETORIAN REGIMES

We have distinguished two basic types of praetorian armies,

196

the arbitrator type and the ruler type. The major differences between them are the time limits they place on their own rule, and their orientations toward controlling the nation's executive. While the arbitrator type army imposes a fixed time limit on military rule and arranges to hand over the government to an "acceptable" civilian regime, the ruler type army believes in prolonged, even permanent, rule. The arbitrator type army, although it does not necessarily relinquish political influence, does believe in returning to the barracks. The ruler type army not only does not set a time limit on military rule; it actually plans to establish itself as the legitimate political ruling group. First, it invents or adopts an ideological stance. Then it creates a political party within the army, a sort of executive committee made up of "free officers". The most significant contribution of Arab army officers to political control of executive power is the Revolutionary Command Council (RCC), an ad hoc military cabinet which runs the government and directs the society. The RCC is also in charge of eliminating opposition within the military and the society. It is the command post of military executive control. This type of instrument has been adopted in all praetorian Arab countries—Egypt, Syria, Iraq, Libya, the Sudan. The ruler type praetorian army belongs to the second political generation since its rise to power is based on its opposition to the "political corruption" of traditional parliamentary regimes, thus encouraging the development of authoritarian non-party or one-party systems. This does not mean that the officers are revolutionary; their sometimes self-proclaimed conversion to revolutionary causes is likely to be much more superficial than their anticonservatism. In fact, of all reformist groups in the praetorian state, the army tends to be the least reformist.

The evolution of executive control in both arbitrator and ruler type praetorianism follows a cyclical pattern, beginning with executive arbitration, developing into executive control, and then turning back to a type of arbitration. The institutional and structural arrangements of each praetorian regime type differ according to its orientation. Both the arbitrator and the ruler type regimes develop political and structural arrangements appropriate to their roles. The syndrome,

Figure 1: MODEL A*
THE ARBITRATOR REGIME TYPE

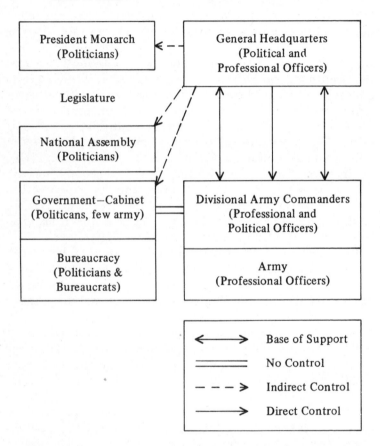

*After I had written about the above model and had designed my charts (models A, B, C) I came across Meir Pa'il's essay, "Patterns of Revolutionary Officers' Regimes in Iraq and Syria" *(Hamizrah Hehadash,* 1969, pp. 181-207) which inspired me to modify my charts following his designs. I am most grateful to Pa'il's ideas and to our long conversations on the above during the summer of 1970.

however, is more complex. Only the first wave of either type is close to the model; the second round of an arbitrator or ruler type becomes more complex, even if the basic principles of the model remain correct. Here we will deal only with the ideal types of executive control—arbitrator and ruler—suggesting a number of case studies to explain the models, and using deliberately generalized examples.

The Arbitrator Regime Type.

This type of regime is a structural accommodation designed by the military to fulfill its role of arbitrator. It might occur when the general headquarters of the army had been taken over by a group of Free Officers, whose major source of support is the military. They would indirectly control the political and civilian institutions, without dominating the executive, the government or the bureaucracy. This model creates a dichotomy in executive power, where the real executive (cabinet and government) is indirectly controlled by an executive behind the scene (the general headquarters, ruled by the Free Officers). This model of military rule may disintegrate when members of the general headquarters, as well as others within the army, combine with the bureaucracy or with the government and thus are able to overthrow the military regime.

The arbitrator regime type was first introduced by the military regimes of Iraq between 1936 and 1941 and by three of the Syrian military regimes in 1949.[2] In the Middle East, parliamentary regimes and party structures were so entrenched that they did not collapse at the outset of the coups directed against them. The monarchy in Iraq and Syria's parliamentary regime demonstrated a remarkable capacity to survive for some 30 years, while in a state of permanent crisis. Iraq's military leaders did not even contemplate overthrowing the monarchy until 1958, nor did the Syrian army seriously consider arresting parliamentary government before 1966. In fact, the Ba'th party, Syria's sponsor of military interventionism, advocated sustaining parliamentary and party rule at least until 1966.

Middle Eastern military leaders have generally found the arbitrator regime model unsatisfactory, for two major reasons.

Indirect rule over the executive does not permit the military to control completely the failures or antagonisms that occur within the government and the bureaucracy, and between these and the military. Second, because of their semi-independent rule, political parties, civilian institutions and the bureaucracy can successfully challenge the military leaders. Ironically, the arbitrator type regime, which was designed to strengthen political authority and create order in the Middle East, actually helped strengthen the radical, nationalist groups and parties, while it weakened military authority.

The short-lived coalition of the arbitrator regime, between progressives, politicians, ideologues and the professional military, usually evolves into a military dictatorship which ousts all civilians from executive power and establishes an army executive arm such as the ALM (Arab Liberation Movement) in Syria, between 1952 and 1953, and the RCC in Egypt and other Arab military regimes, since 1953.

The Ruler Regime Type

The ruler type of regime, represented in Figure 2 as Model B, is a modification of Model A (the arbitrator regime), designed to overcome the latter's failures. Here we find the perfect domination of the military over the executive, as the Revolutionary Command Council is established as the instrument for controlling the executive. In this ruler type of praetorianism, the head of the RCC is also both president and prime minister of the country, while the major source of support is still the general headquarters of the army. In this model, however, the RCC is composed entirely of non-political officers, to avoid any chance of a coalition between the politicians and the military-bureaucratic alliance. The head of the RCC can sometimes relinquish his position as president to a civilian but only under the condition that direct military rule over the bureaucracy will continue. There is a good chance that the legislature will be abolished, or else be completely dominated by the military. Once this type of regime becomes fully established, as we shall see in the diagram of Model C, it will pack the legislature with former officers and members of its own political party. Thus the cabinet-government and the bureaucracy each become a mixture of soldiers and bureaucrats, both of them firmly controlled by the RCC. This type of ruler regime first appeared in Syria under Colonel Adib Shishakly, who in 1952 transformed the military regime from Model A to Model C by uniting the army's general headquarters and the government under the control of a Revolutionary Command Council.

Figure 2: MODEL B
THE RULER REGIME TYPE

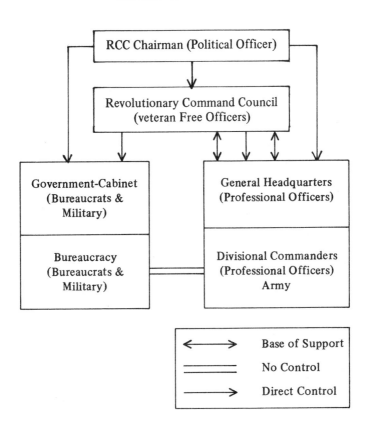

Figure 3: MODEL C
SECOND ARBITRATION REGIME TYPE:
RULE OF MILITARY PARTY

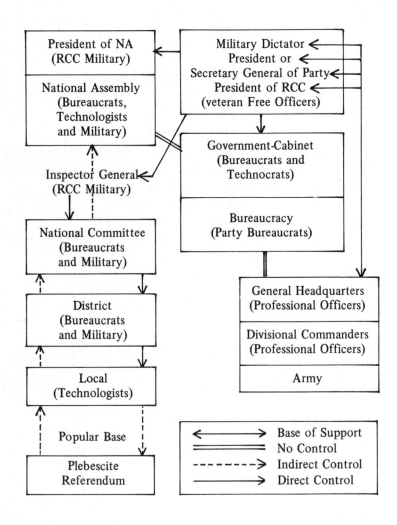

Back to the Arbitrator Regime.

In the case of Model C, the military dictator, the head of the RCC, still totally dominates the executive. His major source of support remains the military high command. The RCC head then appoints loyal professional and patrimonial-oriented officers to general headquarters; and the military is rewarded with corporate autonomy. Thus, the relationship between the military dictator and the high command is both corporate and patrimonial.

If the military dictator is successful both in establishing order and in respecting the military's corporate orientation, the army returns to the barracks and switches from the ruler to the arbitrator role. The praetorian cycle is now complete: from arbitrator to ruler type regime, and then back to the arbitrator type. If the military intervenes again, it may face both the opposition of the successful military dictator turned head of state, and the political organization at his disposal. Thus, the military is still divided, even though it is back in the barracks.

The second source of direct control and support for the Model C regime is a political movement or a political party dominated by the RCC. In the Arab Middle East, the military either initiates such political movements, or takes over established radical nationalist parties, in order to legitimize its own rule.

THE EVOLUTION AND DYNAMICS OF NASSER'S POLITICAL PARTIES

Before we discuss the specific political structures established by Nasser, it may be useful to explore Nasser's aversion to party politics structures. A radical nationalist, Nasser felt that the government should not be tampered with. "We should be entirely irresponsible," he said, "if we allowed our enemies to tamper with the government machinery."[3] He considered government machinery to be the responsibility of the "internal" Egyptian group of himself and his cohorts. Political parties, in Nasser's view, are tools of capitalistic democracy, of bankers and pashas; they are partisan instruments of the feudal classes. "The dictatorship from which we have suffered under the name of democracy," says Nasser, "was the dictatorship of capital, feudalism under the name parliament." He continues:

> Political democracy cannot be a reality unless there is social justice and social democracy and unless there are equal opportunity between the capitalist and the worker and between the feudalist and the agricultural laborer. One has plenty of money and can have a good dinner and one has no money to pay for dinner. Capitalists and feudalists want to hold general elections according to Western methods adopted by capitalist countries in which the minority enjoys all the influence and has an abundance of money. The political parties serve the interests of feudalists and capitalists.[4]

The function of the RCC was to establish political influence over the Nasser group. Nasser was aware that the Officers Corps were on the whole not political,*that the few who were politically oriented were also isolated and divided; and that most of the politically oriented officers were merely the political agents of radical and social parties and movements heading the military cells of their respective groups. Nasser established the FOC (Free Officer Corps) to provide these politically oriented officers with an autonomous political organization. The FOC was an executive committee made up of 11 members: Nasser, Sadat, Zakariyah and Khaled Muhi al-Din, Abdel-Hakim 'Amer, Gamal and Salah Salem, Tawrat 'Ukasha, al-Mun'im a-Ra'uf, Hasan Ibrahim and Latif al-Baghdadi. Three of these men—Nasser, 'Amer and Zakariyah Muhi al-Din—acted as the core group.[6] The FOC established a miniature political organization with five departments: Manpower, Terrorism, Propaganda, Finance and Welfare. The first political act credited to FOC was the defeat of Faruq's candidate for the presidency of the Officers Corps.[7] They also organized guerrilla action against the British in the Suez.

The FOC served another purpose as well—loyalty screening. Nasser would periodically meet with the group in seminar fashion, to discuss Egyptian history and politics.

---

* The number of politically active officers in the Egyptian army before 1952 was never over 300, with less than 50 officers who were real activists, out of an Officer Corps of some 20,000 members.[5]

Thus he was able to do the screening personally, while observing the viewpoints, character, behavior and expectations of the participants.[8] Thus these "seminars" were designed to encourage group cohesion and to distinguish friend from foe, dependable from frivolous candidates for FOC membership and action. Hence the FOC was the first officer's consolidated-kinship group in the history of modern Arab military intervention.*

The need for an executive committee of the FOC immediately became apparent. The struggle for power against Nagib, the Wafd and above all the Muslim Brotherhood[9] and dissident officers called for an executive body to plan, consolidate and operationalize the July coup. The Revolutionary Command Council originated part of the FOC group in 1949 and became an autonomous and cohesive cabal in the regime of Nagib between July 1952 and April 1954. The RCC was the political instrument which established the Nasser group in power in April 1954. Between 1952-1954, the RCC was also established to recruit support for the FOC and Nasser, and to abolish the University Students' Union—with the help of the radical MBs (Muslim Brotherhood Members). The RCC, under Nasser's supervision, had already demonstrated the pattern of Nasserite rule: clandestine, quiescent manipulation of competing rivals (Wafdist, MB and assorted FOC officers), the end product of which was Nasser's personal dictatorship over Egypt, via the RCC.

The RCC as an executive committee for the Liberation Rally after 1953 functioned not unlike the FOC, as the sole representative of the military coup makers. Nasser himself participated in its design and worked closely on the organizational details of the Liberation Rally-RCC.[10] The major functions of the RCC were to eliminate opposition parties and personalities, to organize the masses, and to establish a political organ for Nasserite legitimacy and support.[11] The basic structure of the Liberation Rally was patterned after that of the RCC. Its President, General Nagib, was intended

---

* 'Abd al-Qasim of Iraq (1958-1963) and the 'Alawi group of Asad-Jadid (February 1966-1970) succeeded in emulating the FOC. But Shishakly's Arab Liberation Movement of 1952 failed to serve the same purpose and he was unable to sustain his military dictatorship.

to be a figurehead. The Secretary General, the all-powerful man dominating policy and appointments, was Gamal Abdel Nasser. There were also a Deputy Secretary General and an Inspector General: the Deputy was the operating arm of Liberation Rally, and the Inspector General was in charge of Liberation Rally's political cells and local organs.[12] The Central Executive Committee of the Liberation Rally was composed of the same personnel as the RCC, to ensure FOC ideology and domination over the central bodies of the Liberation Rally. The RCC was successful in dominating the Liberation Rally, and in duplicating the functions of Liberation Rally's Central Executive Committee. Nasser preferred a political organization such as the Liberation Rally, as an organ for rule and for "revolutionary" activities. Basically, Nasser opted for the formation of a mass party with extremely limited political functions. In fact, his concept of the Liberation Rally mobilizing and "revolutionizing" Egypt was necessitated by the political needs of the military dictatorship at the time. Not until the collapse of the UAR in 1961 would Nasser modify this concept of party organization and function.

The Liberation Rally proved a failure as a mass organization, and it also failed to achieve the popularity of its major rival, the Muslim Brotherhood, the only legal party between 1952 and 1954. The Liberation Rally proved incapable of recruiting a leadership group to operationalize its goals. Thus the Egypt Nasser inherited was politically divided, fratricidally torn and socially fragmented. The Liberation Rally did not become a link between the center and the periphery, as intended. In fact, the Liberation Rally, designed as a participating party, proved virtually a total failure. Now the RCC had to make changes in its structure, in order to assume the responsibility for the Liberation Rally's functions. Having failed to gain mass support, Nasser now opted for widening the scope of the RCC and of his personal role and office. Between 1953 and 1955, the RCC was purged of its "ideologues" on both the left and the right.[13] Several new members joined the RCC: including members of the "second generation" Free Officers, the formerly non-political officers and new recruits. The growth of the RCC was parallel to the percentage of officers in the cabinet, which declined from 45 per cent in April 1954, to 32 per cent in September 1956.[14] The military establishment and especially the army's high command were also purged of RCC's political opposition; and new professional non-political senior officers (several of them from pre-1952 groups) were elevated to the high command. Divisional commanders were clearly non-political, professional soldiers. This new composition weakened the RCC and strengthened the power of the *Rais*. A special office, that of president, was established in 1956, thus elevating Nasser above the RCC. The president reserved sole power of appointment and dismissal of the prime minister, the cabinet, the commander-in-chief of the army, and the senior officers. Supporting power was still derived from the army, but was not entirely dependent on senior officers. Civil servants were also recruited to the RCC, thus further weakening the influence of the military and the FOC veterans, and therefore that of the RCC. At least until 1961, the military remained the major source for recruitment to RCC, the cabinet, the government and the bureaucracy. Thus, prior to 1961, the military provided Egypt with most of its political, bureaucratic and industrial elites. To strengthen his personal power and weaken the RCC, Nasser then established a new political participatory structure, the National Union.

THE NATIONAL UNION AND THE SOCIALIST UNION:
TWO NASSERITE ANTI-POLITICAL EXPERIMENTS

On June 19, 1956, Premier Nasser proclaimed the end of martial law, an act symbolic of the consolidation of the Free Officers' power. With the opposition crushed, Nasser and his group were ready to enforce the project for Egypt's future formulated in the constitution which had been presented to the country earlier that year. On June 23, the voters approved the constitution by plebiscite, and elected Gamal Abdel Nasser president. As the only candidate, he received all but 2,857 of the 5,508,291 votes cast; of 5,498,271 total people voting on the issue, only 10,046 voted against the constitution. Three new ministries, reflecting the regime's new social and economic objectives and managerial orientations, were set up: Industry (under 'Aziz Sidqi, an engineer); Agrarian Reform (under Sayyid Mar'i, an agricultural engineer); and Communications (under Mustafa Khalil Kamal, a railroad engineer).[15]

At the same time, three former members of the RCC and of the Liberation Rally cabinet moved to non-cabinet positions: Gamal Salem to head governmental organization and the Civil Service; Hasan Ibrahim to become Director of the National Planning Council; and Anwar al-Sadat, one of Nasser's closest associates, to act as Secretary General of the Islamic Congress. The placement of Nasser's trusted associates in these positions indicated the increased importance of the tasks the holders of these offices were to perform, and the emergence of a new attitude toward public policy.

The constitution also provided for the establishment of a political organization. Chapter Six ("Transitional and Final Provisions"), Article 192 reads: "The people of Egypt shall form a National Union [*Ittihad Qaumi*] to accomplish the aims of the Revolution and to encourage all means to give the nation a solid foundation in the political, social, and economic realms."[16] The formal decree creating this party was issued in mid-1957, and the National Union participated in the elections in the summer of that same year. Anwar al-Sadat was appointed its Secretary General.

During 1958, Sadat published the National Union's principles and aims, first in a series of articles which appeared in the daily *al-Gumhuriyyah* (The Republic) and then in a pamphlet, *Qa'idah Sha'biyyah* (The Popular Base).[17] It had been apparent since the 1952 coup, he argued, that the RCC lacked the "necessary link" with the people. The National Union was now to supply this link, with a new political unit called *Qa'idah Sha'biyyah*. The National Union was meant to be a popular instrument, a party of solidarity. It was not supposed to be either a governmental organ—although, in fact, it became one—or a representative party, since it did not recognize classes, groups, or competing ideologies. Al-Sadat states that:

The National Union is not a party or an abstract idea; it is a way of protecting the spirit and there is no other way. It is not an expedient freely adopted, but a necessity forced upon us, dictated by our new conditions and our new responsibilities.[18]

Nasser also announced the aims of the National Union, both at home, to establish a democratic social welfare society; and abroad, to achieve independence and freedom for Arabs, and to pursue Arab unity under Egyptian auspices.

The international objectives of the National Union were embodied in the union with Syria, announced on February 1, 1958, and constitutionally effected on March 5, 1959. This emphasis on Egypt's "Arabness" was not limited to discussions about the National Union. The 1956 Constitution itself had proclaimed Egypt "a sovereign independent Arab state," and "the Egyptian people [were] described as an integral part of the Arab nation."[19] It is doubtful that a union of the type attempted with Syria was specifically intended at the time the constitution was written; nor was it an original goal of the National Union. Rather, Egypt's intentions at that time were international only in the sense that it wanted a united Arab foreign policy, with Egypt setting the pace.

It was the Syrian Ba'th party, rather than Nasser, which ffanted the union in the form it took. The Ba'th thought it could strengthen itself through the union, but Nasser wanted the Ba'th dismantled, with the National Union acting to unify the two counries. In fact, any discussion of the United Arab Republic is impossible without a simultaneous discussion of the National Union. But before examining the extension of the National Union to Syria or its actual organization, further discussion of its ideology and proposed objectives is necessary.

THE IDEOLOGY OF THE NATIONAL UNION

The National Union was intended to accomplish the Triple Revolution, as stated by Nasser in his speech before the National Union Congress of July 9, 1960. The first of these was the "national" revolution of all Arab countries struggling against colonialism.

The second [was] the Arab revolution which urges its nationals to pass the artificial barriers and knock down the hurdles that represent false frontiers invented by invaders who spread dissension and suspicion. And the third, the social revolution which calls for an honourable living for every member of Arab society in fulfillment of social equality which is the mainstay of every national structure.[20]

Thus Nasser still felt that the Arab countries were threatened by the imperialists, who fomented divisions in the Arab world. Consequently, *Al-Isti'mar* (imperialism) was the chief national villain for all Arabs who subscribed to National Union principles. To combat imperialism and its instruments of divisiveness, such as competing political parties, Arabs were obliged to unite. However, this process of unification was specifically intended to be led by Egypt, for as the creator of the National Union, Egypt took upon herself the responsibility of defending the Arab world against the imperialists.[21]

In effect, the accomplishment of these goals—i.e., the national and anti-imperial revolutions—would have meant Egyptian hegemony in the Arab world. In the case of union with Syria, the actual result was domination by Egypt. Since the National Union was to be the instrument of unification, and since parties were considered divisive instruments, Nasser attempted to eliminate the Syrian parties, especially the Ba'th and the Communists.

The specific diplomatic and international power gains that Egypt was attempting to obtain by taking up the banner of Arab unity, were, of course, played down in official speeches. And as Egypt's actions became increasingly and more obviously self-aggrandising, the official line more stridently proclaimed the ideal goals, with special emphasis on the ever-present threat of imperialism. The foreign devil theory was used more and more often in Syria, as the failure of the unification scheme became more and more apparent.[22]

In the third revolution, the social one, two basic themes can be identified: the theme of social democracy and economic equality, and the theme of the uniqueness of the Arab world, which requires special solutions for its problems.

Nasser, speaking on the theme of social democracy on the ninth anniversary of the July coup, said:

We should establish a new democracy and a new state with new political, economic and social systems. We must prove that our socialism means the Liberation of man [sic] from bondage in all its forms. The socialism we are working for means both social and political democracy. We must build a new state in all its aspects, to be based on justice and equal opportunities.[23]

This new state was to be built through national planning and by the rational allocation of resources, so that the fruits of the people's labor would be used for the general good of the people, and not for the benefit of a small group of persons. The responsibility for the just distribution of rewards was to be placed on the officials of the state; but there was relatively little emphasis on the mobilization of the people, so that they could effectively observe and control the officials' conduct. Along with this emphasis on management and planning, Nasser attacked the remnants of feudalism as well as capitalist practices, claiming that both worked to the advantage of the few by using the labor of many. Nasser and his propagandists emphasized that, without the initial creation of social democracy, political democracy would not be possible.

Egyptian and Arab social democracy, its proponents claimed, must be different from European socialism. This difference was defined by Kamal Rifa't (ideologue of the Arab Socialist Union until 1967)*:

> Arab socialism is diametrically at variance with European social democracy, particularly from the practical point of view, inasmuch as our socialism finds its level with societies not as yet developed in the political and economic spheres.[24]

Socialism, a phase that developed from capitalism both historically and philosophically, was coupled in Europe with the gradual rise of the industrial system. In Egypt, as elsewhere in the underdeveloped world, it is appearing already in the pre-industrial stage, that is, during the stage of modernization.

The National Union was formally created in May 1957. In February 1958, a joint communique was published by Nasser and Shukri al-Quwwatli, the President of Syria, announcing the formation of the United Arab Republic. Following this,

---

* Kamal Rifa't was an influential writer on Nasser's Arab socialism; he played an important role in the regime during the UAR period.

the Supreme Executive Committee of the National Union was formed, to prepare for the creation of an intricate organization for the accomplishment, in both Egypt and Syria, of the national anti-imperial and social revolutions' objectives. The United Arab Republic's elections of July 1959 were held to establish the "popular base" for the National Union—the organization of popular provincial, regional and supreme groups. The N.U. was divided geographically, into the Southern Region (Egypt), and the Northern Region (Syria). The party structure paralleled that of the U.A.R.'s government, and was almost indistinguishable from it, beginning at the village level, continuing through the town district level, and going up to the province or governorate, the regional congresses, the United Arab Republic Congress, and the President of the National Union.

This complex and cumbersome organization was more a blueprint than an operable and functioning mechanism. Thus, in describing and analysing this intricate, web-like structure, it is not possible to identify precisely which organs were actually put into operation and which were merely on the books. However, in general, the supreme organs and higher echelons of the National Union structure were put into operation. The status of the middle and lower organs of the National Union ranged from that of tentative plans to ineffectively operating units.

At the bottom of the National Union pyramid was the Popular Base (*Qu'idah Sha'biyyah*), an elective body. This organization was intended to provide the key link between the leaders of the regime and the lower orders, and therefore to mobilize support for the regime. The link between the Popular Base and the party's upper level was to be the Local Government Central Committee (*al-Lajnah al Markaziyyah lil-Idarah al-Mahalliyyah*). This committee was to consist of a group of ministers appointed by Nasser, the National Union's *Rais*.[25]

The Union's national organs were to be divided into three administrative areas: regional congresses, General Congress, and the Supreme Executive Committee. For the northern and southern regional congresses, membership was fixed by presidential appointment from Cairo. The regional congresses were responsible for reviewing both local and regional activities, each congress being headed by an inspector general who also directed the Ministry of Local Government. The inspectors general, Marshal 'Abd al-Hakim 'Amer for the North and Kamal al-Din Husain for the South, were appointed by President Nasser. To carry out its goals, each regional congress had 17 functional committees for dealing with youth, labor, women, public services, industry, finance, health, art, science and other fields. These were tripartite bodies which included representatives of local committees and various functional organizations, as well as the directors of regional departments.[26] The national organ of the U.A.R.'s National Union was to be the General Congress (*al-Mu'tamar al-'Amm lil-Jumhuriyyah al-'Arabiyyah al-Muttahidah*). The membership of this organization was to include persons nominated by the president and the regional inspectors, and persons nominated by town and village committees. Thus, direct nominations and ex-officio nomination were combined. The General Congress was to meet once a year at the direction of the *Rais*, and it was to be a key in implementing the three revolutions: national, Arab and social.

The highest organ of the National Union was the Supreme Executive Committee. It was composed of the president, the inspectors general of the two regions, a secretary general, and the United Arab Republic cabinet, consisting of 18 Egyptian and Syrian ministers. The Supreme Executive Committee also linked the party to the U.A.R. government. It was the United Arab Republic's highest executive instrument and that of the party as well.

The U.A.R. government's middle level, the Executive Committee of the Governorate (*Lajnah Tanfidhiyyah lil-Muhafazah*), was composed of the executive committees of district and town quarters and members of the General Congress. In the effort to have uniform structures in both regions, the U.A.R. government dissolved the Syria Majlis (Chamber of Deputies) and set up one National Assembly to serve both regions. The dissolution of the Majlis effectively placed legislative power in the hands of the U.A.R.'s president, and his consultants. The National Assembly had no effective independent power;

it was a creation of the executive, and essentially a ratifying body. The Presidium of the Assembly, however, must be taken into consideration in any discussion of policy formulation in the United Arab Republic, for the Presidium's president was Nasser's trusted friend, Anwar al-Sadat. Representatives from the army, from trade unions, and from Cairo's rival city, Alexandria, were also prominent in that organization.[27]

Both the leaders of the United Arab Republic and the National Union ignored the letter of the law establishing the National Assembly's constitutional functions and powers. In a similar fashion, and with the same intention, to increase the importance of the executive, the members of the General Congress of the U.A.R. were actually chosen by government nominations which had to be approved by the regional inspectors. Attempts at local and popular organization were thwarted by similar approaches and consequent policy changes.

Egypt's concern with integrating the Syrian provinces into the United Arab Republic and mobilizing local support in both regions was exemplified by the proclamation of the Law of Local Government (*Qanun Nizam al-Idarah al-Mahalliyyah*) in March 1960.[28] Originally, the law was to apply only in Egypt, but by early 1961 it was being enforced in Syria as well. At that time, the inspector general of the Southern Region (Egypt) was appointed Minister of Local Government. The Local Government Central Committee (which was to advise the inspector general on policy matters) was supposed to be a committee formed of ministers appointed by Nasser. It was meant to be divided in such a way that the Ministry and the Inspector General could closely supervise the directly elected village and town councilships.[29] The Ministry was to issue all policies, and to form the lower councils. This was another manifestation of centralization of power in the executive organs, although the original intention behind the creation of local councils had been to activate the local populations.[30]

In Syria, this law was designed to cut through the nation's traditional interests, and harness local energies to the newly formed machinery of the National Union.[31] For example, it

Figure 4: EXECUTIVE AND REGIONAL ZONES OF THE NORTHERN UAR REGION (SYRIA)

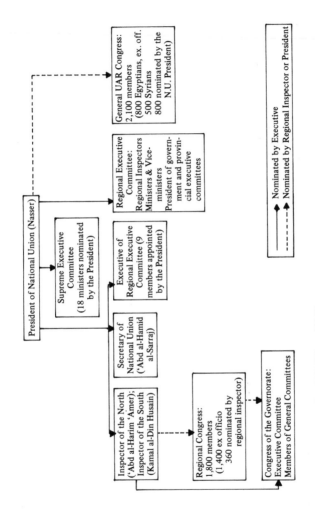

Source: Adapted from *MER* 1960, pp. 467-468.

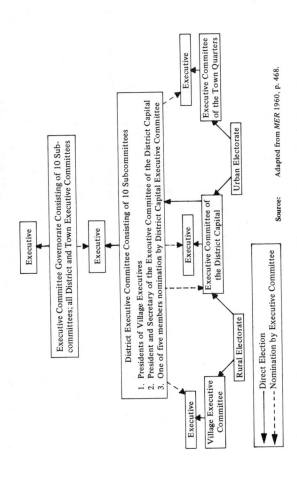

Figure 5: POPULAR BASE AND MIDDLE LEVELS OF THE NATIONAL UNION PARTY
IN THE NORTHERN REGION (SYRIA)

Executive

Executive Committee Governorate Consisting of 10 Subcommittees; all District and Town Executive Committees

Executive

District Executive Committee Consisting of 10 Subcommittees

1. Presidents of Village Executives
2. President and Secretary of the Executive Committee of the District Capital
3. One of five members nomination by District Capital Executive Committee

Executive

Executive

Executive Committee of
the District Capital

Executive Committee
of the Town Quarters

Urban Electorate

Rural Electorate

Village Executive
Committee

Executive

Direct Election
Nomination by Executive Committee

Source: Adapted from *MER* 1960, p. 468.

was intended to isolate landlords from their local constituencies. Various government ministers and journalists wrote articles in *al-Ahram* and *Ruz al-Yusuf*, to explain that the interests of the new Local Government System and the Popular Base were identical.[32]

The attempt at mobilizing popular support in the Northern Region was unsuccessful, and conflicted with the aims and interests of the Syrian political forces that already existed there. Specifically, such policies hurt the Ba'th, which had promoted and supported the formation of the United Arab Republic. The Syrian elements initially favorable to union were further alienated by the Egyptian attempt to abolish party government and parties, which Nasser considered "Divisive elements [of] foreign implantation, [and] an instrument of the imperialists."[33] The very concept of the National Union as an instrument of unity above parties, created dissatisfaction in Syria. Because the Ba'th, Syria's popular Socialist party, was under attack, Nasser was forced into alliances with the conservative elements whose elimination had been the declared objective of the regime. Thus, as the socialist objectives of the Union were being stridently proclaimed, their actual supporters were driven underground.

In 1968, the *Economist* judiciously described the problems and failures of the National Union scheme:

> The formation of the United Arab Republic in February, 1958, put an abrupt end to Syrian politics and also to the rather timid experiments that were then being carried out in Cairo. The new Constitution specified an assembly, but in terms so confused that even Egyptian lawyers quail at the thoughts of interpretation. The first sign of movement on this front was last summer, when both regions elected village committees of the National Union; these committees were then supposed to elect provincial councils which, in turn, were to elect a general congress. But the pyramid has been slow in building. The idea of weaving, from the outer edge inward, a spider's web of committee reaching to Cairo at the center could be attractive and even useful. The trouble in the United Arab Republic is that little gets done and even less is understood by the people concerned. Thus the villages, called upon to vote, voted for the same families who have always been dominant, and the web breaks off long before it reaches the center.[34]

Thus the instruments which were supposedly designed to break the chains shackling the poor to their traditional exploiters, were not used. And by attempting to impose a new unity, the Union actually created new divisions.

Neither the National Union leaders nor local government members had enough experience in organization—or, perhaps, enough desire—to forge strong links with the *Sha'b* (people). Education in the ways of revolution requires well-trained party workers and organizers. Nasser first tried to organize cadres four years after the consolidation of his power, whereas Lenin had started preparing "professional revolutionaries" as early as 1903, 16 years before he assumed power. Chairman Mao spent nearly a quarter of a century—from 1927 to 1949—enforcing an articulate and complex system of tutorship in self-government in China. While the National Union and the United Arab Republic lasted, Nasser organized no popular nuclei of support, failed to integrate Syrian elites and Egyptian cadres, and trained no future political officers. Thus the National Union organization remained merely a bureaucracy, with few links to the people, and Nasser's cadres collapsed before the creation of the United Arab Republic.

THE FAILURE OF UNION

Egypt's failure in Syria was not purely administrative. Syria's people could have been emotionally and politically recruited to serve a central government which they saw as "their own", but Nasser's Egyptianized Arabism (which saw Egypt as the dominant power in the Arab world) found no response in a country long associated with Arabhood (*Al-Urubah*). The Egyptian authorities and National Union officers soon faced opposition from the Ba'th, particularly from its non-military supporters and members.[35] When the socialist program launched in Egypt was finally extended to Syria—against the protest of Marshal 'Abd al-Hakim 'Amer, the Egyptian Proconsul in Syria, the U.A.R. began to dissolve. This Egyptian nationalization of Syria was the last act of alienation; within a few weeks the Syrian army revolted, and in mid-1961, the United Arab Republic came to an end. With the disintegration of the UAR, the National Union, which even in Egypt had been merely a paper organization, also dissolved.[36]

THE SOCIALIST UNION: A PARTY IN CHARGE OF ECONOMIC MODERNIZATION

After the failure of the attempted union with Syria, the Egyptian regime launched a new program. The old "social revolution", and Egypt's attempts at territorial and ideological integration had also failed. So a new program of economic modernization was launched under the auspices of a new government party, the Socialist Union, and the new orientation was definitely managerial at the expense of popular mobilization.[37] (In other words, this was a party dedicated to the creation of economic and social cadres, rather than political or electoral mobilization.)

The RCC's failure to integrate the Muslim Brotherhood into the first mass party, the Liberation Rally, had caused it to consider forming a government political party. The Popular Socialist Party (*al-Hizb al Jumhuriyyah al-Ishtarakiyyah*), which was advocated by RCC Vice-President 'Abd Latif al-Baghdadi, and Ikhsan 'Abd al-Qudus, the editor of *Ruz-al-Yusuf*, was such a party.[38] The total failure of the second mass party, the National Union, modified Nasser's conception of the type of political organization best suited to Egypt.* Thus the Arab Socialist Union represented a compromise between Nasser's conception of a popular party centrally controlled, and a cadre party supported by the masses.[40]

The new party was to be formed on the basis of two

---

* It is most significant that the term "political organization" (*Tanjim Siyasi*) was not used for either the Liberation Rally or the National Union. The Arab Socialist Union was the first political organ in Nasserite Egypt to be called a political organization. Later, the Liberation Rally and the National Union were both termed *Tanjim*, that is organizations. The term *Hizb* (party) was purged from the Nasserite political terminology.[39]

principles: limiting the RCC's control over the party, that is, narrowing the organizational scope of the party's top-level structure; and forming a permanent party base at the level of party activists, to give the latter significant political influence, particularly in the modernization programs, structures and activities of Egypt.

Thus, neither the popular base of the *Sha'biyyah* (People) the foundation stone of the National Union, nor al-Qudus's concept of cadres, was adopted. Instead, party activists were to be given some political leverage on the functional level, that is, regarding factories, public authorities and government corporations established to advance modernization projects.

Agitation had not sufficed to get the *Sha'biyyah* to work for social justice: neither the Liberation Rally nor the National Union had been able to base the state's power on the allegiance of the population's lower economic strata. Rather than continuing to obtain support from these strata, the new program, called "State-Ensured Justice", was to be directed from the top, with a minimum of popular involvement.

A new political theory was proclaimed: Egypt's socio-economic revolution was to be based on a state run by military men and technocrats. In explaining this new orientation, 'Ali Sabri, Minister for Presidential Affairs wrote: "Historical experience has shown that the government is the most valid representative of the people where factors and politics have kept a broad mass backward, ignorant and depressed."[41] The new era was to begin with a campaign against vested interests and social injustice; in effect, this meant a more intensive nationalization program and a growing bureaucracy, protected by the regime, to manage the state-run enterprises and lead social programs. 'Ali Sabri concluded: "The emergence of a public factor in industrial entrepreneurship in this country, projected against the background of the national experience, of private business and its connections with the past, together with its role as an instrument directed at the disruption of the nationalist front was an inevitable consequence of the march of events."[42]

The junta now began to assume complete economic control

of Egypt. The years 1952-1957 were marked by the military leaders' efforts to aid Egyptian industrialists and private entrepreneurs, in the hope that private enterprise could demonstrate vigor and initiative and thus enhance Egypt's industrialization and development efforts. But these efforts were to no avail, since Egypt's entrepreneurs were politically impotent.

Ten years after the coup the wheel had turned full circle, and the government was pressed by its ideological and nationalist commitments to turn toward a so-called socialist economy. Officially, Egypt's new economic system is a command economy, planned and co-operative. Institutionally, however, it is a mixed system, and O'Brien's designation of it as a centralized market economy system is probably the most accurate evaluation of Egypt's economic system since 1960.

The Economic Development Organization, which had been established early in 1957, was given greater authority and eventually became the major instrument for nationalization.[43] The new system's main objective was the creation of a technocratic-industrial cadre by the military elite. Muhammad Hasanain Haykal, Editor-in-Chief of the nationalized *al-Ahram* and one of Nasser's most trusted political pamphleteers, wrote in 1964 that the Aswan High Dam project was "one of the most conspicuous achievements of the July 23 Revolution".

The administration that Haykal praises is a bureaucratic one, that discusses its current problems in terms of need for new technocrats and managers who can implement the hopes of the poor, but without mobilizing the poor. Thus, Haykal feels that the immediate need is for a new and efficient technocracy to regulate the High Dam, the Suez Canal, and the Desert Reclamation Authorities.

Slight conciliatory gestures were made toward the people. To guarantee the loyalty of the new bureaucracy, the "supervision of the people" was entrusted to cadres. There were to be two levels of government, the cadres and the experts. The Socialist Union served to recommend carefully selected political candidates, later to become the cadres. Thus elections in the U.A.R. would be handled by the only election broker, the Socialist Union, whose purpose was to determine the quality of candidates, their loyalty and their potential as cadre material. A Preparatory Committee was appointed to determine the method by which the Congress of Popular Forces would actually name the candidates; it was this committee which managed elections for the National Assembly. If the Socialist Union's primary aim was to form a nucleus of loyal and dedicated cadres, it has completely failed in its task. Since the Socialist Union was largely designed to eliminate old political rivals, it recruited politically impotent and pliable members, rather than establishing a cadre of dedicated party professionals and ideologues. To secure the praetorian political system, Socialist Union representatives were selected on an occupational basis—thus isolating what were to be the cadres from their raison d'être, the political "shock troops" of the Socialist Union.

The instrument established to prevent the activists from becoming an ideological-political cadre was the Political Bureau (*Hizbah Siyasi*), which was not mentioned in either the July 1962 Charter or the December 1962 Arab Socialist Union Directive. The Political Bureau began as neither a party nor a cadre, but rather a group of super-activists.[44] The left envisaged the Bureau as a revolutionary cadre, but Nasser refused to give the Bureau his official sanction. In the end, it was neither a cadre nor a committee of activists, but a group of functionaries similar to the Executive Committee of the National Union. There were two levels of political domination: the functional level, handled by the Bureau; and the other, real level, managed by the government. The second level of government was the cabinet, and the governmental bureaucracy. Nasser selected his new cabinet in 1961, without consulting the National Assembly. This cabinet did not act as a committee of the National Assembly, as in the case of competitive party systems under parliamentary political systems. The Nasser cabinet became an administrative and technocratic body, selected and approved by Nasser and his close cohorts. With the exception of 'Ali Sabri, between 1961 and 1965, no member of the cabinet has possessed executive powers. The cabinet is only responsible to the Premier and, through him, directly to Nasser.

In 1961 'Ali Sabri was appointed Prime Minister of a

corporate directorship which would control the economic ministries. His 11 deputies were directed to attract qualified professionals, even members of the old administration, by paying higher salaries. If the old machinery drew personnel from the "theoretical faculties", this one would draw from "the technical faculties". Haykal claims that 45 per cent of the new directorate were engineers.[45]

Of the seven newcomers heading economic, scientific and communications corporate ministries, six were engineers, and one was a chemist.

Thus, the technical aspects of economic modernization were made the concern of a professional bureaucracy; at the same time, the political modernizers were protected somewhat from the emergence of uncontrolled rival elites. These useful, highly paid professional directors presented no threat to the regime's Executive Committee.

Sabri's new cabinet bore some resemblance to the Soviet Supreme Council of the National Economy, the *Veshenka*. As an operational unit designed to administer the new economic system, the Egyptian cabinet, like the *Veshenka*, provided administration, rather than leadership. Sabri's cabinet was supposedly responsible to a General Assembly; while the *Veshenka*'s successor, the Council of Ministers, was completely subservient to the Supreme Soviet. But the U.A.R. president did not give Sabri's cabinet even the minimal autonomy that the Soviets gave to the Council of Ministers. Its only substantial functions were those of management. Egypt's Socialist Union gave birth to experts, not cadres; and the cadres were neglected, to the advantage of the experts. The ideological indoctrination of the experts was not the Socialist Union's primary function; the Socialist Union was intended to create and supervise the two types of elites—what Chairman Mao would term the Reds and the Experts.

Egypt's Socialist Union provided supervision, censorship and control, acting on behalf of the government to keep the economic modernization programs, technocratic machinery, and the new cabinet separated from the process of restricted political participation. The administrative-functional cabinet was directly responsible to the *Rais*; the representative assembly was also under his direct supervision. The policy of restricted political participation was a concomitant of Nasser's modernization policy, intended to slow political mobilization while promoting economic modernization and growth.[46] This policy was co-ordinated with the Socialist Union's policy of candidate selection. Originally, only people whose loyalty was well known could become candidates. However, the candidates were later selected by occupation, and again were carefully screened in terms of loyalty. Thus, in the 1964 parliament, there was a predominance of candidates who possessed skills and were engaged in occupations which could promote change in a modernizing polity.

Sabri's cabinet came to an end in 1965, when Nasser's old friend, the veteran Free Officer Zakariyya Muhyi al-Din, became cabinet head. Sabri's rapid modernization plans had been thwarted by tying down the government programs too closely to supervision. Sabri's attempts to combine governmental modernization with functional political representation did not fare well. In 1966, Nasser relieved Sabri of his post as prime minister, to concentrate on building the Socialist Union; and appointed an engineer, Sidqi Sulaiman, to head the economic-administrative and functional cabinet. At this point, the processes of economic modernization had been separated from ties with the political party. The Socialist Union still functions only as a representative of occupational and technical groups. The cadres have been replaced by experts and technocrats, and ideological indoctrination is no longer a goal. The cadres never served the purpose for which they were supposedly created; and were soon superseded by the "scientific" model of experts.

The Arab Socialist Union Between 1965 and 1967.

Before 1965, the ASU did not serve as the mobilizing political structure of Egypt's growing bureaucratic elites. The political functions of the Liberation Rally, the National Union and the ASU were extremely limited and their social impact was severely restricted. Nasser's political structures served as governmental parties, to eliminate opposition and to diffuse the Nasserite ideology throughout Egypt's masses. These political structures became ad hoc instruments for resolving critical political issues concerning internal, domestic and economic policies. The *Rais*, and a few of his trusted lieutenants. dominated without interference in the areas of foreign affairs and security.

The relationship between the government and the ASU became extremely complex. Each level of the ASU (see Figure 6) was dominated by the respective governmental structures, thereby ruling out vertical mobility. Control was horizontal, but not total. For instance, between 1965 and 1967, 'Ali Sabri succeeded in mobilizing into part of the ASU pyramid locals who were neither governmental bureaucrats nor under the domination of their respective echelon in the government side of the structural pyramid. It is true that Rank A of the ASU was closed to the masses, for it was composed of veteran FOC loyal elites newly recruited from the Nasserite army, senior governmental executives (military and civilian) and the professionals—lawyers, engineers and doctors. The strategic elite, Rank B, was appointed mainly by Rank A and the Executive Committee of the National Union or the ASU. The members of Rank C, supposedly elected from below, were in fact appointed by Rank B. Thus, for our purposes, the political influence of Rank C members was nil. Since 1965, Rank B of the ASU has been widened, and its political influence significantly increased; but Rank C has totally collapsed. To make the political influence of Rank B more effective, Sabri abolished the district structure of the ASU and established a network of functional units of factories, public authorities, and unions. These were given considerable autonomy in the ASU middle echelon level. Domination over the functional units was by the Activists.[47]

The Socialist Union was designed to achieve Egypt's modernization and industrialization without popular mobilization. (The cadres do not threaten the expert.) However, this regime was structured to protect the current ruling elite of the military bureaucrats, scientists, technocrats and former capitalists.

The vague acceptance of so-called "socialist" doctrines on the part of the regime may be the result of a commitment to a managerial organization, rather than any commitment to a radical revolutionary position. Modernization and quasi-socialization were consequently pursued, so that this class of managers could adapt itself to a post colonial era, remain in power during the process, and guide Egypt in an antiliberal direction. This group has been aware that its political fortunes lie in directions different from those of Egypt's historical middle class; its commitments and expectations were governed by an astute evaluation of the sources of power in post colonial developing states. Thus it has introduced a form of socialism that is adaptable to bureaucratic and étatist practices.[48]

When the search for political solutions on the Arab level failed, Egypt's hope for the future took the form of a classless system, administered by inflated bureaucracies. Rather than

Figure 6:
ASU—REGIME SYSTEM OF CONTROL

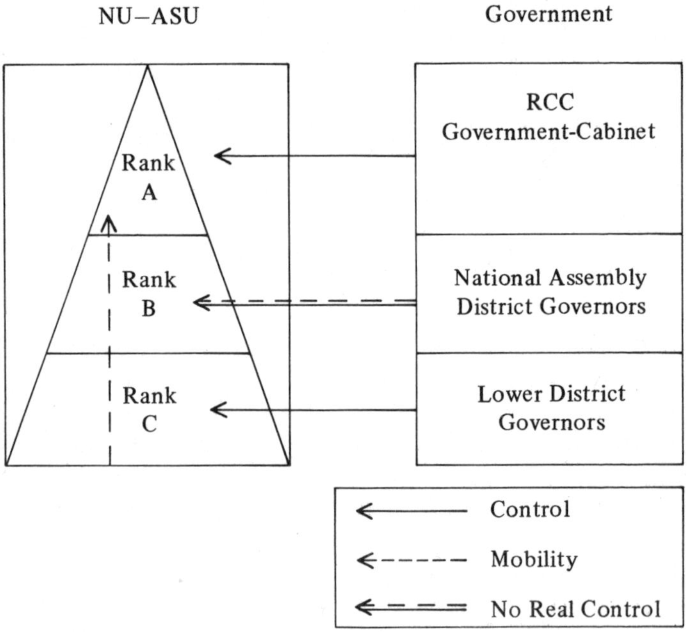

Source: S. Lulko: "The Popular Structure of the Nasserite Regime: unpub. mss. (Tel-Aviv, 1971), p. 10.

attempting to build webs of political relationships and loyalties, Egypt tried to build an organization. Egypt was searching for political utopianism, in attempting to amalgamate the people of Syria into the union. When that attempt failed, the Egyptian bureaucrats and planners returned to Cairo to concentrate on Egypt. This time they offered a new bureaucratic model meant only for Egypt; that model was the Socialist Union. Sabri and his activists sought to establish their regime's legitimacy in the ASU, eventually turning the latter into a Soviet-model party, and to eliminate the political content of government structures like the National Assembly and the Cabinet. They also hoped to infiltrate if not eliminate the RCC, and to limit the influence of the military. It was hoped that Nasser would support these orientations after the 1967 disaster. In fact the period from 1967 to Nasser's death could be accurately described as the radicalization of Egypt. During this time, the ASU gained in influence, as did Sabri and his ASU activists. But Egypt's radical period was not to last for long.

NOTES

1. Samuel P. Huntington, *Political Order in Changing Societies* (New Haven: Yale University Press, 1968), Chap. 5. Amos Perlmutter, *Political Institutionalization* (Cambridge: Center for International Affairs, Harvard University, no. 25, 1968).

2. Majid Khadduri, *Independent Iraq* (London, Oxford University Press, 1968). Amos Perlmutter, "From Obscurity to Rule: The Syrian Army and the Ba'th party" *Western Political Quarterly* vol. 22, no. 4 (December 1969).

3. *President Gamal Abdul Nasser's Speeches and Press Interviews,* January-December 1961, published by the Egyptian government, 1961, p. 395.

4. *Ibid.,* p. 396.

5. Eliezer Be'eri, *The Officer Class in Arab Politics and Society,* Praeger (New York, 1970), and Jean Lacouture and Simmone Lacouture, *Egypt in Transition* (New York: Criterion Books, 1958).

6. Be'eri, *The Officer Class,* p. 75.

7. Jean and Simmone Lacouture, *Egypt in Transition,* pp. 141-45; Be'eri, *The Officer Class.*

8. Ihsan Abdal-Qudus in *Al-akhbar,* 1954.

9. Richard P. Mitchell, *The Society of the Muslim Brothers* (London: Oxford University Press, 1969); Be'eri, *The Officer Class;* Lacouture and Lacouture, *Egypt in Transition.*

10. Shimon Shamir, "Five Years of the Organization of Liberation Rally in Egypt", *The New East* vol. 8, no. 32 (1951), p. 263.
11. *Ibid.,* p. 264.
11. *Ibid.,* p. 278.
13. Be'eri, *The Officer Class.*
14. *Ibid.*
15. *Al-Ahram,* June 24, 1956.
16. Article 192 of the new Egyptian Constitution as published in *Al-Ahram,* January 1, 1956. Author's translation. The clause may also be found in the *U.A.R. Yearbook,* 1960 (Cairo: Information Department, 1960).
17. Anwar al-Sadat, *Qa'idah Sha'biyyah (People's Base)* Cairo June 1958), quoted in *Middle East Review* (1960): 478.
18. *Ibid.,* p. 37.
19. Curtis Jones, "The New Egyptian Constitution", *The Middle East Journal* 8, no. 4 (Summer 1956): 300.
20. *Egyptian Gazette,* July 29, September 4, and December 12, 1960, quoted in Itzchak Oron, ed., *Middle East Record, 1960* (hereafter cited as MER) I (London: Weidenfeld and Nicolson, 1962), pp. 467-68.
21. See, for example, the speech delivered in Damascus, February 24, 1961, in Nasser, *Speeches and Press Interviews,* pp. 53-57.
22. *Ibid.*
23. *Ibid.,* p. 51.
24. *Egyptian Gazette,* December 12, 1960.
25. *MER,* p. 479.
26. *Al-Ahram,* June 12, 1960, pp. 2-3.
27. *U.A.R. Yearbook,* 1960, pp. 31-32.
28. *Al-Ahram,* May-June 1960.
29. Colonel 'Abd al-Hamid Sarraj, a pro-Nasser Ba'thist, was appointed Secretary General, relieving Anwar al-Sadat, in 1960.
30. The Majlis was dissolved despite Syrian opposition. See *Al-Hayat,* January 5, 1960; also *al-Ayyan,* January 30, 1960.
31. Full text in *al-Ahram,* March 27, 1960, pp. 3-4.
32. MER 1960, p. 491; *U.A.R. Yearbook,* 1960, pp. 31-32.
33. Nasser, *Speeches and Press Interviews,* p. 83; al-Sadat, *Qa'idah,* pp. 22-27.
34. *Economist* (March 12, 1960), pp. 974-77.
35. This began as early as spring 1959, during a general convention of Ba'th delegates from all the Arab States. In September 1959, the Ba'th leader and U.A.R. Northern Region Minister for Culture and National Guidance, Riyad al-Maliki, resigned. The Ba'th itself split; in mid-1960, 'Abdallah al-Rimawi, the party's Secretary General in Jordan, established a rival National Command in Damascus, denounced the Syrian Ba'th, and hailed the UAR as champion of all Arabs. In December 1960, Akram al-Hawrani, then Minister of Justice, in the U.A.R. central government, resigned. Mass resignation of Ba'th ministers, at both levels of the UAR, followed. *Middle East Record* (1960): 497-507.
36. Since we are dealing here mainly with the National Union, the

U.A.R. merger is discussed only in passing. For a recent interpretation of the union, its merger, and collapse see Patrick Seale, *The Struggle for Syria* (London: Oxford University Press, 1968), pp. 307-26; Malcolm Kerr, *The Arab Cold War 1958-1967,* 2nd ed., (London: Oxford University Press, 1967), pp. 97-137; Kemel Saleh Abu Jabar, "The Arab Ba'th Socialist Party; History, Ideology and Organization", Ph.D. diss., Syracuse University, 1965, pp. 106-50.

37. The new program was directed by Nasser's trusted Minister for Presidential Affairs, 'Ali Sabri.

38. Sarah Lulko, "The Popular Organization of the Nasserite Regime", mimeographed, Tel-Aviv, 1970, p. 5.

39. I am most grateful to Sarah Lulko of the Shiloah Institute of Tel-Aviv for suggesting this to me.

40. *Ibid.,* p. 7.

41. 'Ali Sabri, "State Ensured", *Egyptian Gazette,* p. 6.

42. *Ibid.*

43. The entire July 1961 issue of *Egyptian Economic and Political Review* (EEPR) is devoted to the *Economic Development Organization* (EDO). For a summary of economic activities, see Malcolm Kerr, "The Emergence of a Socialist Ideology in Egypt", *The Middle East Journal,* 16, no. 2 (1962): 127-44. For the best concise evaluation of the Egyptian economy since Nasser see Patrick K. O'Brien, "An Economic Appraisal of the Egyptian Revolution", *The Journal of Development Studies,* 1, no. 1 (October 1964): 93-113, and his *The Revolution in Egypt's Economic System* (London: Oxford University Press, 1966).

44. Lulko, "The Popular Organization", p. 8.

45. *Al-Ahram,* July 3, 1964, pp. 2-3.

46. Leonard Binder, "Political Recruitment and Participation in Egypt", in Joseph La Palombara and Myron Weiner, *Political Parties and Political Development* (Princeton, N.J.: Princeton University Press, 1966), p. 234.

47. I am grateful to Sarah Lulko for this invaluable information. See Lulko, "The Popular Organization", pp. 8-13.

48. On the lack of balance between political policy making institutions and bureaucratic policy implementing structures, and the conflict between military officers and civilian officers see Fred Riggs, "Bureaucracy and Political Development", in La Palombara *Political Parties* (Princeton, N.J.: Princeton University Press, 1963), pp. 120-67; also S.N. Eisenstadt, "Bureaucracy and Political Development", *ibid.,* pp. 107-08.

CHAPTER 9

Political Power and Social Cohesion
in Nasser's Egypt

The thrust of the argument concerning a praetorian orientation is that protracted political institutionalization, a low
level of social cohesion and the persistence of military rule all
enhance praetorianism. In non-praetorian states, the above
conditions could initiate the movement toward praetorianism. Thus, in the next three chapters we will examine the
relationship between political power and social classes in
Egypt, the processes of political institutionalization of
Nasser's Egypt; and the persistence of Nasserite praetorianism
in Egypt.

THE TWO ELITE CLUSTERS OF EGYPT

The connection between Egypt's social classes and its political power is based on the country's power pyramid, with two
ruling elites sharing the top, and the rural middle and skilled
urban workers' classes distributed through the lower part.

The concept of elites has developed greatly since Mosca,
Pareto, and Michels first formulated their theories at the turn
of the century. More recently, Harold D. Lasswell's formulation stressed elite research on the empirical level.[1] However, a
review by Dankwart Rustow[2] of the research done thus far
reveals that recent quantitative and empirical studies of elites
have not established a proper "correlation between political

power and social status".[3] Therefore Rustow, supporting R. Bendix and S. M. Lipset's contention that the facts of politics must be studied in their own right and not merely inferred from the politician's social background, is critical of most recent empirical elite studies.[4]

Nasser's Egypt contains two clusters of elites, one acting as a ruling class, the other as a strategic elite primarily concerned with administration and technocracy.

The Ruling Elite

We can identify Egypt's top echelon of political power by using a modified definition of Pareto, Mosca and Michels's ruling class. The ruling class, thus modified, is not a natural aristocracy; it need not be associated exclusively with authoritarian or democratic regimes; and it could be located anywhere on the left-right continuum. A ruling class does not need to be cohesive, or politically effective, or restricted in size.

The stratocracy that dominated Nasser's Egypt was not merely another elite category among a variety of elites.[5] It was a ruling group because it had a "group identity derived from sources other than their political function".[6] Its scope of authority was relatively wide and diffuse,[7] and its sources of recruitment and internal organization differentiate it from the strategic elites in Egyptian society. It was the political leadership in power.[8] A ruling group could be distinguished by its long-term rule, its inaccessibility and its relatively small and concentrated size. Yet it can also thrive in a transitional state.[9] It also restricts the formation of other political groups from which competing political elites could spring.

Nasser's elite was a ruling group not only because it was "suffused with strong sentiments of moral indignation and social protest",[10] but also because its members had significant political authority. They are an example of the classic governing elite, although they lack the requirements of birth and wealth attached to the Pareto natural aristocracy. According to Ralf Dahrendorf, the Michels-Mosca-Pareto definition of an elite has serious weaknesses—at least in highly complex, democratic and industrial societies. I prefer to modify their definition for the praetorians: "the politically governing elite". According to Dahrendorf, the Michels-Mosca-Pareto definition of an elite fails "to relate [conflict groups] to the crucial category of imperatively co-ordinated associations".[11] Thus, "ruling groups are . . . no more than ruling groups within defined asociations. In theory, there can be as many competing, conflicting, or coexisting dominating conflict groups in a society as there are associations."[12] This elite definition prevents us from identifying the ruling class as the only political elite in circumstances where other associations exist, containing other defined ruling groups or elites within them. The first echelon of Egypt's political pyramid is the most influential political elite in that society; the echelons below consist of strategic elites, some with clearly defined and highly restricted political functions, others recruited only to participate in political decision making.

The political power of the ruling elite must also be measured by the existence or absence of organized political opposition. Thus, the absence of a mass political party and organized political associations in Egypt increases the political power of its ruling class.

The amount of political power the ruling group shares with other elites also determines its level of political power. In Nasser's Egypt, several measures were adopted to decrease the power of competing political bureaucracies and their elites, in a conscious effort to promote Egypt's single political elite. Among these measures are: the diffusion of the officers' class into new bureaucracies; the use of the Arab Socialist Union as a clearing house for selecting "acceptable" candidates for the government bureaucracy; the co-operation of the old entrepreneurial and economic classes; the emulation of professional classes; the cautious land reform programs; and the higher proportions of key political offices in relation to the Civil Service. Sadat, on the other hand, uses the permanent purge to limit political competition. Sadat's regime is much more restrictive, and thus more praetorian, than Nasser's.

The ruling elite model has been unpopular among political and social scientists since the criticism of Robert Dahl and others.[13] According to these critics, the ruling elite model of the old Michels-Mosca-Pareto school is ambiguous; while the models of C. Wright Mills and Floyd Hunter are fallible and, at best, "interpret complex ruling elite formations, political systems essentially as instances of a ruling elite".[14] However, Dahl's critique only applies to complex political systems in highly industrial societies. So does C. Wright Mills' elite theory. Based on Mills' concept of institutional and corporate linkages i.e. the industrial military-multiversity complex, the theory is that the directorship-general of society or power elite is linked at the above institutional level. This elite theory also implies a conspiratorial aspiration on the part of the power elite, that is, the power elite is continuous, cohesive and possesses a common will for action to dominate society *politically*. In fact, the existence of a praetorian ruling class as the political elite demonstrates the transitional nature of Egypt's political system. This is further shown by the fact that Egypt's ruling class can be well defined and easily identified; that its preferences regularly prevail; and that it is not complex and linked via large-scale corporate institutions.[15] As James Heaphey demonstrates, the Egyptian decentraliza- tion of government is "non-political" in character, and the absence of "uncertainty relationships" between the governors and the people demonstrates the former's political impotence and the latter's meager demand and political input.[16] Nasser's elite is certainly not the same as Mills' power elite.

Domination by a political ruling group or, in the case of Egypt, by a ruler type praetorian group is also an indication of advanced praetorianism. The restricted ruling political elite is a most useful criterion of the study of developing states in the presence of local polarity, low political institutionaliza- tion and inadequate distribution of political power. A ruling class need not be highly cohesive to be able to dominate under praetorian conditions. That group which has the most dominant political power will rule, regardless of its cohesive- ness, although some form of cohesion is necessary to govern in a praetorian state.

In Egypt, from 1953-1970, at the top of the pyramid of political power stood the *Rais*, Gamal Abdel Nasser. He was the most important decision maker, wielding almost un- limited executive and legislative power. Aiding the Rais were former members of the Free Officers and of the Revolution- ary Command Council, which had been abolished as an organization in 1956.[17] Officers, and particularly veteran Free Officers, held the highest positions in Nasser's cabinets until 1966.

Identification of the ruling elite begins with the study of Egypt's formal and effective political power structures, the government and the cabinet. Since Egyptian political parties and interest groups had been reduced to playing the role of governmental instruments, the real power holders were the senior members of Nasser's cabinets. During the eight Nasser cabinets, the percentage of officer members fluctuated from 45 per cent in the 1952 cabinet, to 32 per cent in the 1956 cabinet, to 47 per cent in the 1965 cabinet.[18] The June 1967 disaster finally caused the ouster of Veteran Free Officers from Nasser's 1968 cabinet—although only one Shafi'i had ever held a political office.

Between 1952 and 1967, each of the four top governmental positions—President, First Vice-President, Prime Minister and Senior Vice-President—was held by only one civilian.*[19] The army as a ruling group was diffused into the crucial governmental (and Arab Socialist Union party) positions, in economics, industry and diplomacy. Be'eri estimates that this ruling group constituted 1,000 loyal officers, headed and directed by the small group of veteran Free Officers.[20] In the classic manner of the ruling group, it is replenished by the same group, in this case the army. Since 1952, no group has enjoyed a greater increase in its share of the highest political offices. The regime of Sadat is completely dependent on the military.

The most comprehensive analysis (although it uses a small sample) of the social origin and family background of Egyptian army officers has been conducted by Be'eri.[21] His analysis of 87 Egyptian officers killed in the Palestine War of Liberation from 1947-1949 (2.9 per cent of the total officers class in 1948-1949) illustrates the conspicuous position of the rural middle class and its urban offshoots in the Egyptian Officers Corps, from which the Free Officers sprang.[22]

The similar social origins and family background of Free

---

* Between 1967 and Nasser's death in 1970, the post of First Vice-President was abolished, and the *Rais* was the only civilian officeholder.

Officers, especially the senior members, could demonstrate the potential of the ruling elite to act as a cohesive class. However, this is not equivalent to a political class, although it could be a crucial factor in elite political formation and influence.

The close and clandestine nature of the ruling elite, as well as its members' common background, encourages common social action, but does not guarantee common political action or ideology. On the whole, Nasser's officer group was a closed group which, despite its primary group bonds, was not cohesive politically. It could be argued that the Free Officers, having emerged from an identifiable stratum of the Egyptian army, having experienced the Palestine campaign together, and having endured the surveillance of Faruq's secret police, developed political cohesion and some form of common political action. But it was a short-lived era of political cohesion. Events after 1952 show that the rise of the Free Officers was less dependent on social origins than on common bonds connected with the army, as conspirators. Another weakness in the argument that the political power of the Egyptian officers came from their common social background is the fact that they acted as individuals, not as a class. Common descent, social class and economic interest have not been sufficient to make the Egyptian rural middle classes, and their urban offshoots, a ruling elite. The army elite did not become a ruling class and did not create at least some form of political cohesion because it had a common social class, family background and group identity. Nor did it do so because of its clandestine nature, or the hostility of the senior officers of the old regime, or even the traumatic lessons of Palestine. Rather, the army elite became a ruling class through antagonism to the civilian politicians, and, above all, through the longevity of its rule and its independent control over political power, which has excluded all other elites in Egypt since 1952. The ruling elite now has a monopoly on political power since it has vanquished its antagonists old and new. Although Nasser purged many army officers from his government after 1967, the chances for the future return of the military to political power are better than ever, part-icularly as Egypt's army, under intensive training by the

Soviets, prepared for the next round of the "Liberation of Palestine" in October 1973. Social origins and political cohesion do not explain the political behavior and elite formation of either Nasser's or Sadat's regime. Both are restrictive praetorian ruling classes—the former more secure and the latter precarious, but praetorian nonetheless.

The Strategic Elite

The second type of elite in Nasser's Egypt, the strategic elite, is distinguished by its members, consisting of "specialists in excellence".[23] It is an elite of merit, representing Egypt's professional and technocratic group. Yet some influential members of this elite have been accepted into the ruling class, because of the political recruitment means employed by Nasser's inner circle. The strategic elites were recruited on the basis of function, rather than group and kinship, as is the case with the ruling group. Because the Free Officers are the ruling group and many members of the strategic elite are recruited from, or co-opted by, the army, this type of recruitment helps diffuse the ruling group into all the key centers of political power. Thus, former army officers have certain privileges which other members of the strategic elite do not enjoy. For example, Free Officers among the strategic elite have ruling class advantages and enjoy specific types of political influence which their functional equivalents, the strategic elite, do not.

Among the strategic elites, the officers are assigned to co-ordinate governmental departments, to run industries and economic enterprises, to inculcate the "Egyptian Revolution" or Nasserite concept of politics into the bureaucracy, and to administer land reform. Although performing as an elite of merit, they also behave as a ruling class. In this case, the army, as a ruling class, and the reservoir from which this core group of the strategic elite is recruited, are the same.[24] This stratum of the strategic elites wields great political power, not because of its economic function, but because it is recruited from the ruling class. The military under Sadat clearly demonstrates this argument. Another stratum of the strategic elites, not recruited from the army, represents the technical, professional and economic groups and is composed of lawyers, physicians, engineers, university professors and former financiers and businessmen considered untainted by the "corruption" of the former regime. This technical-professional-economic elite, unlike the political elite of former Wafdists, journalists and politicians, does not represent a threat to the political elite. The members of this technical elite are mostly retained for their valuable skills, which could not be replaced by the ruling class or other elites of merit. Under Sadat this group has declined.

On the whole, since Sadat's coup of May 1971, officers have headed Egypt's political departments: the Defense Ministry, the Ministry of National Guidance and the Foreign Office. The non-ruling elite of merit is spread throughout the functional and economic departments—the Ministries of Finance, Economics and Industry. The major circulation of elites under Sadat is between and within the military.

Even in the latter ministries, former army men had top positions, and the key governmental enterprises are still headed by former officers. This is true of the Suez Canal project, the Aswan High Dam and Desert Reclamation authorities, as well as the directorship of Bank Misr (the National Bank), and the directorship of the Nile Navigation Company. Thus, in the key economic and public enterprises, the managerial and financial elite of the previous regime is subordinated to the military officers.

The Foreign Office was dominated by the officers; Mahmud Riad was in charge of foreign affairs between 1967-1972, and has been in the Foreign Service since before 1952 (he was also a member of the Egyptian delegation to the Rhodes Egyptian-Israeli armistice in 1949). In 1952, 25 of the 58 Egyptian ambassadors were former officers; in 1964, 43 out of 73 were former officers.[25] The Secret Police is similarly staffed by the military, although its leaders—including several officers —were purged and tried during the 1968 Cairo military trials. With the purge of the army in 1967, the strategic elites were expected to gain a temporary ascendance, until the army regained its influence. Since the Sadat coup, the army has regained its influence. However, we do not yet know about any major changes in the strategic elite composition, except for the fact that more military men will be recruited.

The Free Officers soon found that the principles of the Egyptian Revolution were not promptly accepted by civil servants. Later, when the regime became more confident of the bureaucracy's loyalty, the problem of providing positions for the junior officers arose. This was solved by moving them into the foreign service. There they felt well rewarded, since the status of diplomats is high in Egypt, and because their tasks in the Foreign Service were less difficult than those available in the Ministries of Interior, Social Affairs, Agrarian Reform or Education.

To establish the fact that the military is the political ruling group in Egypt does not explain why this is so, or the consequences of its rule. Praetorian rule is elitist, narrow and concentrated. This military ruling group is small; its roots are in the rural middle classes; its education is not above the high school level (except courses in foreign military academies);[26] it is a closed group, acting as a caste; and it is secretive. An analysis of the military as a ruling political group should explain what type of political actions this elite prefers; to what extent it is committed to the public good and modernization; to what extent, in short, praetorian rule serves public welfare in Egypt.[27]

Answering some of the questions of what ruling elites do rather than what they are[28] requires an investigation of the social classes which benefited from the Egyptian Revolution and a determination of whether the ruling class has established, in combination with these groups, a wider spectrum of political power.

THE RURAL MIDDLE CLASS AND THE URBAN WORKERS

In 1956, the leaders of the Egyptian Revolution proclaimed that, once the political revolution was achieved—ousting the imperialists, the political parties and the court—the social revolution would inevitably follow. This "social revolution" was meant to include social and land reform, and end feudalism and the remnants of social inequality in Egypt.

Two classes benefited directly from Nasser's social revolution: the rural middle class and its urban offshoots, and the skilled working class.

The Rural Middle Class and the Revolution.

The real beneficiaries of Nasser's two unsuccessful agrarian reforms, in 1952 and 1961, have been the owners of between 10 and 100 *feddans** of land. Tables 1 and 2 indicate six strata of land ownership. Three of them make up the rural middle class: the owners of 5-10, 10-50, and 50-100 feddans. Table 2 shows that, since the first agrarian reform of 1952, the average amount of land owned by those in the 5-10 feddans group had increased from 8.8 per cent to 10.1 per cent. In the second group, the owners of 10-50 feddans, the average land ownership decreased from 18.7 per cent in 1952 to 14.9 per cent in 1964; however, the amount of land this group possessed increased from 21.6 per cent to 21.9 per cent during the same period. Although the third group, the owners of 50-100 feddans, decreased from 71.5 per cent to 65.3 per cent in average ownership of land, the overall percentage of land owned by this group barely decreased—from 7.2 per cent to 6.4 per cent in that same period. In fact, this group profited by the agrarian reform of 1952, for in 1961, it had owned a higher percentage of land (10.5 per cent).

These figures indicate that the rural middle class was retained after the Revolution, and that in fact members of some strata in this class were able to improve their economic lot. The economic stability of this group, unharmed by agrarian reforms, is a highly significant political factor in Nasser's Egypt.

The percentage of Egyptians in the poor peasant group (owners of less than 5 feddans) increased from 35.4 per cent to 54.7 per cent between 1952 and 1964. Yet, during the same period, the average land ownership of this group only rose from 8.8 per cent to 10.1 per cent.

Nasser's agrarian reforms did not eliminate the rich peasant category of people owning 100 to 200 feddans. Members of this group possessed 7.3 per cent of the total land in 1952, and had suffered a loss of only 0.4 per cent by 1964: while their number increased from 3,000 to 4,000 (see Table 2). Baer points out that neither of Nasser's agrarian reforms

* A *feddan* equals 1.038 acres.

TABLE 1

Division of Landed Property in Egypt, 1943-1964

Classification of Ownership (in feddans)	No. of Landowners (in thousands)				No. of feddans owned (in thousands)			
	1943	1952	1961	1964	1943	1952	1961	1964
0-5	2,376	2,642	2,870	2,965	1,944	2,122	2,660	3,353
5-10	85	79	79	78	570	526	530	614
10-50	62	69	69	90	1,204	1,291	1,300	1,342
50-100	7	6	11	6	459	429	630	392
100-200	3	3	3	4	438	437	450	421
200+	2	2	2	—	1,245	1,117	430	—
Totals	2,535	2,801	3,034	3,143	5,860	5,982	6,000	6,122

SOURCE: Gabriel Baer, "New Data and Conclusions about the Effects of Egypt's Land Reform," *Hamizrah Hehadash (The New East),* Jerusalem, Israel, 16, no. 2 (1966): 176-78.

TABLE 2

Individual Average Ownership of Land and Percentage of Land Owned
by Each Group, 1943-1964

Classification of Ownership (in feddans)	Average Ownership of Land by Each Landowner (% in feddans)				Percentage of Land Owned by Each Group			
	1943	1952	1961	1964	1943	1952	1961	1964
0-5	0.8	0.8	0.9	1.1	33.2	35.4	44.3	54.7
5-10	6.7	6.7	6.7	7.9	9.7	8.8	8.8	10.1
10-50	19.4	18.7	18.8	14.9	20.6	21.6	21.7	21.9
50-100	65.6	71.5	57.3	65.3	7.8	7.2	10.5	6.4
100-200	146.0	145.7	150.0	105.2	7.5	7.3	7.5	6.9
200 +	622.5	558.5	215.0	—	21.2	18.7	7.2	—
Total	2.3	2.1	1.9	1.9	100.00	100.00	100.00	100.00

SOURCE: Gabriel Baer, "New Data and Conclusions about the Effects of Egypt's Land Reform," *Hamizrah Hehadash (The New East)*, Jerusalem, Israel, 16, no. 2 (1966): 176.

made non-owners of land into owners, although some 900,000 feddans were distributed among a million small landowners possessing 0.8 per cent to 1.1 per cent feddans.[29] Essentially, agrarian reform benefited the Egyptian rural middle classes,[30] enhancing their economic stability. The real victims of the agrarian reform were the owners of 200 feddans or more, whose land was taken away completely after the 1961 reform. The elimination of these feudal classes created a political and economic power vacuum in rural Egypt, which the rural middle classes filled.

While the rural middle class did not assume the role played by the former feudal lords and rich peasants, it did assume a significant role among Egypt's strategic elites. The economic perseverance of this class demonstrates how little the Egyptian countryside had been disturbed by Nasser's social revolution. But the political influence of the rural middle class is severely limited in comparison with that of the ruling group; it may actually be equal to or below that of the strategic elites. The rural middle class is not much more politically potent than it was prior to 1952. The fact that many army officers are still drawn from this class does not mean it is a source of political power; it simply indicates the social origin of much of the Egyptian military. The source of the ruling group's political power is not the rural middle class, but the army. The rural middle class merely serves as a supporting group. Here lies the confusion of many writers who identify the army with the rural middle class and therefore consider that class a major source of political power in Egypt.

If we accept Leonard Binder's statement that the Preparatory Committee of 1961, which selected and nominated candidates for the Congress of Popular Forces in 1962, "provides a fairly good picture of the kind of people who run the Egyptian polity",[31] then the rural middle class only represents 8 per cent.[32] Some analysts argue that the rural middle class is better represented than this percentage indicates, because many village notables (*'umdah*) have relatives among both the ruling elite[33] and the strategic elites. But this still does not mean that the rural middle class is the source of political power in Egypt. That argument confuses a social elite with a ruling class. Suzanne Keller says:

> Most discussion of . . . ruling classes and elites fails to distinguish between two dimensions: the processes leading to the development of a core group . . . and the reservoir from which this core group is recruited.[34]

Such a confusion of political function and group identity leads to an exaggerated picture of the political role of the rural middle class in Egypt.

The Skilled Urban Workers.

O'Brien claims that "those who have clearly and tangibly gained from the Egyptian Revolution are industrial workers and the beneficiaries of land reform".[35] Although the skilled workers were not politically mobilized in the 1950s, great changes occurred in the 1960s, with the rapid nationalization and heavy investment in industry. Their numerical increase is shown in Table 3.

The numbers for 1952-1961 are based on the yearly censuses in enterprises employing more than ten workers. After 1962, they are based on quarterly accounts and are only listed for industries employing more than 50 workers.

The addition of a force of 100,000 workers between 1950

TABLE 3

Number of Skilled Workers in
Egyptian Population from 17,000,000 (1952)
to 31,000,000 (1971)

Year	Workers
1952	272,156
1959	293,434
1961	399,998
1962	352,188
1963	384,490
1971	500,000*

* estimated

SOURCE: *National Bank of Egypt Economic Bulletin,* No. 1 (1964), p. 115. Quoted in Avraham Ben Tsur, *Arab Socialism* (Tel Aviv: Kibbutz Movement Press, 1966).

and 1963 accounts for the end of the stagnation of the 1950s. According to Charles Issawi, workers in modern industry comprise a little more than 3 per cent of the total Egyptian population and 10 per cent of its urban population; the unskilled, domestic servants, handicrafts workers and the *lumpenproletariat* comprise 56 per cent of the urban proletariat and 16.6 per cent of the total population.[36] Significantly, the 3 per cent of the population represented by Egypt's skilled workers have improved both their economic conditions and their political representation.

The rise of Egypt's skilled working class is also reflected in the governmental structures—in the Socialist Union, the Parliament and the Congress of Popular Forces. The representatives of this group held 13.5 per cent of the seats in the 1964 Parliament.[37] The trade unions played a key role in Nasser's rise to power between 1952 and 1954. In fact, they were one of the few organized groups supporting him at that time; they helped him topple Nagib's "old parties" government coalition in 1954. Later, to control the potential power of labor and especially that of the skilled groups, Nasser recruited workers into the government-controlled unions,[38] and banned strikes.

Along with the rural middle class, the skilled workers have improved their economic lot; but they have not increased their political power at the same rate, because representation in Nasser's Parliament does not constitute political power. The working class had a proportionally higher representation in the 1961 Preparatory Committee (11.2 per cent) than did the rural middle class (8 per cent).[39] The reason for the higher figure is that many so-called "workers" (officials of the Arab Socialist Union and of trade unions) actually belonged to the professional and governmental employee groups[40]—a stratum of the strategic elite.

The United Arab Republic's official division of political groups follows an occupational classification which distorts class origin and exaggerates the political power of those social classes that benefited economically from the Egyptian Revolution. In the absence of categories based on criteria other than occupation, it is impossible to assess the political power of the various social and economic groups. Political power in

Egypt depends on the Officer Corps as a ruling clique and on the strategic elites, both of which draw heavily on the upper strata of the rural middle class and on the skilled workers. However, neither Egypt's rural middle class nor its skilled working class serves as a major source of the country's political power.

The relationship between the rural middle classes and the army needs clarification. In some underdeveloped countries, the politically influential classes are closely related to the powerful economic groups. This was the case in Egypt before 1952, when senior positions in the bureaucracy, in the army and in the civil service were allocated to the ruling class— then a combination of the landed aristocracy, urban upper bourgeoisie and rich professionals. Members of the rural middle class only occupied those positions in the army and in the bureaucracy that corresponded to their own more modest political power. Thus, a direct relationship existed between core political elites and the reservoir from which they came. Since 1952, however, the sons of the rural middle class (especially its two upper strata—owners of 10-50 and 50-100 feddans) should have become the ruling political elite. But, contrary to many people's expectations, this did not increase the political power of the rural middle classes. The army, having developed into the effective equivalent of a class, became the instrument of political power. Individuals were recruited to the ruling elite through the army, rather than through the rural middle class, whose political power had remained the same even though the Revolution's economic reforms had improved its economic lot. These conclusions reiterate my thesis on praetorianism: that military rule is politically restrictive and fails to integrate new men and economically and socially liberated groups and classes; that the level of political institutionalization is restricted, rigid and non-adaptive; that economic changes do not affect social cohesion on the distribution of political power; and that, above all, praetorian rule enhances the political power of the military and a persistent praetorian enhances praetorianism which, after a certain period of time, develops a momentum of its own. Furthermore, the utility of military rule is maximized under the ruler type of praetorianism,. the type which has ruled Egypt for close to a quarter century.

The U.A.R. government officially represented all of Egypt's political and societal functions—government, party, class interests—and skills, but it by no means included all the various social and political groups. Rather, the U.A.R. government avoided these differences, by simply denying their existence. The elite's base had been broadened by the dominance of the senior army officers, the former Free Officers and the better salaried professionals in the government bureaucracy. The government was still tightly controlled by former Free Officers and their bureaucratic-technocratic allies. The absence of political institutions or structures in Nasser's Egypt representing class and political cleavages does not mean that class, interest, social, political or ideological conflicts had disappeared. Rather, dissension resulting from decisions made at the top of the power pyramid had been silenced.

To sum up, Nasser's agrarian reforms were only partially successful. Although the power of the big landlords was curtailed, the landless and the owners of less than 1 feddan did not benefit from the reforms.[41] The rural middle class and even the rich peasants (owning 100-200 feddans) have benefited economically from the agrarian reforms. During the period 1966-1967, a third agrarian reform, designed to restrict the power and wealth of people owning 20 feddans or more, was suggested in the Egyptian press,[42] indicating increased pressure on the regime to effect revolutionary change in the countryside. However, since the Six Days War of 1967, agrarian reform has been abandoned; thus, no third reform took place.

The 'umdah, the second stratum of the rural middle class, who owned 50 feddans or more before the Revolution and now own 10—20 feddans, have been sustained in powerful positions on the local level through Nasser's agrarian reforms. O'Brien observes that the Revolution has made little difference to the mass of Egypt's poor peasants, agricultural laborers and employees of non-corporate enterprises.[43]

The 1952 Nasser coup was planned, organized and executed entirely by the army, strictly for its own benefit, and with little or no support from other movements or classes, although the officers were inspired by a variety of nationalist, religious fundamentalist, fascist and antiforeign groups. The 1958 Qassem coup in Iraq was also conceived, planned, organized and executed exclusively by the military, with no outside support. Iraq's military coup makers were supported by the United National Front (the bloc of anti-Hashemite, antimonarchist parties), but the latter's help was not crucial for the coup's success.[44] In Syria, likewise, we know of no coup that was conceived, organized or executed by other class than the military, even if several coups were encouraged by the Ba'th party. The three successful coups in 1949 were planned by the army's high command, as was Adib Shishakly's coup in 1954. The 1961 coup against the U.A.R. was conceived, planned and executed by the army as were the coups of 1963, 1966 and 1969. In none of these countries did the military represent the interests of the middle class (either old or "new"), or of any other class. Military rule in the Middle East indicates the chaos of social structure and the decadence of politics, two of the most significant characteristics of praetorianism.

Nasser's ruling elite apparently sought a formula for modernization and restricted political mobilization. It sought to sustain power without dealing with the problems of alienation and cleavages. This group was seeking to avoid the penalties of functional differentiation, without fragmenting Egypt's social order, or, for that matter, without encouraging pluralist community and political tendencies.[45]

The removal of foreigners and imperialist powers, the political and economic elites of colonial Egypt, left a vacuum into which the army moved, as the new ruling group. Members of the native Egyptian ruling group, the court and the aristocracy, which also depended on foreign rule and finance, were expropriated, although some co-operated with the new army regime. The rural and urban middle classes, the small working classes and the urban intelligentsia work at cross purposes; thus their rivalry only furthers the army's position as the political elite of Egypt.

Such conditions prompted Nasser and the Free Officers to turn the army into a reservoir of political power, at the expense of the strategic and other elites, and at the price of restricting political mobilization of any group besides the rural middle classes and the urban industrial workers.

The regime's policy of restricted recruitment is intended to help it control change. Huntington argues that "the strength of political organizations and procedures varies with their *scope of support* and their level of institutionalization".[46] The military junta prefers a limited and highly restricted scope of support: from the military itself, the bureaucracy, the skilled workers and the rural middle classes. This formula of restricted and controlled political participation is not unique to Egypt; it has also been adopted by several other developing regimes, among them Indonesia and Pakistan.[47] The restriction of political participation is often related to sustained institutionalization, because the wider and more permanent the popular support, the more durable the political institutions.

Slowing down political mobilization can be a strategy of institutional development. Huntington suggests three methods of harnessing political mobilization: to increase the complexity of social structures; to limit or reduce communication in the society; and to minimize competition among various segments of the political elite.[48] Only the third measure has been used in Egypt. The failure of a concomitant growth in the complexity of social structures and of their political autonomy, and the continuous creation of false expectations of a wider political participation for new social groups while the power pyramid remains essentially unchanged, makes the motives of Nasser's followers in restricting political mobilization seem suspect. The restriction of political participation may be interpreted as a desire on the part of the military junta and its rural and urban allies to perpetuate themselves in power. This can be deduced, not from the failures of the regime, but from its achievements. Either Nasser failed to meet the participation crisis with a concentrated effort at recruiting political support, or the curtailment of participation was simply another measure for keeping the praetorian elite in power.

NOTES

1. Harold D. Lasswell and Daniel Lerner, eds., *World Revolutionary Elites* (Cambridge, Mass.: M.I.T. Press, 1965), chaps. 1 and 2, pp. 29-96.
2. Dankwart Rustow, "The Study of Elites: Who's Who, When, and How", *World Politics*, 18, no. 4 (July 1966): 690-717.
3. *Ibid.*, p. 701, see also pp. 715-16.
4. Dankwart Rustow, "Political Sociology", *Current History*, 1, no. 3 (1957): 85.
5. See Carl J. Friedrich, *The New Image of the Common Man*, 2nd ed. (Boston: Little Brown and Co., 1950), pp. 257-58, 370, fn. 12; and Meisel's critique of Friedrich's interpretation of the Mosca-Pareto elite concept in James H. Meisel, *The Myth of the Ruling Class: Gaetano Mosca and the Elite* (Ann Arbor: University of Michigan, 1962), pp. 356-60. See also T.B. Bottomore, *Elites and Society* (New York: Basic Books, 1964), pp. 1-15.
6. Rustow, "The Study of Elites", p. 711.
7. I have borrowed some of Professor Keller's criteria for the ruling class, without accepting Keller's universality of elite types—the strategic elites, or strategic types.
8. The difference between a bureaucratic class and a ruling class is that the latter is made up of the political leadership who rise to power by exercising their political ability. See Bottomore, *Elites and Society*, n. 78.
9. *Ibid.*, pp. 86-104.
10. Rustow, "The Study", pp. 715-16, feels that elite theorists from Marx to Michels "formulated comprehensive statements about ruling classes . . . sustained by inadequate evidence. . . . "
11. Ralf Dahrendorf, *Class and Class Conflict in Industrial Society* (Stanford, California: Stanford University Press, 1959).
12. *Ibid.*
13. Robert Dahl, "The Concept of Power", *Behavioral Science*, 2, no. 2 (July 1967): 201-18; "A Critique of the Ruling Elite Model", *American Political Science Review*, 52:2 (June, 1958): 463-69; *Who Governs?* (New Haven, Connecticut: Yale University Press, 1961), pp. 1-12, 271-325. See also Daniel Bell, *The End of Ideology*, rev. ed., (New York: Collier Books, 1966), pp. 47-74; and Talcott Parsons, *Structure and Process in Modern Societies* (Glencoe, Ill.: Free Press, 1960), pp. 199-225.
14. Dahl, "A Critique of the Ruling Elite Model".
15. *Ibid.*
16. James Heaphey, "Organization of Egypt: Inadequacies of a Non-Political Model for Nation-Building" *World Politics*, vol. 18, no. 2 (January 1966): 186-88.
17. See Eliezer Be'eri, *The Officer Class in Arab Politics and Society*, (New York: Praeger, 1970).
18. The following statistics are taken from Eliezer Be'eri, *Ha-ktsuna Ve'hashilton B'Olam Ha'aravi* (Hebrew) (Merhavia, Israel: Sifriat Poalim, 1966).

19   With the exception of the U.A.R. government, 1951-1961.

20. Be'eri, *The Officer Class,* pp. 287-93.

21. *Ibid.,* pp. 293-350.

22. *Ibid.,* pp. 24-40.

23. Suzanne Keller, *Beyond the Ruling Class: Strategic Elites in Modern Society* (New York: Random House, 1963), p. 32.

24. *Ibid.*

25. *Ibid.,* p. 290.

26. Be'eri, "Social Origin."

27. We are grateful here to ideas provided by Reinhardt Bendix and Seymour Martin Lipset's "Political Sociology", in *Current Sociology,* 6, no. 2 (1957): 83-87.

28. *Ibid.,* p. 84.

29. Gabriel Baer, *History of Landownership* (New York: Oxford University Press, 1962), pp. 177-78.

30. Patrick O'Brien, "An Economic Appraisal of the Egyptian Revolution", *The Journal of Development Studies,* 1, no. 1 (October 1964): 99.

31. Leonard Binder, "Crisis in Political Mobilization", in *Political Parties and Political Development,* ed. Joseph La Palombara and Myron Weiner (Princeton, N.J.: Princeton University Press, 1966), p. 235.

32. *Ibid.,* Table 3, Category 5, pp. 237-38.

33. *Ibid.,* p. 237; Be'eri, *The Officer Class,* pp. 297-98.

34. Keller, *Beyond the Ruling Class,* p. 32.

35. O'Brien, "An Economic Appraisal".

36. Charles Issawi, *Egypt in Revolution: An Economic Analysis* (New York: Oxford University Press, 1965), Table 12, p. 120.

37. Binder, "Crisis in Political Mobilization", Table 3, p. 237.

38. Binder argues that this was an improvement over the old regime. For now, labor has political access to the official establishment of the government. Through their legitimation as government employees, workers can secure redress which they could not obtain in the past; *Ibid.,* p. 232.

39. *Ibid.,* Table 3, Category 6, p. 237.

40. *Ibid.*

41. Baer, *History of Landownership.*

42. The 1965 volume of *Ruz al-Yusuf* describes feudal corruption in villages and states that some *'umdahs,* through legal procedures, can deprive peasants of their land. They do this through their administrative powers as governmental representatives and, in some cases, as directors of co-operatives. *Al-Ahram* and *al-Gumhuriyyah* issues of May 1966 give full descriptions of the trials and errors of land reform in Egypt, and "the struggle against feudalism".

43. O'Brien, "An Economic Appraisal", p. 99.

44. Uriel Dann, *Iraq Under Qassem* (Jerusalem: Israel Universities Press, 1969), pp. 19-32.

45. On the crisis of political participation in Egypt see Leonard Binder, "Political Recruitment", in La Palombara and Weiner, *Political Parties,* pp. 217-40.

46. Huntington, "Political Development", p. 419.
47. For a similar argument on the Maghreb based on attitudinal and psychological insights, see Douglas E. Ashford, *Elite Value and Attitudinal Change in the Maghreb* (Bloomington, Indiana: Indiana University Press, 1966).
48. Huntington, "Political Development".

CHAPTER 10

Perspectives on Praetorianism

PROSPECT AND RETROSPECT

Praetorianism is both a descriptive term and a dynamic explanation for three types of authority relationships. These are 1) the government and the Roman Praetorians, or historical praetorianism; 2) the regime persistently found in societies undergoing change and lacking legitimate political order and support; 3) a type of civil-military relations prevalent in praetorian regimes.[1] Both Huntington and Perlmutter have linked these latter two: a weak (praetorian) political order produces an interventionist military.[2] My concern here will be to focus on these interrelated modern phenomena.

1 STABLE POLITICAL SYSTEMS AND CIVIL-MILITARY RELATIONS

The most significant fact about civil-military relations is the modernity of the concept. It is a post-1789 political problem.[3] Authority in pre-democratic pre-nation-state eras and in the pre-bureaucratic state was feudal, mercantilist, and imperial. Political intervention meant the intervention of a tyrant, a dynasty, a feudal lord, an imperial governor. In other words, politics was the study of the dynamics of rulers and rulership.

The only type of intervention which was historically legitimate was that of a ruler. The Coup d'Etat is an example. As Herbert Gooch's perceptive study demonstrates, this was chiefly associated with an act of government undertaken by a sovereign.[4] It was not conceived as an illegitimate act. Nor was it a praetorian regime.

The modern age of democracy, constitutionalism, mass authoritarianism and the nation-state deals with a new sovereign, the "people". In modern popular democratic and totalitarian systems, authority relationships between the civilian and the military are delineated as clearly as are the discrete structures, functions, and procedures of government, the legislatures, executives, and judiciaries. However, the balance of civil-military relations in modern times is more dependent on the stability or instability of the political order than on affiliation with a ruler, as was the case with the Coups d'Etat and military regimes in the pre-modern age. Just as the political concept of civil-military relations is related to modern nation-states, praetorianism is linked with the two most significant structures and powerful instruments of modern unstable political order, the bureaucracy and the military. Without moderation, I argue that the modernization-mobilization revolution of modern times in states with weak regimes created and enhanced two prominent structures of the classical eighteenth-nineteenth centuries' nation-state, the bureaucracy and the military establishment. The conspicuous growth of the military as against the relative impoverishment of political parties, pressure groups, organized socio-economic groups and classes, and even an articulated and organized public opinion, characterizes the praetorian syndrome: a weak state, an interventionist regime, kaleidoscopic changes in authorities, and permanent and guaranteed insecurity and political illegitimacy.

The purpose of intervention is to accomplish mission impossible—create stability, order and legitimacy. The goal is to replace a troubled government. Instead, in fact, praetorianism begets praetorianism. Nevertheless, the concept of popular sovereignty, the political signpost of the modern age, calls for allegiance to office not to men, even in praetorian regimes.*

The creation of offices, of bureaucracies and of a state apparatus marks the end of pre-bureaucratic empires and the emergence of the modern bureaucratic state.[5] The state apparatus, constitutionalism and the procedures of authority, the relationship between separate and functional political structures brought into focus a new and crucial political relationship between civil-political authorities and bureaucratic and military functions and establishments. The problem was one of constitutional and political responsibility. To whom are the military responsible—the monarch, the executive, to both the executive and the legislature; and what differentiates the governmental bureaucracy from the military, if anything? Is the military establishment another bureaucratic organization of the modern nation-state or is it a special structure with an esprit, virtue, and a mission orientation? Is the military establishment of the modern nation-state an exclusive corporate and special instrument of the state with special privileges bestowed on it, or is it, once more, a bureaucratic and subservient civil servant structure in mufti?[6] The prevalent exclusivist and corporatist orientations, especially of continental[7] armies, but also of the British aristocratic officer corps, actually *created* the issues of modern civil-military relations.[8] The type of civil-military relations that prevailed in nineteenth-century Europe and America, identified by Huntington as the professional objective type of civil-military relations, was characterized by the distinctions made between the state, the military and the bureaucracy.[9] Military professionalism, a sense of mission, and responsibility to clients distinguished soldiers from some state bureaucrats and politicians in the modern nation-state. The professional

---

*For the benefit of the readers I distinguish State, government and regime as follows: *State*: a body of people living within a defined territory in historical times. It is also known as a body politic. The sovereign territorial group. *Government*: the mechanism though which the state acts. The administration of the state. The legitimate power-holding group. The instrument of society which centralizes political and legal authority. *Regime*: a system of rule of government, a system of management of government.

model of civil-military relations (Huntington's objective model) is, thus, the product of a stable political regime that dominated the modern nation-state whose supreme legitimacy, in the case of the U.S., was "the people", and in Prussia, "the dynasty". Both democratic American and authoritarian Prussia shared one fundamental political asset—legitimacy. Unquestionably, the responsibility of the classical professional soldier was not always to the state. In the case of Prussia-Germany, he was responsible to the War Lord and the dynasty,[10] while in France the officer, on the whole, accepted Republican regimes.[11] The few cases where the French army defied constitutional authority and/or the Republican regime, certainly suggests an early form of Twentieth Century praetorianism. But there was no inherent conflict between civil-military authorities as long as both structures functioned in the prescribed manner: both the military and the bureaucracy were to defend the government and/or the state. The nation-state, the regime, and the authorities (the government) were legitimate. The military was not inclined to change this arrangement, of which, anyway, they formed a respectable part. Also, political stability and a strong regime could easily, as they did, resist military insurrection, interventionism and praetorianism. It is the instability of a government that is the crucial factor bearing on civil-military relations. The classical model of military professionalism, linked as it is to an historical place and time—the rise of the modern nation-states in Europe—is an intrinsic part of a stable political structure. Conflict between civilian and military authorities, in the classical model, was not over political supremacy. The civilian supremacy was unquestioned. The conflict between civilian and military authorities in stable authoritative and legitimate political systems has become one over *policy* not power. The military was not expected, nor was it oriented in the classical model, to intervene (except in very exceptional cases) in electoral, constitutional politics and arrangements.

Since the function of the military was to defend authority, and not society, it almost always came to the support of the state in suppressing political dissidents, democrats, socialists and others. The function of the military, to defend stability at home, was almost consistent with its function to defend the state from its external enemies. The function of the military was, therefore, to improve the condition of authority, not to challenge civilian authority. The nineteenth-century military was dedicated to the defense of the sovereign, not popular sovereignty. Military support was expected under stable conditions. Under unstable conditions, the military was expected to support the state, not necessarily the regime; this was the case with the early but fundamental praetorianism of Spain in the nineteenth century.[11a] The par excellence model of praetorianism was Latin America at the same period. In Spain the military supported Royalty, but refused to support the Republic and challenged Republican, democratic, central authority. Intervention is almost guaranteed under conditions of political instability, as was the case of Spain and Latin America in the nineteenth and early twentieth centuries. What was not studied nor even identified were the conflicts that arose between the civilian authorities and the military establishments.[12]

Historians, sociologists, political theorists and military strategists were concerned with the analysis of the modern military establishment, the history of warfare and military campaigns, the study of the generalship of the great captains, and with strategy and reform of the military establishment. Few, if any, directed their attention to the conflict between civilian and military authority. Gaetano Mosca was one of the few to analyse the role of standing armies in the making of European civilization and of the importance of civilian supremacy for the maintenance of European civilization.[13] Carl von Clausewitz, the most illustrous military philosopher of modern times, who demonstrated the symbiotic linkage between war and peace and grand strategy, i.e., the combination of policy and military science, failed to perceive the conflict between civilian and military authorities. Clausewitz, who introduced the concept of policy as strategy—such a volatile and impressive political concept—failed even to identify the conflict between the civilian and the military, even if the essence of his reform was the differentiation of military functions from the political.

The politics of the reform of the Prussian Army, in which

Clausewitz was involved, were directly connected with the problems of professionalism, skill, and responsibility, requisites of the classical model of civil-military relations. The absence of attention and interest, theoretical and otherwise, paid to the conflict between civil and military relations, stemmed from a corresponding absence of interest in democratic theory and the concept of popular sovereignty. As long as the sovereign's authority and its institutions prevailed, and the military establishment was conceived as an instrument of the sovereign in Anglo-American constitutional theory, and in Prussia, as an organic part of the patrimonial dynasty, then the issue of both constitutionalism—the division of authority, and of democracy—popular sovereignty, were not intellectually necessary to define the sovereign's relations to his instruments. Only theories of public administration, and of management, defined the scope of analysis of civil-military relations. Additionally, normative theory, so prevalent among political and legal minds in the nineteenth century and early twentieth century Europe and America, failed to identify the behavioral and dynamic aspects of politics, thus overlooking the fertile field of civil-military relations. The issue of legitimacy was related to the sovereign's control rather than to popular check. It is interesting in passing that republican theory is embodied in the American constitution, and the concept of popular sovereignty embodied in its preamble, while Article II of the Constitution that created the President as Commander in Chief is not related to democratic, but to popular sovereignty theory. In other words, the republican requisite embodied in the Commander in Chief was embodied in the Constitution in connection with the presidency, not with democratic theory. The Civilian Supremacy clause demonstrated the Founding Fathers' concern with a popular and Constitutional, not monarchical, executive rule.[14] The President was established as Supreme Commander not to solve conflicts of civil-military relations (until so interpreted by the Supreme Court and President Lincoln), or out of concern for the professional integrity of the military, but as a matter of contitutional theory, of the separation of powers and the division of labor between the three branches of the newly established democratic republic.

The professional military, in the modern nation-state, intervenes in national security and foreign policy. In the second half of the twentieth century, especially among the two superpowers, the military has become, at times, co-equal, (as in the U.S.S.R.), and a senior partner (in the U.S.) with civilian and bureaucratic authoritites in the formulation and implementation of national security policy. Once again, true to its legacy of clientship, the military's responsibility to sovereign and constitutional authorities was unchallenged. Civil and military relations in the classical model are irrevocably connected with the clear proviso of civilian supremacy and military political responsibility, and significant participation in policy making.

2. UNSTABLE POLITICAL SYSTEMS AND CIVIL-MILITARY RELATIONS

The most conspicuous model of civil-military relations in weak regimes or unstable states is the praetorian model.[15] Types of civil-military relations do not necessarily coincide with the classification of political systems into Western, Communist, and Developing Nations, nor is the classification of civil-military relations divided along an ideological continuum of conservative, liberal, and radical, or a classification anchored in geography. Modern praetorianism is the most conspicuous political arrangement of weak states.

Praetorianism is a type of civil-military relations with high incidence in regimes and states lacking political legitimacy and supportive political structures, groupings, and organized interests. Praetorianism is the mark of the weak and non-legitimate regime; it is the only type of civil-military relationship prevailing in the weak polities. It is the political system that is continuously patrolled by the military. This type of civil-military relations conforms to F.M.Watkins' classic definition of praetorianism (1933), "a situation where the military class of a given society exercises independent political power".[16] Praetorianism is, therefore, linked to instability, to the absence of a powerful executive, or a reasonably representative legislative authority, and the absence of group consciousness or excess that lends itself to support authority.

Above all, it is symptomatic of political decay and the inability to harness and transfer social change into political order.[17]

The praetorian state (where governments are frequently weak) and the praetorian civil-military type are convergent. The latter thrives in weak states, i.e. where weak governments are prevalent. The modern weak state has become a victim of military interventionism. The modern weak government is characterized as much by a rigid and ineffective executive as it is by lack of instruments and structures to channel political support. Above all, the characteristic of the modern weak states is the *disproportionate* growth of the historical instruments of the classical nation-state, the bureaucracy and the military, over political structures, institutions and parties. The most powerful instruments of weak states are precisely those structures which traditionally and constitutionally, in the classical model, are subservient and instrumental, i.e. the military and the bureaucracy. Obversely, the weak government generates, by virtue of its popular institutional impotence, the rise of non-political and extra-political structures. In the praetorian case the military and the bureaucracy are not conspicuous. In fact, those who argue that the administrative state creates legitimacy are misperceiving the praetorian nature of such a state. Legitimacy cannot be secured from the barrel of a gun or from the administrative apparatus. Legitimacy of the modern state can be secured only from the popular organized and representative sovereign—the party system, the interest group network, the organized articulation system, the media and, of course, group and collective support. Legitimacy derived from the barrel of the gun that dominates the weak state is passively supported. Thus, praetorianism begets praetorianism. In the weak state and non-legitimate regime the chances are that civil-military relations are skewed in the direction of military domination if not supremacy. Military corporatism then supersedes professionalism. The only instrument that possess the instrument of force—the military—has the opportunity, which it often uses, to seize power and turn the classical civil-military arrangement upside down.[18]

Characterizing praetorian civil-military relations, then, is an intense competition for power over the weak state between the two modern and relatively more efficient and institutionalized structures of the praetorian state, the military and the bureaucracy.[19] The two are supposedly functional and service organizations and are, constitutionally and otherwise, subservient to the state, but this is not the case in the weak states. There civil-military relations are a continuous and unequal struggle for domination between the military and other interests, including weakly organized political groups on the one hand, and between the military and the bureaucracy on the other.

In fact, what produces the different types of praetorianism are the kinds of coalitions they create to sustain themselves in power. The coalitions could be with one another, or between the bureaucracy and the military and another political group. Praetorian civil-military relations are clientelistic not regime oriented. On the whole, the militaries of praetorian states become rather rigid corporate non-cohesive alliances of ambitious and interventionist officers, bureaucrats and opportunistic politicians.

The case of Bonapartism is worth mentioning here. Bonapartism was a nineteenth century concept synonymous with military intervention. What Bonapartism actually represented was Republicanism on horseback.[20] Bonapartism was a regime dominated by some type of interventionism, generally military. Although this regime, argues Zeldin, was a truly Republican one, i.e. subscribing to popular sovereignty, it was, nevertheless, a product of the struggle over the domination of the Republic by several political and bureaucratic forces, and in the Bonapartist case was a regime dominated by the military. Bonapartism and the Spanish *Pronunciamento* regimes are the antecedent of praetorianism: the struggle for domination of a regime that subscribes to the ideology of popular sovereignty but whose political order is weak or disrupted.

3.   PRAETORIANISM AND AUTHORITARIANISM

I have already argued that praetorianism is both a condition of political instability and a type of civil-military relations. I will subsequently distinguish three types of praetorian civil-military relations—Autocratic, Oligarchic, and Corporate —each producing a different type of authoritarianism. Before I delve into an analysis of these relations, I make the following categorical statement: the modern praetorian state represents a new type of authoritarianism.

Although the classical definitions and explanations of autocracy and authoritarianism are quite similar, "autocracy" and "tyranny" describe the nature of the ruler while "classical authoritarianism" describes the nature of the regime. *Autocracy* may be defined as rule by a single person wielding absolute executive power. Autocratic government contains no provisions for legal limitation of powers, accountability or orderly succession. Rule is arbitrary and maintained by force. *Tyranny* is the arbitrary government of "no king by law". In it, authority is secured by conquest and maintained by fear. An authoritarian regime may be a collective dictatorship, an oligarchy, or a stratocracy; the term connotes collective rule. However, supreme power may still be embodied in a single person, as it was in Rome, for example, when one tribune took temporary possession of unlimited power. Significantly, classical definitions and explanations of autocracy are restricted to personal rule and assume the lack of a permanent and institutionalized structure of power. Classical definitions are incomplete in the sense that authority is identified with personal leadership, that is, domination-submission, leaving out institutional arrangements which regularize super-ordinate-subordinate relationships.

There is a clear distinction between modern and classical authoritarianism.

The classical version was rule by the few in the name of the few; modern authoritarianism is rule by the few in the name of many. Modern authoritarianism is further differentiated from classical authoritarianism by the scope, level, and type of political (a) support, (b) control, (c) mobilization, and (d) ideology. Thus I prefer to use "authoritarianism" rather than "autocracy" in describing the modern examples and to use "autocratic regimes" rather than "tyranny" or "dictatorship". Parenthetically it is significant that the Encyclopedia of Social Science, 1931-1933 edition, has no entry for authoritarianism (although entries exist for authority, autocracy, absolutism, tyranny, and dictatorship). However, the author of the "dictatorship" entry does note that "the modern dictator never omits to win popular support." Modern authoritarianism depends upon popular support and on some type of political mobilization, however limited, exclusionary, and restrictive.

A.   The Ideology of Praetorianism

a.   Nationalism

Unquestionably, nationalism represents the only ideological link that exists between the military praetorians (tyrannical, oligarchic, and corporate). Comtism and positivism, adopted as doctrine by the early praetorians at the end of the nineteenth century in Argentina and Brazil, was superseded in the 1930s by fascism, which captured the imagination of radical nationalists in the military in Chile as well. Most, if not all, coups in Latin America were and are nationalist and corporate in orientation. However, since the 1960s, nationalism has blended with anti-communism and anti-Castroism to produce the form of authoritarianism common to Brazil, Argentina, and Chile. Xenophobic and radical nationalism is still the platform of modern oligarchic praetorians in the Middle East and North Africa. Over 95 per cent of the military interventions in the Middle East (1936-1978) were initiated or executed by a civil-military coalition of radical and anti-foreign nationalists. The most rabid arch-nationalists in modern times are found among this area's military coup-makers (and their civilian mentors). The xenophobic strain began with the numerous Iraqi coups between 1936 and 1941 and continued through the Nasserites, the PPS, and the Ba'thi-Syrian military regimes in the 1950s and 1960s. Syria and Iraq are still under the influence of virulent xenophobes.[21]

b.   Antiliberalism

Antiliberalism might almost be called the twin of radical nationalism. In fact, the only distinction between antiliberals and radical nationalists is that they are committed to different types of authoritarianism. The tie between radical and xenophobic nationalism and modern authoritarianism is very close.

Liberalism, by its nature, implies struggle against the despotic state, the pedestal of modern authoritarianism. The liberal concepts of minimal state intervention and economic laissez-faire are equally unacceptable to modern authoritarians. It is most significant that modern authoritarianism has prospered in states whose tradition of liberty and the political ideology of liberalism was essentially non-existent (Czarist Russia), fragile (monarchical and Bismarckian Prussia), or tainted by corruption (Giolittian Italy). It is needless to belabor the weakness of the liberal tradition in Latin America. In the Middle East and sub-Saharan Africa, liberalism has never gained a foothold, and praetorian authoritarianism has flourished. Although Egypt and Syria did have liberal-constitutionalist parties between 1920 and 1950, their political relevance was slight. I know of no liberal tradition in any portion of sub-Saharan Africa.

c. *Antiparliamentarism*

The major characteristic of modern praetorianism is its deep contempt for parliamentarism and the party government. The Arab Middle East is an example. Parties, parliaments, and political democracy, are all considered the tools of colonial rule. Because they are seen as the instruments of clientelistic pashas, parties and parliamentary rule have been denounced as corrupt, irresponsible, reactionary, and contrary to the "Arab spirit". This attitude is reflected, for instance, in the words of one of the leading Arab praetorians, Gamal Abdul Nasser. Political parties, in Nasser's view, are tools of capitalistic democracy, of bankers and pashas; they are partisan instruments of the feudal classes. "The dictatorship from which we have suffered under the name democracy," says Nasser, "was the dictatorship of capital, feudalism under the name parliament." Nasser continues:

> Political democracy cannot be a reality unless there is social justice and social democracy and unless there are equal opportunity between the capitalist and the worker and between the feudalist and the agricultural laborer. One has plenty of money and can have a good dinner and one has no money to pay for

dinner. Capitalists and feudalists want to hold general elections according to Western methods adopted by capitalist countries in which the minority enjoys all the influence and has an abundance of money. The political parties serve the interest of feudalists and capitalists.[22]

4. TYPES OF AUTHORITARIAN PRAETORIANISM: THE MODELS

A praetorian state has non-institutionalized political authority and its social or ethnic-religious system is fragmented. Relative to other political, social, class, group, and economic structures, the structure with the greatest degree of institutionalization in a praetorian state is the military establishment monopoly on violence, and therefore it is the group with the potential to dominate the state. Nevertheless, the major causes of military praetorianism are not the non-institutionalized authority and fragmented society that provide the conditions for it. Instead this type of praetorianism occurs when the military elite (or a segment of it) is seeking to maximize its *political* influence. To reiterate: *the orientation of the modern military in the praetorian state is to maximize its influence and involvement in politics.*

Military influence in modern polities takes at least three forms: (1) military coups, (2) military regimes; and (3) the drive for influence in the making of national security policy. By military coups I mean those defined "as occurring whenever members of the regular armed forces remove or attempt to remove a state's chief executive through the use or threat of the use of force."[22a] By military government regimes I mean regimes dominated by a military or by a fusionist. Modern military regimes are not purely military in composition. Instead they are fusionist, that is, they are military-civil regimes. However, what distinguishes the modern military regime from the historical version is that the former seeks "mass" political support. Such regimes could be personalist, oligarchic, or corporate.

I distinguish three praetorian models. One, the personalist type dominated by a despot-tyrant (Amin's Uganda, Bokasse's Central African Republic) or the despot-patrimonial type (Samoza of Nicaragua, Trujillo of the Dominican

Republic and Haiti). The system heavily depends on graft. This system is actually a *Kleptocracy*[22b] (the government of the rip off artists) totally dominated by the despot. The tyrant arbitrarily dominates the army. He needs the support of loyal regiments, not all the military which is however small. (See Figure 1)

FIGURE 1

The Praetorian Tyranny: The Kleptocracy

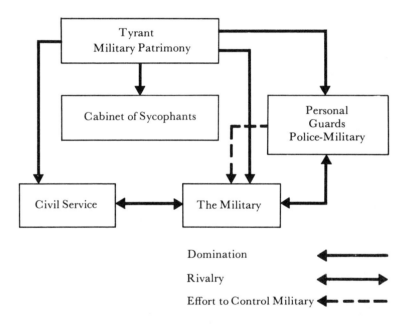

In Central America, the patrimonial-military tyrant establishes a constabulary-guard system to sustain the oppressive regime. The *Guardia Nacional* is a marine trained elite praetorian military designed to protect the Samoza family. The *Guardia* is a combination of military and constabulary personal loyalty as in the sub-Saharan type and is a major requirement for the well-being of the *Guardia's* officer clan.[22c] The oligarchic-praetorian type is structured along the lines of the tyrannical type with the exception that the military in the oligarchic system is autonomous and, in the case of Egypt, Syria and Iraq, is always in a position to overthrow the military oligarchy. Here the military oligarchy is dependent on the military which is, in fact, its major source of support. The single party, or the non-party, is a pure instrument of the oligarchy (Figure 2).

FIGURE 2

The Praetorian State Structure: Oligarchic

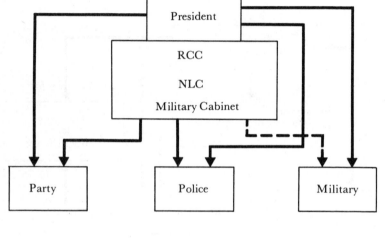

Recruitment is mixed, as in the corporate authoritarian state; it comes mainly from the bureaucratic, technocratic and functional groups.

The corporative praetorian model is based on corporativism and clientelism. The structure of government is based on the clientelistic-corporate form; it is the patron of patrons i.e. the patron of the corporative system. The government is composed of military, technocratic, and expert patron groups which dominate the corporative system. The corporative system is not composed of equally powerful corporations. The military, the church and the governmental ministries (bureaucrats and technocrats) are autonomous corporative groups while the functional-economic corporative groups are

FIGURE 3

The Corporate Praetorian Model: Bureaucratic and Populist

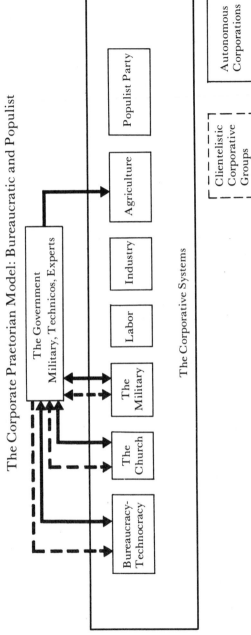

hierarchically and clientelistically dominated by the government. The military, the church and the technicos are serving as the regime's source of support where once more the military are more powerful than are other corporative functions. The military in fact acts as the arbitrator of corporative system. The functional-economic corporations are internally and externally clientelistic and dependent on the government and the more powerful autonomous corporative groups. Since the middle 1960's Argentina, Chile, Peru and Ecuador governments have depended on the military. (Fig. 3)

a. *Types of Modern Military Praetorianism*

When we speak of modern military praetorianism, we distinguish between three forms (or subtypes): autocratic, oligarchic, and corporate. Military autocracy is simple military tyranny, unchecked personal authority embodied in a military officer. Military oligarchy is a political system in which executive power is wielded by the few, who are mostly military men. The chief executive is either a former military man who is now a civilian or a civilian figurehead whose support comes exclusively from the military. Intrinsically, the only difference between the military oligarchy and the military tyranny is the number of rulers involved.

Corporate praetorianism is characterized by a military-civilian fusionist rule. Governmental authority resides in a coalition of military and civilians (bureaucrats, managers, and technocrats) governing with little or no external political control. In the executive, either civilians or officers may be in the majority and the supreme head may be a civilian, who may not even possess military skills. The distinction between oligarchic and corporate praetorianism reflects different socio-economic and political conditions. The corporate type on the whole is a regime that rules over a relatively developed society, where socio-economic groups are corporatively organized and are linked to the corporative state. The oligarchical type represents a poorly stratified society and the absence, or near absence, of organized autonomous economic interest groups and political articulation and interest aggregation structures.

The corporate praetorian regime makes it costly for society

to resist the interests of corporative groups supported by the state and especially the military. Political bargaining is conducted between organized groups where the military either arbitrates or dictates policies. The oligarchical type represents a military more powerful than other organized groups and a bureaucracy with which it allies, the latter either its silent or junior partner. Power becomes dependent solely on the military in oligarchic praetorianism.

Corporate praetorian regimes are types which link society with state. It is a product of industrialization and modernization and exists in South American states.[22d] Corporate praetorianism is a political system or regime where organizations officially represent "private" interests and where the range of state activities are wide, managerial, bureaucratic, technocratic, repressive and efficient. (Rational organization).

The corporate state is an exclusionary system, i.e. one that excludes and restricts the popular sector (urban working classes). The element that stabilizes (or to use O'Donnell's awkward term "statizing") the corporate state in South America is the military. The state as authoritarian "patron of patrons" (the patron of the corporative conglomerate) is arbitrated by the military. This is the corporate-praetorian state. It is identified with (a) a weak regime (b) state penetration into society (c) corporative (d) the army as a ruler that arbitrates the corporative alliance. The state is praetorian and so is the army. The former is weak, the latter interventionist. It is corporate and authoritarian. According to O'Donnell (who classifies South American political systems according to modernization) there are two types of corporate authoritarianism, bureaucratic and populist. To my mind the distinction is useful but insufficient, since it excludes the praetorian intervening crucial variable that makes all such regimes, at least in Latin America, corporate but praetorian. Corporate-praetorianism is a political system or regime where the autonomy of the corporative group is dependent on the state and the military being the arbiter of the corporative conglomorate is more autonomous than other corporative structures in the sense that it is the most persistent interventionist.[23]

b.   *Political Support, Mobilization and Auxiliary Instruments*

The single most important source of political support for the praetorian regime is the military establishment. In the case of praetorian tyranny, only part of the military is necessary for support. In corporate praetorianism additional support can come from such groups as the bureaucracy, the church, labor unions, and the technocracy, but it remains secondary. Clearly, without the support of the military establishment or its major section, no praetorian regime can survive.

As mentioned earlier, the type of political support is the factor that differentiates corporate-oligarchical from tyrannical praetorianism. The tyrannical variety seeks or expects only the support of the military. The corporate-oligarchical seeks to widen its base of support. On the whole, the corporate praetorianism of Brazil, Argentina, and Chile, the major states of this type, engage in restricted and highly disciplined political mobilization. However, in the area of economic modernization, the corporate and oligarchic types are actively committed to industrialization and economic transformation, although again they pursue these goals while restricting the growth of alternative political groups. The praetorian systems in these major South American states, and in Peru as well, are committed to agrarian and industrial modernization and even to social and tax reforms. To some extent, this is even true of Nasser's and Sadat's Egypt. Other regimes, however, are less committed to economic modernization.

Modern praetorianism's two most interesting structural political innovations are the military party (a party created by harnessing the popular or radical party to the military regime) and the military executive. Both are auxiliary structures designed to widen the base of political support, help sustain the praetorian regime, and create structures and procedures for regime legitimization. They are not instruments of mobilization.

These two creations are part of the experience of oligarchic praetorianism, which is most prevalent in the Arab Middle East. In the Middle East the control executive is the Revolutionary Command Council, the instrument of conquest and power; in other words, the executive committee of the coup. Once in power, the RCC assumes different forms, calling itself variously the presidential office, the cabinet, or council. The motivation in all cases, however, is the same—the continuance of political monopoly. Although the new regime may find a political party or conquer an established popular party, this party will be kept weak so that the RCC can exclusively dominate the regime. The weak single party's function has never been to mobilize the masses, as demonstrated by the history of Ayub's Basic Democracy, or Nasser's semibureaucratic-cadre Arab Socialist Union. The function of such groups is clearly to assist the praetorian oligarchy in running the state, whether by dominating the state's elephantine bureaucracy (Egypt) or by subduing traditional opponents and splinter groups (Syria). The Liberation Rally, Nasser's major nascent single party effort, at first was to serve as the juntas' chief propaganda vehicle. Primarily occupied with pamphleteering and proselytizing for the Nasserite "Egyptian revolution" in the countryside and in mosques, it ended in failure in 1954. In propaganda, however, Arab military regimes have been more successful than other praetorians, such as the African regimes.[24]

With the exception of these two innovations—the RCC and the weak single party—no other parallel and auxiliary structures have been introduced by modern praetorians. In fact, the general inability to institutionalize political structures was closely linked to praetorian oligarchy's failure to institutionalize the military executive and the military party. Thus, even the military oligarchies are autocracies that depend on one man's charisma (Nasser) or on the political skills of a Sadat, Asad or Ghaddafi. The military tyranny of Amin's, Mobuto's and Bokasse's sub-Saharan African style made no contribution to parallel or auxiliary structures of modern praetorianism, although they introduced considerable refinements in the practices of torture and terror.

5.   THE POLITICAL DYNAMICS OF MODERN AUTHORITARIANISM

Unquestionably, a static model is inappropriate in explaining any political system, however rigid and conservative it may be. The most remarkable fact emerging from almost a century of authoritarian experimentation is that, despite the autocratic regimes' vocal espousal of revolutionary change, they have made considerable strides toward conservatism in their consolidation of political power. Political institutionalization and regime legitimization create a new condition for the authoritarian leaders who in turn move to stabilize the revolutionary momentum, and thereafter establish more rigid procedures and fixed institutional political arrangements. The earliest manifestation of such tendencies accompanies functional changes in the structures of political mobilization and of parallel institutions, such as the military party, the Revolutionary Command Council, the political police etc. As time passes, the authoritarian regime is oriented more and more toward maintaining a durable (but flexible) relationship between the military party, state, corporate groups, and elites—at the expense of the original ideology and the society as a whole.

The comparative definitional and typological analyses so far have demonstrated that we cannot generalize about modern authoritarianism and autocracies in a meaningful way unless we distinguish types and analyse each cluster independently. Thus, to explain the political dynamics of authoritarian regimes we again divide them into two major groups: (1) the strong and stable authoritarian regime, the Bolshevik, Nazi, and Fascist types; and (2) the weak and unstable regime, the praetorian type. Samuel Huntington argues that the one-party system is the chief characteristic of modern authoritarianism. Thus, he distinguishes between strong (Bolshevik, Nazi, Fascist) and the weak (praetorian) one-party system. Huntington also distinguishes authoritarian parties on the basis of their relative capacity to expand political power. The strong-weak continuum involves three variables: (1) the legitimization of the system; (2) recruitment of political leadership; and (3) interest aggregation and policy-making.[25] I shall take advantage of this classification to explain the dynamics of praetorian-authoritarian types.

1. *Non-Institutionalized, Praetorian and Corporate Authoritarianism*

  a. *Political Dynamics*

The politics of oligarchy is at the heart of corporate and praetorian politics. The nature and structure of the regime is oriented toward substituting autocratic oligarchic coalitional corporate arrangements for an otherwise institutionalized Parteistaat, or state-dominated authoritarianism. Thus, all corporate-praetorian regimes restrict political mobilization and seek political support from only national and *relatively* institutionalized structures: the corporate coalition of military, church, labor unions, and industrialists.

The typical praetorian oligarchy in the Middle East has been hailed by some authors as a military-populist regime heading a mass political party. Nothing could be further from the truth. Nasser's three attempts to build a political party of the army demonstrate that not only was he opposed to a cadre party but also that he could never make up his mind whether the Arab Socialist Union (ASU) should be a populist party. In fact, the ASU (and the Ba'th Party conquered by the Syrian and Iraqi military) is in actuality an auxiliary instrument of the military oligarchy.

Corporative theory and ideology in the case of Portugal (1931-1975) calls for corporative institutions whose function is both control and change. The corporative structure is a statist-bureaucratic design to resolve two problems, modernization and the maintenance of stability. The corporative chamber consists of representatives chosen by the major functional and corporate interests (agriculture, commerce, industry) as well as by historical and classical corporate institutions, the military, the church and nuclear organic groups, the family and the local-regional federations.[25a]

To substitute for the type of mobilization that was developed by Nazi-Bolshevik-Fascist types, corporative grass roots organizes the guilds (gremios).[25b] The association is clientelist and the relationships, for instance, between workers and employers, landlords and peasants are that of patriarch and client. Mobilization is hierarchical, patrimonial and clientelistic. The corporations are the capstone of the entire corporative system. But their most powerful corporative structures are the military, the governmental bureaucracy and ministries and the church. They are not equal to the economic-functional corporations.

In Latin American corporate and authoritarian praetorianism, the corporative system which seemingly is the supreme political structure of the state is actually a system of unequal and hierarchical relationships between autonomous and non-autonomous corporative groups. The state dominates only with the active support and intervention of the autonomous corporate groups, the military, the technocrats and the church. The populist political party is one of the weakest non-autonomous corporate groups as are the economic-functional groups. The police is both the instrument of the state but also of the military.

The corporate praetorianism, the dictatorship, shares power with a coalition of political bureaucrats and technocrats representing organized groups; the praetorian oligarchy would share its power with individual bureaucrats and technocrats and former loyal army officers; and the tyrannical military refuses to share power, conducting politics through fear and assassination. The most interesting fact about corporate and praetorian regimes is that *all* have emerged when weak political systems (monarchical, imperial, republican, or parliamentary) were being replaced. The praetorians, however, could not handle the demands of modern politics; they could not create a new political system in the old colonial territories. A continuous, unresolved controversy among political leaders of a praetorian tyranny and their opponents is whether these regimes have really achieved *more* than the non-praetorian regimes in the areas of political development, economic modernization, and social change. (There is little doubt that they *have* provided the symbols of newly acquired nationhood for these people.) Nevertheless, there is a consensus among social scientists and historians that the praetorian regimes, on the whole, are unstable, authoritarian, non-institutionalized and restrict political mobilization. There is no such consensus on the dynamics of economic modernization in corporate-praetorian autocracies.[26]

b. *Economic Dynamics*

Oligarchic and corporate praetorian states seek the establishment of a modern economic system, whether partial or complete. They have, however, no consistent economic orientation and policy. One finds a mixture of socialism and state capitalism with atavistic economies. The emphasis on growth and technocratic skills is prominent in the most advanced corporate praetorian regimes (Brazil, Argentina, Chile, and Peru, for example). Egypt is a borderline case. Other oligarchic and tyrannical praetorian states are essentially variations of relatively primitive agricultural systems. In the absence of a party or a state that can set goals and maintain firm control over the economic system, the praetorian executive and its semitechnocratic elites engage in a permanent struggle for control. In most of the praetorian systems the role and influence of foreign investment is considerable. This dependence on foreign support restrains the reformists (who may favor some form of socialism, for example) among the praetorians. This point should not, however, be overemphasized; the very praetorians who depend on foreign aid also constantly engage in foreign intervention. The politics of foreign aid parallels the praetorian-oligarchic nature of the system. Thus, the corporate and praetorian classes are the favored beneficiaries of foreign capital and investment. Kleptocracy, government by rip-off artists, is not an uncommon phenomenon in Sub-Saharan Africa and in the Arab praetorian states (as is parasitism in military regimes in Latin America).[27] Economic modernization, in my view, only feeds praetorians and their oligarchic allies and prolongs the praetorian condition, most conspicuously in corporate-praetorian systems.

c. *Social Dynamics*

Clearly, in the absence of either a strong party or state and lacking economic diversity and political structures of any permanence, social classes cannot be expected to cluster within party or state auxiliaries as they did in the Bolshevik or Nazi systems. Apparatchiks are insignificant in number and the civil service is impotent. The social system in a praetorian-corporate system is atomized, and dominated by a few scattered political and economical classes. Praetorian political structures have little or no stable social and economic foundations. Nevertheless, the oligarchic corporate and developed praetorian regimes encourage and support the growth of middle classes and skilled workers, while seeing that the aristocracy and unskilled workers do not go economically unrewarded. However, the arrest of social and political mobilization, as in Brazil for instance, means that sectors of social and economic life are unequally encouraged to engage in political participation.

In Egypt, Nasser encouraged the emergence of military bureaucratic effendis while Sadat brought back the bankers and the pashas. Institutional instability does not encourage the emergence of any classes other than the bureaucratic-technocratic allies of the regime. In Brazil neither the old classes nor the new left provide effective opposition, nor are they actually tolerated. In Chile and Argentina, they are brutally repressed. The regime becomes the arbiter of class conflict. This was true in Nasser's Egypt, which repressed the middle classes, and in Sadat's, which does the same to the bureaucratic-socialists. In Syria and Iraq, the radical military oligarchy tolerates no classes at all and suppresses everyone (including the military in general). In tyrannical praetorian regimes the policy of assassination of the opposition has removed the factor of the social class or group from politics.

6.   THE GOVERNING OF PRAETORIAN STATES:
THE FUTURE OF PRAETORIANISM

In the last two decades we have witnessed the emergence of few praetorian states that are relatively effective or enduring. Unquestionably, the most stable of the unstable types are the corporate-praetorians. The cases of Brazil since 1966, Argentina since 1966, Peru after 1970, and Chile since 1973 demonstrate that the praetorian regimes that represent a coalition of modern groups and structures—military, bureaucracy, technocrats, industrialists and union managers —stand a better chance for political longevity, not necessarily for legitimacy. No praetorian-organized and dominated coalition, however authoritarian, repressive and "efficient", could transfer political assets into political legitimacy. What is guaranteed is more stable order, but the price is stagnation of social dynamics.

In sub-Saharan Africa we have witnessed the rise of more praetorian tyrannies: Uganda, the Central African Republic, Chad and Togo. In each we have witnessed the emergence of tyrants whose chief motivation is to stay in power and eliminate and annihilate opposition within the military and outside it. We clearly witness Decalo's model prevail: that several African armies are non-cohesive, tribal, non-Westernized, non-professional and personalist; that they are as corrupt and inefficient as civilian regimes they have replaced; that recruitment and promotion is not based on skill or on merit, but on personal idiosyncracies of tyrants' tribal connections; that the military is neither interested nor capable to raise the momentum of modernization-mobilization; that grievances are not corporate but personalist and that competing ambitions are of greater value than so-called national aspirations; that army rule is corrupt (at least not less than former civilian rule) and economic development policy is bankrupt, and that not political, but personal, institutionalization is of the utmost concern for the competing ruthless and venal officers and that the hallmark of praetorianism—instability—reigns. And that corporate fragmentation, personal strife, instability, and authoritarian rule are indeed high.[28]

Nor does subscribing to popular sovereignty *ipso facto* render corporate praetorianism into a popular and legitimate political system. Various recent studies on the political dynamics of actual oligarchic and corporate praetorian regimes, Nigeria, Peru, Brazil, Indonesia, Egypt, Burma, and Thailand[29] demonstrate that the essentials of praetorianism are inherent in its political order: instability, illegitimacy, absence of collective group action, of representation of effective political parties and interest groups, and above all, inability to close the gap between the aspirations and the realities of popular sovereignty. A coalition between the military and bureaucracy, as is the case in corporate and oligarchic praetorianism (Brazil, Argentina, Egypt, Burma, Thailand) helps sustain the regime but not to legitimize it, or for that matter to stabilize society, order and politics. In fact, one major purpose of all praetorian types is to harness social change and political dynamics. The difference between one praetorian regime and another is just the scope and level of effective manipulation of temporary order and social discontent, dissent and alienation. The prospects for praetorianism today are therefore:

1. More praetorian regimes, states and militaries. The World Coup Zone[30] is increasing as is the number of more unstable political orders, some states are without even a semblance of order and/or stability and some regimes are only passing affairs.

2. The rapid increase of new nations and mini-states which are inherently unstable enhances praetorianism. This is especially true of sub-Saharan Africa as well as the new (and old) Arab states extending from the Persian Gulf along the Arabian peninsula, over the Red Sea to the Horn of Africa.

3. The breakdown of some of the precarious federated new states and the deeply rooted conflict within multi-ethnic states (Lebanon, Malaysia, Ethiopia, Chad, Congo Kinshasa, Pakistan, Nigeria (1966-1969), Sudan (1966-1970), Iraq to 1973) contributes to instability of the political order. Some of the above could not control revolution among ethnic populations and eventually became praetorian. The penetration of weak states into one another also contributes to praetorianism and to instability of new states, as for example Libya into Chad, P.L.O. into Jordan and Lebanon, Uganda into Tanzania and Kenya, the U.A.R. during Nasser's time into South Arabia and India into Pakistan. The revolutions of black peoples in Southern Africa certainly guarantee more praetorian regimes.

4. The futility on the part of several new states of aspiring to adopt a revolutionary ideology and at the same time a stable system of politics also insures praetorianism. The founding fathers' aspirations to adopt Democracy, Socialism and, in my view, also vulgar Communism (Angola, Mozambique, Ethiopia) have been dismal failures and only lead to disappointment, recrimination,

massacre, and racination. I predict that the fate of the so-called Marxist South Arabian states of PDRY and Somali will be similar to the "Democratic" and "Socialist" experiments of Egypt, Syria, and Iraq—more praetorianism. The dilution of ideology buttressed by the rise of ethnicity and religious fundamentalism will produce a greater Coup Zone, more praetorian states, more unstable regimes and greater internal and regional international conflict.

5. I also predict the eventual disappearance of a great number of so-called new states, mini-states and perennially weak and unstable regimes. And a number of states that will increase due to centrifugal fractionation and succession. Weak ethnic groups in new states will be suppressed and the military-political intervention of small states into one another (Ethiopia-Somali, Egypt-Libya, Lebanon-Palestine) will decrease the number of weak states by elimination and increase praetorianism.

Praetorianism is an incomplete political system. The praetorian and oligarchic tyrannies may not disappear and the corporate praetorian regimes will survive, not by virtue of consensual political order or societal satisfaction, but by the brute uses of sophisticated and highly technological military force combined with bureaucratic corporative organizations that will substitute order for chaos, but at the same time reduce the quality of life, and achieve strictly coercive legitimacy and ruthless political order.

NOTES

1. On the concept of praetorianism see: David C. Rapoport "Praetorianism: Government Without Consensus", Ph.D. dissertation, University of California, Berkeley, 1960. S.P. Huntington, *Political Order in Changing Societies*, New Haven, Yale, 1968, pp. 192-163. Amos Perlmutter, "The Praetorian State and the Praetorian Army", *Comparative Politics* 1969, 1: 382-404. S. Andreski, *Military Organization and Society* 2nd ed., London, Routledge & Kegan Paul, 1968. For criticism see William Thompson "Explanation of the Military Coup", Ph.D. diss. University of Washington, Seattle, 1972, pp. 161-167. Eric Nordlinger, *Soldiers in Politics: Military Coups and Governments*, Englewood Cliffs Prentice Hall, 1977, pp. 1-30. G. Ben Dor "Civilianization of Military Regimes in the Arab World", *Armed Forces and Society* Spring, 1975.

The concept is successfully employed by Rene Lemarchand "Civilian-Military Relations in Former Belgian Africa", C. Welch ed. *Soldiers in Politics*. Samuel Decalo, *Coups and Army Rule in Africa*, New Haven, Yale University Press, 1976, pp. 5-87. G. Ben Dor, *op.cit.* Eric Nordlinger, *op.cit.*

2. S.P. Huntington, *Political Order in Changing Societies* New Haven, Yale University Press, 1968.

3. Amos Perlmutter, *The Military and Politics in Modern Times* New Haven, Yale University Press. 1977.

4. Herbert Gooch, "Coup d'Etat: Historical and Ideological Dimension of the Concept", Ph.D. diss. University of California, Los Angeles, 1977, p. 293.

5. S. N. Eisenstadt, *The Political System of Empires*, New York, The Free Press, 1963.

6. Some of the above are analysed in S. P. Huntington, *The Soldiers and the State,* Harvard University Press, 1957, Cambridge, 1957. See also Max Weber, *Economy and Society* ed. G. Roth, C. Wittich, New York, The Bedmirates Press, Vol. III, pp 1006-1071. Martin Kitchen, *The German Army Officer Corps.* 1890-1914, Oxford, Clarendon Press, 1968.

7. Perlmutter, *The Military, op. cit.*

8. G. Harris-Jenkins, *The Army in Victorian Society,* London, Routledge & Kegan Paul, 1977.

9. S. P. Huntington, *The Soldier, op. cit.*

10. M. Kitchen, *op. cit.* F. L. Carsten, *The Reichswehr and Politics* 1918-1933, Oxford, Clarendon Press, 1966.

11. D. Ralston, *The Army of the Republic,* The Cambridge MIT Press, 1967.

11a. Perlmutter, *The Military op. cit.* Chapter 6, pp. 166-204. R. Carr *Spain* Clarendon Press, Oxford, 1966. E. Christiansen, *The Origins of Military Power in Spain*, Oxford University Press, 1967.

12. D. C. Rapoport, *op. cit.* and H. Gooch, *op. cit.*

13. Gaetano Mossa, *The Ruling Class,* ed. & rev. by Arthur Livingston, New York, McGraw-Hill, 1939, pp. 222-243.

14. David C. Rapoport, "Praetorianism".

15. For an elaborate theoretical disquisition on praetorianism see Amos Perlmutter, *The Military* pp. 89-114, and also footnote 1.

16. Quoted in Perlmutter, *The Military*, p. 89.

17. S. P. Huntington, *Political Order.*

18. Perlmutter, *The Military*, p. 93.

19. R. Dowse, "The Military and Political Development" in Colin Leys ed. *Politics and Change in Developing Countries,* London, Cambridge University Press, 1959, p. 227.

20. Theodore Zeldin, *France 1848-1945,* Oxford, Clarendon Press, 1974, Vol. 1, pp. 504-505.

21. Perlmutter, *The Military*.

22. Amos Perlmutter, *Egypt, the Praetorian State* (New Brunswick, N.J.: Transaction, 1974), p. 139.

22a. William Thompson, "Explanation" p. 6.

22b. The term, not necessarily the concept, is borrowed from Stanislav Andreski, *African Predicament*.

22c. One of the finest studies of this type is Richard Millet's *Guardians of the Dynasty*, ORBIS Books, Maryknoll, N.Y., 1977 pp. 251-261.

22d. On corporatist, authoritarian-bureaucratic, praetorian-corporative and populist-corporatism in Latin America see Guillermo O'Donnell, *Modernization and Bureaucratic-Authoritarianism*, Institute of International Studies, Berkeley, 1973; James Malloy ed., *Authoritarianism and corporatism in Latin America*, Univ. of Pittsburgh Press, Pittsburgh Press, Pittsburgh, 1977. See especially the essays by Malloy, O'Donnell, Kaufman, Skidmore, Mericle and Dietz and Phillippe Schmitter, "The Portugalization" and Alfred Stepan, ed., *Authoritarian Brazil, op. cit.* See also Peter Cleaves, *Bureaucratic Politics and Administration in Chile*, Univ. of California Press, Berkeley, 1974, John S. Fitch, *The Military Coup D'Etat as a political process,* the Johns Hopkins Univ. Press, Baltimore, 1977; Susan Kaufman Purcell, *The Mexican Profit Sharing Decision*, The Univ. of California Press, Berkeley, 1975; Kenneth Erickson, *Corporatism in Brazil*, Univ. of Calif. Press, Berkeley, 1977.

23. O'Donnell's model in *Modernization op. cit.* pp. 113-114.

24. For the literature on military praetorianism in the Middle East, see Eliezer Be'eri, *Army Officers in Arab Politics and Society* (New York: Praeger, 1971); P. J. Vatikiotis, *The Egyptian Army in Politics* (Bloominton, Ind.: University of Indiana Press, 1966); R. Hrair Dekmejian, *Egypt Under Nasir* (Albany, N. Y.: State University of New York Press, 1971); Perlmutter, *Egypt, the Praetorian State* and Raymond Baker, *The Uncertain Revolution under Nasser and Sadat*, Harvard 1978.

25. S. P. Huntington, "Social and Institutional Dynamics of One-Party Systems," In *Authoritarian Politics in Modern Society*, (New York: Basic Books, 1970), pp. 3-4.

25a. These ideas are taken from Howard Wiarda, *Corporation and Development; The Portuguese Experience*, The University of Massachusetts Press, Amherst, Mass., 1977 pp. 55-127.

25b. Wiarda, ibid., pp. 110-112.

26. For a summary of the controversy, see Perlmutter, *Military and Politics in Modern Times*, preface and Chaps. 4 and 5. In defense of oligarchic praetorianism, see John J. Johnson, ed., *The Role of the Military in Underdeveloped Countries* (Princeton, N. J.: Princeton University Press, 1962); and Morris Janowitz, *The Military in the Political Development of New Nations* (Chicago, Ill.; University of Chicago, 1964). The opposition's view is presented in S. P. Huntington, "Political Development and Political Decay". *World Politics* (April 1965) 18:386-430 and Amos Perlmutter, "The Arab Military Elite", *World Politics* (January 1970) 22:269-300.

27. The concept of parasitism is developed by Stanislav Andreski. *Parasitism and Subversion in Latin America* (Pantheon, 1966) describes a political system whose major political behavior is bribing politicians and officials, politics being a major resource for the latter's accumulation of wealth.

28. The finest study demonstrating the corruption of authoritarian and praetorian military rule in Africa is Samuel Decalo's *Coups and Army Rule in Africa: Studies in Military Style*, New Haven, Yale University Press, 1976. See especially pp. 5-39 and pp. 231-255. See also S. Andreski *African Predicament*, London, Joseph, 1968, Kenneth Grundy, *Conflicting Images of the Military in Africa*, Nairobi, East Africa, 1968 and S. Decalo, "The 'Imperial Style' in Africa" forthcoming, 1977.

29. Henry Bienen "Nigeria", Abraham Lowenthal, ed., *Peru*, Princeton University Press, Princeton, N. J., 1976. Amos Perlmutter, *Egypt: The Praetorian State*, New Brunswick Transaction, 1974, R. H. Dekmejian, *Egypt Under Nasir*, Albany. The State University of New York Press, 1971. Alfred Stepan *The Military in Politics: Brazil*, Princeton University Press, 1971. Alfred Stepan, *The State and Society: Peru in Comparative Perspective*, Princeton University Press, 1977, Moshe Lissak, *Military and Modernization in Burma and Thailand*, Russel Sage, Chicago, 1976. John Maynard, "A comparison of Military Elite Role Perceptions in Indonesia and the Philippines", Ph.D. Diss. The American University, 1976, pp. 117-151.

30. On Coup Zone See William Thompson, "Explanation", *op. cit.*, pp. 10-21.

CHAPTER 11

Military Incompetence and Failure

I must, first of all, caution the reader that this essay is experimental in nature. My aim is to develop a conceptual framework and a partial explanation concerning the output of professionals, rather than to put forth a general theory of professional behavior. I have chosen the military professional because several years of study and research in the field of military and politics have given me familiarity with this manifestation of professionalism. I have avoided for the time being the technique of allowing axioms or postulates to serve as a basis for explanation. I find it premature at this stage. I will restrict myself to historical-political explanations. I also avoid much of the ground already covered in sociological explanation (that is, the application of modern organization theory to the military). In my view, this endeavor has reached its logical limits, and few new ideas have been added since the 1960s. In this paper, if only indirectly, I wish to challenge such purely organizational and psychological explanations of the behavior of the military, even as I make different uses of the terms the sociological school has employed successfully but not comprehensively. Thus, when I speak of skills, performance, and attributes of officership, my explanations will not be restricted by the narrow confines of organizational behavior theory. Instead, I feel that the performance of a military organization must be judged on the basis of its competence, which in turn is linked to the clients it serves—regime and state—to the historical era in which it exists, and to the type of war it is conducting or expects to conduct. The explanation for military incompetence and failure will be sought in the political linkage and behavior between military men and political leaders.

1.   THE FUSIONIST THEORY: POLITICS AND WARFARE

War is no longer the elegant game of knights or an exercise in mass hand-to-hand combat. The science of violence has replaced the amateurism of the past. Leadership is no longer a necessary skill for contemporary generals, because military leadership, since 1914, has been assumed by politicians. Strategy is fusionist,* both a political and a military skill. Thus, military incompetence is no longer the sole property of generals, but results from the combined efforts of inept strategists, in and out of uniform. Modern generalship is judged mainly in terms of managerial and administrative skills and by command of troops, rather than strategy. Thus, a general who is highly skilled and competent in command, planning, and intelligence, may easily fail as a result of political incompetence. Military incompetence is restricted to unimaginative and rigid command and tactical planning, failure to inculcate morale, poor organizational ability, and bad reading of the rapidly changing conditions in the modern kaleidoscopic battlefield, whether through reliance on faulty intelligence or misinterpretation. In modern complex organizations, it is extremely difficult to place blame on a single person. Military incompetence is no longer the result of poor leadership or the loss of sense of *virtu*. *Virtu* and the inculcation of values into citizens (and, therefore, troops) is the task of *political* leadership. It essentially depends upon the structure of society, ideological committment, and the dedication of citizenry to national values.

The separation of functions between military and politics,

* The term is Huntington's. He deploys it to explain the fusion between politicians and bureaucrats. I employ it to explain a major variable of military failure.

and its hyphenated relationship, explains why modern generals are prone to both managerial and strategic incompetence. Generals, whose errors can only be managerial, are subject to failures that stem from political misjudgment. Haig, French, Hindenburg, and Gonen demonstrated managerial incompetence. Strategic incompetence was the work of cabinets. The British (1914-1916),[1] German (1916-1918), Egyptian (1967), and Israeli (1973) political leadership demonstrated strategic incompetence, misperception, or both. Sometimes a remarkable political leadership that possesses *virtu* and is capable of bold strategic thinking may err through misperception (as the Meir-Dayan leadership did in 1973), but, again, this is not military but civilian or political incompetence.

Military incompetence is also manifest in militaries that have enjoyed a string of successes—some Israeli generals in 1973 and German generals in 1916-1918 and 1942-1943 suffered from a damaging overconfidence. Over-confidence can be a civilian vice, too, of course. On the other hand, military success may be produced by generations haunted by the memory of traumatic defeats, like those experienced by the Prussians in 1806, the Germans in 1918, and the Egyptians in 1967. Yet past defeats clearly cannot be used to predict future successes. The Egyptian generals, on the fourth day of the 1973 war, demonstrated once more that they had failed to establish norms of high competence. The German generals demonstrated a very high level of competence during World War II (their considerable defeats in Russia related to Hitler's poor strategic decisions), and, in fact, there were fewer competent Allied generals than German generals in that conflict. Thus, one might say that generals do not simply refight their last battle, but their last successful battle. Past history cannot be used to predict competence.

The last strategic genius in the West may well have been Napoleon. Napoleon combined personal magnetism (charisma), sheer intellectual ability (strategic-political qualities), and a phenomenal capacity for hard work and unremitting toil ("work is my element"),[2] despite his slight physique and numerous ailments. Yet he was not infallible. He was defeated not because he was professionally incompetent, but because he became politically overconfident. His successes led him to dysfunctional behaviors like delusions of grandeur, gambling, misperception, distrust of subordinates, and an excessive demand for efficiency that exhausted his troops and officers.[3]

Thus, Napoleon was endowed with supreme leadership and managerial qualitites, intuition, a fertile imagination, an infinite capacity to take pains, and firmness, but all were negated by his boundless overconfidence.[4] The case of Napoleon clearly defines for us the parameters of our investigation. We do not investigate the military competence of the genius—but of those for whom genius is superfluous, i.e., the managers of armies. Leonardo da Vinci was a genius. His architectural creations outlasted those of his contemporaries by centuries. Once the science of engineering became commonly adopted, however, most structures had as much chance of surviving as Leonardo's had. Their aesthetic appeal, however, was at best impoverished. Safety has replaced grandeur. So it is with the modern military. The science of management and of tactics prepares officers to command troops. It is not expected that all or even most will be great leaders of men or strategic geniuses. Thus, we can judge their incompetence solely on their managerial, tactical, and operational skills. The difficulty here is that some generals who are masters of such skills still fail to produce victories. Thus, their lack of performance stems, among other things, from the strategic-political failures of their civilian superiors. Wars may be made by states and battles may be conducted by generals, but the fusion of political responsibility and political-military decision-making makes it exceedingly difficult to identify military incompetence, or military failure that stems from political incompetence.

2.   MILITARY PROFESSIONALISM, COMPETENCE AND FAILURE

By competence I mean skill and ability, expertise and facility. Military competence thus denotes the ability to prepare, train, exercise, and lead troops to war, and to master the strategy and tactics of war (the implication is, of course, that military competence, in contradistinction to legal competence, for instance, is the ability of generals and officers to *win* military campaigns). By expertise I mean economic effi- ciency, i.e., the ability of officers to win campaigns with the least effort and with the minimum loss of equipment, men and territory, while maximizing the enemy's loss of equip- ment, men, and territory. The only meaningful way to deal with military competence is to analyse the performance of senior officers and generals, because, on the whole, it is they who are held responsible for failures.

It would thus seem logical that military incompetence is the reverse of military competence; that is, incompetence in matters military is revealed by lack of skill, ability, and expertise. This is not so, however, for military competence is judged solely on the ability to win battles, campaigns, and wars. Thus military incompetence may stem from an over- abundance of ability and expertise and the excessive confi- dence it engenders—and, on the other hand, a talented amateur may display dazzling military competence.

I shall argue that military failure stems, at least in part, from following the textbooks and manuals of warfare slavishly and without deviation. An air traffic controller who follows his instructions to the letter will create an enormous air traffic jam, and hardly a plane would dare descend. The greatest and most notorious military failures were the work of illustrious and extremely able generals, like Haig, Hinden- burg, Gonen, Joffre, Kitchener, de Lattre, the commanders of the French army in 1940, a considerable number of British senior officers between 1939 and 1941, and several American generals since 1945.

I must stress again that I am speaking of incompetence in terms of military and political-military failure in general; i.e., that military incompetence cannot be identified only when military failure occurs, and military failure is not just the failure of the military. I have little doubt that analysing incompetent officers (according to our definition of compe- tence) who have not reached the top, could sometimes help our understanding of the case. But how can we assess their potential "failure" to win battles? Also, one cannot be sure that understanding would always be advanced. If Liddel Hart had become a commanding general, for instance, it is not necessarily true that he would have won battles.

Thus, while competence can be judged according to established professional norms and criteria, military failure —which is the only reason we are interested in military incompetence—is something more than professional incompetence. In fact, climbing the military ladder depends on the senior officer's strict adherence to specified standards of performance (skill) and/or sets of values, which, if perfectly fulfilled, actually guarantee military failure and/or incompetence. In addition, adherence to an unwritten code of professional behavior and values, which carefully leads the military into docility in its relationship to its client, also assures failure and incompetence.

Because rigid adherence to professionalism plays such an important role in the question of competence, a reconsideration of definitions is in order. Unquestionably, S.P. Huntington has offered the clearest and most precise definition of modern military professionalism: "Professionalism involves a balance among expertise, responsibility, and corporateness."[5] According to Huntington, therefore, what distinguishes professionals is the expertise, responsibility, and corporateness of their special vocation. Expertise is specialized knowledge and skill in a significant field of human endeavor. Specifically, the expertise of military officers involves (1) the organization, equipping, and training of forces, (2) planning of their activities, and (3) directing their operations in and out of combat.[6] Responsibility, since the expert works in a special context, is the performance of a public service; and the soldier's client is the collectivity— the state or the regime. Corporateness means that the members of a profession share a sense of organic unity and consciousness of themselves as a group apart from laymen. Professionals are, furthermore, imbued with a sense of mission.[7]

Yet, in my view, it is the corporate orientations of the officers rather than the other two aspects of their professionalism that in the end dominate the balance between expertise, responsibility, and corporateness. The corporateness, i.e., sense of professional exclusivity and of actual political responsibility, defines the parameters, the standards, and the levels of the former.

Senior officers engage in an effort to influence the selection, promotion, and advance of junior officers. In addition, they incessantly strive to gain reputation and status for the military establishment. Thus, the senior military professionals (like their counterparts in other professional groups) tend to control the orientations, perceptions, and understanding of the purpose and function of the military. The military's image is largely created by this group. Thus, skill and ability do not mean what we objectively consider them to mean, but what senior officers say they mean. Performance, too, is judged and graded by the senior officer group, and promotion is based on the standards of the corporate group. Thus, while "professionalism" still involves the concepts of expertise and responsibility, senior officers (less so in wartime than in peacetime) require their juniors to conform to the orientations and predilections of the profession's experienced standard bearers.

Responsibility to the client also means that those who guide the state, the most influential politicians, do not have inconsiderable input in the choice of senior officers and the appointment of generals. Salonika was devised largely to employ Sarrail, the most republican of generals. Lloyd George failed to get rid of Haig though he did break the Robertson-Haig partnership.* Defense Minister Moshe Dayan, not enthusiastic about General David Elazar, nevertheless appointed him Chief of Staff in 1971 and he failed to help General Ariel Sharon's aspirations for the same job in 1974. Churchill's generals and admirals were not all his choice. This however, does not apply in totalitarian states where Hitler and Stalin elevated and executed scores of generals at will. Here the officer is influenced by the judgment of his political superiors, which has a serious impact on military outcomes—success or failure, competence or incompetence. Skills and values are deeply embedded in the type of society or army from which they arise. The problem is not to discover why some generals are incompetent, but to determine military incompetence and failure.

* I am grateful to my colleague John Gooch for these extremely useful observations.

3. A BRIEF OVERVIEW OF MILITARY TYPES

It has been alleged that the officer in the modern nation state, certainly in those states that possess nuclear weapons, is no longer the heroic but a managerial type.[8]

A.   In Antiquity [9]

It is true that bravery was probably the first attribute of military professionals and fighters. The legends of the Assyrians, Babylonians, ancient Hebrews, Greeks, Romans, and the classical Chinese are replete with stories of bravery and heroism, considered the par excellence skill of warriors. Many passages in the Bible recount tales of kings who assemble brave men for war and the Bible frequently cites cowardice as one of the basest human failings. Greek mythology is full of warriors' heroics and superhuman accomplishments. After bravery, the quality considered most valuable in both antiquity and in some armies in modern times is physical prowess. Warriors in ancient times had to be strong men, for war was mainly a physical struggle and superior height, weight, and strength were obvious advantages. After all, simply carrying heavy armor, shields, and spears called for brute strength. Precision skills like marksmanship were also prized, and so, to a lesser extent, were mobility, speed, horsemanship, and efficient use of animals to wage war.

In other words, the most fundamental human military resource in antiquity was the body, and performance and competence were judged according to one's skill in exploiting his body. The brain, on the other hand, was accorded relatively little importance. Command was assumed by those whose physical attributes were superior to those of their fellow fighters and whose skills were those of hand-to-hand combat. The ancient warrior did use brainpower, as Xenophon's descriptions of the duties of the cavalry officer in siege warfare illustrate, but the use of tactics was extremely limited, even if it was effective.

The only known Greek tactical device, for example, was the ambush (the Trojan Horse). Tactical geniuses like David, Hannibal, Epaminondas, Philip of Macedon, and Alexander the Great with his methodical style of warfare were the exceptions. In Greek warfare, troops were massed in ranks whose depth was reckoned as so many shields. Two forces attacked each other, and the side which broke under pressure surrendered. It was *brutality* and sheer physical power, not the technology of attack, that decided the outcome of war—even when deception and cunning were employed.

The intelligent use of strategy (largely a matter of craft and deception) was the preserve of the generals and the result of individual intellect rather than doctrine, an *untaught* skill. Officer training in antiquity did not take place in the academy, but on the field of battle. Leaders were *ipso facto* considered officers in the Bible. So were former peasants and slaves with physical abilities, who received training on the "job".

Thus, experience and genius, rather than training, determined the status of warriors and their progress up the promotional ladder. Eventually certain tribes and peoples (Galileans, Spartans, South Arabian nomads, people of the Samarai steppe) specialized as "professional" warriors. In several of these cases the regimented military life style began in early life. Thus, for these peoples, training for military purposes was their life vocation. Nevertheless, for these "professional" warriors, too, military competence was judged on the basis of physical prowess and efficient uses of the body.

The Romans were the first to conduct military training, although the art died out with the fall of Rome, and did not reappear until the seventeenth century.[10] "So sensible were the Romans," says Gibbon, "of the imperfections of valor without skill and practice that, in their language, the name of an army was borrowed from the word which signified exercise."[11]

Not until the invention of the musket and the cannon made firepower a crucial element in warfare, was interest in military training revived. Thus, military proficiency in the use of organizational skills was postponed until the time of Frederick the Great's pronounced advances in military training techniques.*

---

* This is not to say that interest in military training and organizational skills were not revived before Frederick the Great in the sixteenth century with Tartagliu's *Quaestri*; de Saxe in his *Reveries* (1732) inveighs against the practice of over-much drilling of recruits previously current. (These illuminating points have been made by John Gooch to whom I am grateful).

B.   *In Medieval Times*[12]

Medieval warfare did involve specialization and specific competence, but these attributes were the exclusive possessions of one class, that of the knights. The crusaders were military innovators whose originality lay in the integration of the ideology of monasticism with warfare. (Not all crusaders were monastic knights, of course.) The Hospitalers linked the Christian conception of mercy, humanitarian deeds, care of the ill with the exclusivity of a high-ranking group of rulers and warriors. Knighthood was wrested away and became autonomous from the Church and the monastery by the Templars, whose daily life implied their military aims as a community of soldiers.

The crusaders changed the brutal requirement of wars. To a Christian, war was an elegant art. Thus, the sanctified warriors of the military orders became the first corporate soldiers. Blessed by the Church, they were also legitimized by their acts of charity. In short, they were warriors whose mission was peace and love. Warfare became a religious and moral commitment. The knights were both an *ordo*, or corporate structure, and an "officium", performing social and political functions. In fact, the Hospitalers became Europe's first standing army, a mission-oriented group dedicated to waging war. War was now ennobled.[13] The traditions of antiquity and medieval times, of both war's physical brutality and its ennoblement, have been passed down to the modern military, and values of bravery and a sense of mission are significant residues still.

C. *In Modern Times*[14]

The military was gradually professionalized; i.e., it established norms of competence and the adaptation of skills. "It is no doubt," writes one of the most perceptive military historians, Michael Roberts, "a historical commonplace that major revolutions in military techniques have usually been attended wtih the most widely ramifying consequences. The coming of the mounted warrior, and of the sword, in the middle of the second millenium B.C.; the triumph of the heavy cavalryman, consolidated by the adoption of the stirrup, in the sixth century of the Christian era; the scientific revolution in warfare in our own day—these are all recognized as major *turning points* in the history of mankind."[15]

Medieval warfare introduced several organizational innovations of which the most important were technological skills and discipline. Discipline became a necessary skill for warriors, in order to ensure that technological and weaponry innovations could be used efficiently in tactical maneuvers. The competence of commanders thus came to be judged by their talent in division of labor, manipulating hierarchical relationships, and specialized unit assignments, rather than on their bravery and physical strength. Their tactical skills and ability to control and deploy subdivisions of their forces (brigades, battalions, and platoons) became crucial.

The major skills of the military in modern times have increasingly become those of management and strategy. The brain has finally taken precedence over the body. But, as we shall see later, the competence of officers would be judged by their corporate peers exclusively on their managerial, strategic and even tactical performance and competence—e.g., the German General Staff. Yet the criteria of physical force and moral ennoblement—inherited from the past— will continue to impair the efficient view of their newly acquired skills.

Although the most significant military revolutions in modern times are the tactical, strategic, and managerial revolutions, the major breakthrough obviously took place with technological revolutions in the use of weapons. Strength, mobility, and marksmanship—all the attributes of the body—were multiplied by the new armaments. The technological revolution called for new organizational requirements.

The rise of the cavalry, the invention of gunpowder, the introduction of the longbow, and the advent of the pikeman, signaled the end of chivalry. War, the knightly game and profession mingling piety and religious enthusiasm with sadism and cruelty, was replaced by the pursuit of *Machtstellung* (political power) of the ruling monarchs of Europe. As Roberts notes, "The stricter discipline, the elaborately mechanical drilling, required by the new linear tactics, matched the tendency of the age towards absolute government, and may well have reinforced it; if discipline proved so successful in obtaining results in the military sphere, it might well be worthwhile trying the experiment of applying it to civilian life."[16] Thus, war was no longer the privilege of a class but the affair of states.

This much too brief an overview on the evolution of the art of war and the nature of the military establishment in the West, is intended to demarcate the profession of soldiering from other professions and, above all, to identify the residual values and skills that still inhabit the military that today sustains modern society.

Expertise, responsibility and corporatism did not figure in the militaries of ancient times. Military men were amateurs—consider Saul and David. Political responsibility was never clear. Political systems were either coalitions of tribes (ancient Israel), polises (Greece), or imperial systems (Assyria, Babylonia and Egypt); all required centralization, which necessitated military power. There was no clear division of political responsibility, because the head of state was usually also the commanding general. In fact, the military commander in times of war became *ipso facto* head of state, or approximating this role in times of peace—the Egyptian pharoahs, David and Solomon in ancient Israel, and the rulers of the Assyrian and Babylonian empires all bear this out. Similarly, the undefined political responsibility of the military class in Rome is the origin of the concept of praetorianism.

Because no military in antiquity was either corporate or professional, competence was clearly a personal attribute, not an organizational function. Competence depended on leadership, administrative and strategic skills of single, talented, and gifted individuals. Except for the children of established royal and imperial houses, where military training was part of a classical curriculum for the ruling classes (although Alexander was tutored by Aristotle, not by a great military theoretician), most generals, like Hannibal and David, learned their skills because their kingdoms were in a state of permanent war, not because they attended military academies. Their officers were their kinsmen, tribesmen, and loyal supporters, and their competence was judged largely on patrimonial performance, although some also happened to be great generals.

Antiquity contains numerous examples of military incompetence, since amateurism and clientelism prevailed. Several kings of Israel and Judea, numerous Assyrian, Babylonian monarchs, and a great number of Roman generals were clearly incompetents. In the absence of a science of war, of regulated systems of strategy, and of acknowledged standards of tactics, the predominance of amateurism, and incompetence, did not mean lack of skill, responsibility, or corporate orientation; simply, it meant lack of genius. Since few military leaders in any age are endowed with genius, military incompetence was the normal condition in antiquity.

Medieval knights were certainly a highly select group, an exclusive corporate club. Their skills were learned, as one would expect, from corporate behavior: admission into the club meant that one had to possess required skills and abilities, and perform a special ritual or ceremony. Such codes of behavior left no doubt as to who was the amateur and who was the skilled knight. Certainly, with the advance of the technology of war and especially its art, genius was no longer required. A corporate belongingness and a learned profession were sufficient to qualify a man for competence. Medieval knights developed a sense of ideological responsibility both to Church and to princes. Thus, judgment of military competence was directly linked to their knights' corporate identity and responsibility, if not so much to skill. The military, tactical, and strategic revolutions made the military essential to the rise of the absolutist state and later to the creation of the nation-state, just as it revolutionized ways of perceiving and judging military competence and incompetence. From its *medieval* origins, the nation-state derived an *orientation toward centralized* administrative authorities,[17] and this development influenced the emergence of large and complex military organizations and changed the nature of warfare.

This was not uniformly true Not all armies, or for that matter states, simultaneously established a centralized administrative authority. There was confusion of rights and privileges in both the armies of France and England at the

end of the sixteenth century. Nevertheless the connecting line
between medieval and modern state and armies is in the end
central administrative authority, even if it was not true in all
cases, since not all administrative or for that matter military
authority did undergo similar scope and level of centralization.

Thus, the classical attributes of leadership and bravery
were no longer sufficient. Professional skills now required
were administrative and strategic: command, operational
planning, intelligence networks, tactical mastery, and strategic thinking. Military incompetence thus can be more easily
identified in complex societies and organizations where
structures and functions are varied and specific. Faulty
command structure, bad planning, poor intelligence systems,
and tactics, are *identifiable*, as is poor or inadequate strategic
thinking (although, as I state later, strategic thinking has
been largely removed from the military's responsibility).
Leadership skill acquired a new value in modern warfare,
that is, the concept that Clausewitz called *virtu*. Already
identified by Machiavelli[18] in the Italian city-states in this
modern type of authority and warfare, *virtu* means good spirit,
citizenship, a new type of civic and military responsibility.
Virtu means that the professional's skills and responsibility
will be dedicated to a well-defined authority.

4.   THE GENERAL STAFF: COLLECTIVE OF EXPERTS AS A SUBSTITUTE FOR GENIUS

Although the origin of the German General Staff is generally
traced to the reign of Frederick the Great in the early
eighteenth century, the Great Elector in 1755 actually took
the first steps toward a modern system of centralized army
administration,[19] which developed later into an *Oberkriegs-
kollegium*,[20] which ceased to function properly by the end of
the eighteenth century. It, in turn, was replaced by Scharnhorst with the *Selekta*—the upper class of the *Kriegsakademie*,
the chief recruiting ground for the General Staff, where such
disciples of Scharnhorst as Clausewitz and Tiedmann were
trained. Here academic training and soldierly qualities were
combined. By the 1870s under Moltke, its most illustrious

chief, the General Staff gained its autonomy from the war ministry and became a supermanagerial institution. The French also adopted the General Staff in the 1870s,[21] although the British did not have one until the early 1900s and the USSR and the United States *still* do not. In the great powers of Europe, therefore, the General Staff became the military institution par excellence. It was by experts and for experts, the perfect military managerial-tactical and strategic collective. Organization had replaced the genius. The German General Staff, in particular, served as the military instrument that sustained military competence, by serving as the highest training institution of the elite corps, and it collapsed only when it was politicized after 1916 under the joint rule of Hindenburg and Ludendorff.[22] In the 1920s it was revived by General Hans von Seeckt and produced most of the brilliant German generals of World War II. The General Staff was the instrument for sustaining military competence—a structural, authoritative, and skillful system of recruitment, training, and advancement. Although there was a relatively high incidence of political simpletons among the General Staff, the institution proved that military incompetence could be identified and then checked. Thus, although the French General Staff was also created in the 1870s, Ralston has clearly demonstrated that the French could not have absorbed the Prussian tradition of sustaining military competence and of using the General Staff as the instrument for skill standardization, and only a general staff of the Ministry of War was established in 1871. A true army General Staff was established as late as 1890.

The unceasing efforts of Lord Esher, Haldane, and Fisher to change the structure and conduct of the British army finally resulted in the creation of a General Staff in 1904-1905.[24] Significant reforms in the Royal Navy were instituted by Lord Fisher at about the same time. Nevertheless, these reforms were not successfully integrated into the senior British High Command. John Gooch has noted that the adoption of the German structure of the General Staff by the British army was incomplete. The innovation was not accepted by the most important British generals. As Gooch states, "Implicit in the development of the General Staff as an intellectual elite within the army was the growing isolation of its members from day-to-day soldiering."[25] Although provisions were made to integrate General Staff officers into the army at the regimental level, they failed. The high command simply did not create the structural conditions for circulation of ideas between the General Staff and the divisional and regimental levels. It is interesting to note Haig's concept of the qualities a staff officer should possess: he felt courage and health were more important than personal magnetism and technical skills.[26] British failure to institutionalize an elite of expertise and to transfer organizational norms of competence down the military hierarchy certainly contributed to the military failures they experienced in World War I. In addition, Lord Kitchener, who was personally unenthusiastic about the General Staff idea, was selected by the politician Asquith as Secretary of War. Kitchener impeded the work of the General Staff from the beginning. Many senior and junior members of the General Staff were assigned to the British Expeditionary Force, but appointments to the BEF were constantly changing. Other General Staff officers were not mobilized, but remained in the War Office. This decision, as well as other Asquith-Kitchener errors, cost the British dearly.[27] The British failed to establish the collective of experts to substitute for genius and reduce the incidence of incompetence.

This short comparative analysis of the German and British General Staffs supports the theory that, as Huntington wrote two decades ago, in the absence of genius, the collective mind could serve to reduce the range available for incompetence. I am not categorically defending the idea that the higher incidence of military incompetence among Allied (as contrasted to German) senior officers in World War I resulted from the absence of an institutionalized high command and standards to judge competence. Nevertheless, its absence must have hurt the Allies, just as the blundering of the Allied political decision-makers did.

5. POLICY, STRATEGY, MISTRUST AND MILITARY FAILURE

The lines of demarcation between policy and strategy are no

longer clear. The military in a complex modern nation state is an important actor in the making of both. Yet political responsibility rests with politicians; and strategic responsibility in the modern nation state is shared between the regime (the politicians, the government), the senior military establishment, and the senior security bureaucracy. The complexity of modern warfare and weaponry and the nature of the modern bureaucratic organization has fused the two functions—policy and strategy—and intermeshed the political and military structures. Lack of definition of the scope of responsibilities has already led to military failure, and may well do so again.

The collapse of Germany in 1918 was the result of the growing disparity in power and authority between a politically pliable cabinet and an ascendant and autonomous military establishment. The Prussian General Staff overruled the German Cabinets. The tragic teaming of Hindenburg and Ludendorff ended in the demise of the Prussian landlords and the collapse of the imperial system. Clausewitz's dictum, which was espoused by the elder von Moltke, that the absence of a policy leads to military disaster finally proved true.

In Britain between the 1870s and 1914 the line between policy, which was determined by the cabinet, and strategy, which was the responsibility of soldiers, was not clear—either in war or in peace—and thus struggles of authority took place in a kind of twilight zone.[28] The commander-in-chief, the representative of the Crown, refused to accept a position subordinate to that of the secretary of state for war. Thus, the ambiguous relationships between military men and politicians within the War Office helped to retard the development of the British army, which, as a result, lagged far behind the continental armies in modernization.[29] The British army was small, anachronistic, and rigid. The politician had no military policy,[30] and the army despised the innovations that delighted the civilian amateurs. The politicians abhorred the innate conservatism of the military. The Secretary of State for War suspected the army because it was a creature of the royalty and not a parliamentary institution, and he therefore shunned the advice of military professionals. The latter opposed the continuous encroachment of political concern in military questions. The legacy of mistrust, even after the reforms of Sir Henry Wilson, did not eradicate the gap between policy makers and strategists, although the times made fusion imperative. Thus, the disasters of the Boer War (1899) were due not only to lack of communication between the military and the cabinet,* but that the Secretary of State, lacking a single authoritative source of advice, could turn to any one of a number of soldiers—and did. The 1914-1916 failures were, among other things, also the consequences of structural weaknesses and constitutional issues.

In Israel the absence of clear lines of responsibility between the prime minister, the defense minister, and the chief of staff, did play a major role in the mistakes of October 6-8, 1973. But the results were even more significant. The Israel Defense Forces' failures between the sixth and the eighth of October created deep estrangement and an open antagonism between the minister of defense, Moshe Dayan, and the chief of staff, David Elazar, and between Dayan and some senior IDF officers. Dayan felt "betrayed" by Zahal's senior command, which had promised, before 1973, no successful Egyptian crossing. As a result of the war, Zahal officers lost confidence in Dayan, and mistrust bred additional personal antagonism and misperceptions. The lines between policy and strategy became totally blurred, and continued to be so until the October 25th cease-fire. Military failure resulted from constitutional, structural, and personal problems, which again demonstrates that such defeats are not simply the result of the incompetence of generals.[31] The failure of policy and strategy is shared, although perhaps not equally, between soldiers and politicians.

6.   THE PSYCHOLOGY OF MILITARY INCOMPETENCE

In his very ambitious study, Norman Dixon, *The Psychology of Military Incompetence* (Jonathan Cape, London, 1976), analyses military incompetence as a function of psychological misperception, the rigidity of the military organization, and the

* Communication with John Gooch October 1977

"inefficient delivery of energy" and dysfunctional communication of information, the latter being the two major types of activity of the military organization. Analysing several "incompetent" military campaigns in the Crimean War, the Boer War, World War I, and World War II, Dixon comes to the rather commonplace conclusions that the intellectual ability of senior military commanders is limited, that military organizations are rigid and authoritarian, and that character, honor, and the cult of masculinity makes genius superfluous to the military.

Dixon's only important contribution to the explanation of military incompetence is his application of the concept of cognitive dissonance, which is currently enjoying a vogue in studies of organizational and decision-making processes. Dixon fails to convince me that misperception causes military incompetence. Incisive perception, after all, provides no remedy for managerial and tactical incompetence. What is valuable, however, is his analysis of the effect of officers' experience, judgment, strength of character, and determination upon military competence. But, of course, his explanation focuses on psychological rather than structural factors. On the structural sources of incompetence, Dixon merely repeats the contributions of the sociologists of the military. His analysis of the best generals (the competent) puts forward once again the genius theory of generalship; i.e., that geniuses are competent. Others are judged on the basis of psychological incapacity, cognitive dissonance, and misperception. Some of his "exceptions" (Field Marshal Montgomery, to name a prominent example) certainly cannot be classed as geniuses without arousing significant dispute.[32]

Elsewhere Dixon depends heavily upon Liddel Hart and A.J.P. Taylor, two scholars who are hardly objective on the subject of the military professional—and unduly uncritical of several political and military leaders of World War I. Certainly, Liddel Hart's and Taylor's judgment on World War I generals stands in need of serious revision. Taylor's *The First World War*, in fact, is no more than an entertainment, written by a master of paradox. I doubt that even Taylor takes seriously his outlandish conclusions on the incompetence of the military and the politicians of World War I.

Dixon's argument on behalf of military "competents" derives from General Chaim Herzog's contention (in *The Day of Atonement*, 1975) that the Israeli army "fearlessly faced the failure of 1973". This is simply untrue. Herzog was not one of Israel's leading generals, nor is his judgment untainted. In fact, Dayan's astonishing disappointment in the performance of his chief of staff and key senior officers in 1973, led him to disregard some of them and to doubt their competence. Few key senior officers were actually willing to face their failure, as the Agranat Commission report conclusively demonstrated. It is certainly inappropriate to accept Dixon's incredible statement that "great commanders are those who can rise above and even criticize their parent organization".[33] If the reference is to Herzog himself, it is totally inaccurate. Herzog was never a field commander, nor did he serve in combat in 1973. As a retired officer since 1965, he feels free to criticize the IDF, but among the senior generals, retired or active, only Sharon and Adan criticized the Israeli military.

Dixon's interpretation of Erik Erikson, as applied to the military, is basically that lack of inhibition (whether by infantile fantasies, guilt, or fear of punishment), is the mark of military competence as well as of adulthood. Thus, in Dixon's argument, competence varies inversely with professionalism. However, this interpretation explains nothing about military professionalism, incompetence, or, perhaps, even adulthood. In fact, there is a long list of brilliant, though infantile, generals—Grant, Patton, and Sharon, to name only a few. In short, Dixon's thesis is unconvincing. Nevertheless, it contains enough to challenge the imagination of those who can successfully discriminate between toilet training and the successful management of warfare. In no place, though, is the author apparently aware that when he speaks of the military he could just as well be discussing any sort of incompetence. To argue that generals always fight the last war is to accuse them of something that all of us are guilty of, except the few who have the gift of genius. Competence, I would assume, to Dixon means genius. Military incompetence is the incompetence of managers and tacticians, and is rampant in occupations in an industrial or post-industrial civilization. Thus, military incompetence has mainly to do with the type of war the generals are fighting and the society and polity under which they serve; and the relationship is between military and politics.

NOTES

1. John Gooch, *The Plans of War* (London: Routledge & Kegan Paul, 1974).
2. David Chandler, *The Campaigns of Napoleon* (New York: Macmillan, 1966), pp. xxxii-xliii. (Quote on p. xxxi.)
3. Ibid., p. xl.
4. Ibid, p. xli.
5. S. P. Huntington, Preface, in Amos Perlmutter, *The Military and Politics in Modern Times* (New Haven: Yale University Press, 1971), p. iii.
6. S. P. Huntington, *The Common Defense*(New York: Columbia University Press, 1961), p. 11.
7. S. P. Huntington, *The Soldier and the State* (Cambridge: Harvard University Press, 1957), pp. 7-10.
8. Morris Janowitz, "Changing Patterns of Organizational Authority: The Military Establishment", *Administrative Science Quarterly* 3 (1959): 473-493.
9. On literature and military in antiquity, I recommend: O. S. Spaulding, ed., *Warfare: A Study of Military Methods from Earliest Times* (1939); Yigael Yadin, "Some Aspects of the Strategy of Ahab and David", *Biblica* 36 (1955): 336-51; Yigael Yadin, *The History of Warfare in Biblical Times* (Hebrew), Ma'arachot, IDF Publishing House (Tel-Aviv, 1964); J. F. C. Fuller, *Training Soldiers for War* (London, 1914); Graham Webster, *The Roman Imperial Army* (London: Adam and Charles Black, 1969); R. MacMillan, *Soldier and Civilian in Later Roman Empire* (Cambridge: Harvard University Press, 1963); Ronald Syme, *The Roman Revolution*(Oxford: Oxford University Press, 1939).
10. Eldbridge Colby, "Military Training", *Encyclopedia of the Social Sciences* (1933), 9-10: 464-471.
11. Quoted in ibid., p. 464.
12. The best modern study of the Hospitalers is Joshua Prawer, *The Crusaders: A Colonial Society* (Hebrew), (Tel-Aviv: The Bialik Institute, 1975). S. Runciman's *A History of the Crusades*, 3 vols. (1950-1951), should be consulted. Also see Hans Delbrück's classic, *Geschichte der Kriegskunst in Rahmen der Politischen Geschichte* (1904), 3: 283-430; and Sir Charles Oman, *A History of the Art of War in The Middle Ages*, 2d ed., 2 vols. (London, 1924). R. C. Smail's *Crusading Warfare (1097-1193)* (Cambridge: Cambridge University Press, 1954), is an excellent general source book and review on medieval and crusader warfare. Also see C. T. Allmand, ed., *War Literature and Politics in the Late Middle Ages* (Liverpool: Liverpool University Press, 1976); and

C. G. Cruickshank, *Elizabeth's Army*, 2d ed. (Oxford: Clarendon Press, 1966).

13. J. Prawer, *The Crusaders*, pp. 330-357.

14. The best introduction to the military in modern times is Michael Roberts, *The Military Revolution* (Belfast: Marjory Boyd, 1955); and his seminal *Gustavus Adolphus*, 2 vols. (London: Oxford University Press, 1958). Delbrück's *Geschichte*, 7 vols. (Berlin, 1900-1936), especially vols. 5-7, is still a major source, as yet not translated into English. Geoffrey Symcox, ed., *War Diplomacy and Imperialism*(London: Macmillan, 1974), is an excellent source for documents concerning the military of this period. See especially Gustavus's manifesto (1630) and Frederick the Great's "Instruction for His Generals". John Child's *The Army of Charles II* (London: Routledge & Kegan Paul, 1976), is a superb study of the Royalist army and military life in seventeenth-century England. For Napoleon, see David Chandler's *The Campaigns of Napoleon* (New York: Macmillan, 1966), which is an exhaustive analysis of Napoleon's art of war. For students of Clausewitz, see the new English translation of *On War*, edited and introduced by such superior scholars as Michael Howard, Bernard Brodie, and Peter Paret. *Clausewitz on War* (Princeton: Princeton University Press, 1976) is an event to celebrate; and I have joyfully learned once more from *the* classic on warfare, rejuvenated in this accurate, modern, and full translation. Of course, the works of Howard, Brodie, and Paret on modern warfare, the military, and military history, are unsurpassed. See especially Howard's *Studies in War and Peace* (New York: The Viking Press, 1959); and his seminal *The Franco-Prussian War* (New York: Macmillan, 1962). See also Peter Paret, *Clausewitz and the State* (Oxford: Oxford University Press, 1976); and Bernard Brodie's *War and Politics* (New York: Macmillan, 1973). A collection on modern military strategy is E. Mead Earle's classic *Makers of Modern Strategy* (Princeton: Princeton University Press, 1943). It is the most definitive collection of essays on the makers of modern strategy, written by the leading historians and political scientists of the first half of this century. Earle's bibliographic note to this work is still the only one available. See also the short essay by Michael Howard, *War in European History* (New York: Oxford University Press, 1976).

15. Michael Roberts, *The Military Revolution* (Belfast: Marjory Boyd, 1966), p. 4.

16. Ibid., p. 20.

17. Joseph Strayer, *On the Medieval Origins of the Modern State* (Princeton: Princeton University Press, 1970).

18. N. Machiavelli, *The Art of War*, trans. Allen Gilbert, Vol.2, *Machiavelli's Chief Works* (Durham, N. C.: Ducke University Press, 1965), pp. 561-726.

19. Gordon Craig, *The Politics of the Prussian Army (1640-1945)* (New York: Oxford University Press, 1956), p. 30.

20. Ibid., p. 45.

21. D. Ralston, *The Army of the Republic* (Cambridge: M.I.T. Press, 1967).

22. Martin Kitchen, *The Silent Dictatorship* (London: Croom Helm, 1976).

23. D. Ralston, op. cit., pp. 138-200.

24. John Gooch, op. cit., pp. 299-302.

25. Ibid., pp. 32-61.

26. Ibid., p. 106.

27. Ibid., p. 84.

28. Hammer, *The British Army: Civil-Military Relations:* 1885-1905 (Oxford: The Clarendon Press, 1970), p. 47.

29. Ibid., pp. 35-37.

30. Ibid., pp. 31-35.

31. Little has been written on the antagonism between Dayan and his key senior officers. But my researches and access to classified information on military (and some political) events of October 6-8 convinces me that this judgment is correct. Reading between the lines of Dayan's autobiography (the Hebrew version) also confirms this view. Moshe Dayan, *Avney Derech* (Jerusalem: Idanim, 1976), pp. 580-582; 599-602. See also Amos Perlmutter, "Israel's Fourth War, October 1973; Political and Military Misperceptions", *Orbis* Summer 1975, 19: 2, pp. 434-460.

32. Alan Chalfont, *Montgomery of Alamein* (London: Weidenfeld & Nicolson, 1976), is a very controversial and the most critical study of Montgomery so far. In defense of Montgomery, see Michael Howard, "Montgomery the Mascot", *Encounter* (August 1976), pp. 40-47; for Chalfont's rejoinder, see A. Chalfont, "Monty in Cross-fire", *Encounter*, pp. 83-86.

33. Dixon, *Psychology*, p. 353.

Index

Abbas, of Egypt (1849-54), 76
Abbas, Ferhat, 47
Abdul Majid, Sultan, 174
Abdullah, King of Jordan, 134
'Aflaq, Michel, 136, 137-8, 139, 140, 141, 142, 143, 146, 148, 151
Agrarian reforms, in Egypt, 74-5, 76, 77, 78-9, 239, 242, 246
'Alawi, in Syria, 30, 132, 133, 136, 140, 147, 148, 151, 152
Algeria, 30, 31, 47, 70n
'Alwan, Colonel Jasan, 140, 144
'Amer, Marshal 'Abd al-Hakim, 204, 213, 218
Andreski, Stanislav, 161
Antiliberalism, 262-3
Antiparliamentarism, 263-4
Antitraditionalist radical ruler army, 29-30
Antitraditionalist reformer ruler army, 29-30
Arab-Israeli wars/conflict, 169, 171: 1949: 134, 135, 140, 191, 192; 1956: 139, 190; 1967: 147, 190, 192; 1973: 5, 6, 131, 285, 300
Arab Liberation Movement, Syria, 32, 136, 137, 200, 205n
Arab Socialist Union, Egypt, 5, 86, 89, 118, 187, 211, 219-27, 232, 244, 273
Arbitrator praetorian army, 24, 25-8, 197, 199-200, 203
Argentina, 18, 23, 25, 30, 32, 126, 262, 268, 270, 275
'Arif, General 'Abd al-Salim, 144, 146, 182, 186

Army Officers in Arab Politics and Society (Beeri), 160n, 174-8, 179
Aron, Raymond, 69n
Asad, President of Syria, 152-6
Aswan High Dam project, 221, 237
'Atasi family, Syria, 132, 133
'Atasi, Col Luay, 145
Authoritarian praetorianism, 15-16, 260-4; types of, 264-71; political dynamics of modern, 271-6; *see also* Praetorianism
Authority relationships *see* Civil-military relations
Autocracy, military, 15, 261, 268, 271, 272, 273
Ayub Khan, President of Pakistan, 30-1, 53, 271
'Azm family, Syria, 132

Ba'th party, 84, 178, 273; in Iraq, 33, 155, 158n; in Syria, 30, 33, 130-1, 136, 137-55, 179, 188, 193, 199, 209, 217, 218
al-Baghdadi, 'Abd Latif, 204, 219
Baghdad Pact, 139, 187
Baer, Gabriel, 74, 75, 239
Bakhdash, Khalid, 138
Beeri, Eliezer, 125, 160n, 171, 174-8, 179, 181, 182, 184, 185, 186, 188, 189, 190, 191, 192, 234
Ben Bella, 30, 31, 84
Ben-Tzur, Avraham, 148
Berger, Prof. Morroe, 65n, 79-80, 84, 85, 91, 111n, 115-16, 119, 128
Binder, Leonard, 242
Bitar, Dr Midhat, 140

307

Bitar, Salah al-Din, 137, 138, 139, 140, 146, 148
Blanksten, George I, 72, 100
Bonapartism, 260
Boumédienne, Houari, 30, 31
Bourguiba, Habib, 47
Bowen, Harold, 74
Brazil, 16n, 18, 26, 30, 32, 126, 262, 270, 275, 276
British, 12, 131, 299-300; occupation of Egypt by, 74, 76-7, 175; General Staff, 297-8
Bureaucracy, 174, 277; and middle class in Egypt, 73-92, 105, 127; civil-military relations and, 254, 259, 260

Chile, 26, 27, 126, 262, 268, 270, 275, 276
China, People's Republic of, 20
Christians, 132, 133, 151
Churchill, Winston, 289
Civil-military relations: theory and literature, 160-91 *passim;* Garrison Soldier model, 162, 163; Professional Soldier model, 162-3; constabulary-force concept, 164; Progressive Modernizing Soldier model, 165-6, 177-8; in underdeveloped countries, 164-7; Hurewitz's *Middle East Politics,* 168-74; Beeri's *Army Officers in Arab Politics and Society,* 174-9; Dann's *Iraq under Qassem,* 179-81, 182; military coups and interventions in the Middle East, 183-7; and military dictatorships, 187-91; stable political systems and, 252-8; and unstable political systems and, 285-90; *see also* Praetorianism
Clausewitz, Carl von, 256-7, 296, 299
Colombia, 31-2
Communist parties, 55, 138, 150, 187, 188
Congress of Popular Forces, Egypt, 222, 242, 244

Constabulary-force concept, 164
Corporatism, 1, 2, 5, 27, 74-5, 167, 259, 261, 266-9, 270, 273-5, 276-7, 288
Cromer, Lord, 76-7, 175
Crouchley, A.E., 76
Crozier, Michael, 119

Dahl, Robert, 232-3
Dhrendorf, Prof. Ralf, 118, 119, 120-1, 231-2
Dann, Uriel, 160n, 179-81, 182, 185, 186, 187, 190, 191, 192
Dayan, Moshe, 289, 300, 302
Dixon, Norman, 300-2
The Doctrine of Inevitability, 177
Druze, in Syria, 132, 133, 136, 137, 140, 147, 148, 151, 152

Earle, Edward M., 161
Easton, David, 184-5
Eckstein, Harry, 170
Economic Development Organization, Egypt, 221
Egypt, 69-70n, 82, 131, 150, 169, 175, 190, 192, 263; military praetorianism in, 3-7, 172, 196, 203-27; arbitrator army in, 26; and ruler army, 30, 31, 32, 33-4, 35; search for NMC in, 47, 53, 59, 65n, 71-96, 103; bureaucracy and middle class (1805-1919), 73-9, 105, 127; the military and political mobilization in, 85-92; military coups in, 125, 186-7, 246-7; Syrian relations with, 138, 139, 146, 153, 189; and U.A.R. (1958-61), 139, 141-3, 144, 209, 210, 211-12, 218-9; evolution and dynamics of Nasser's parties, 203-7; and National Union, 208-19; and Socialist Union, 219-27; political power and social cohesion in, 230-48; ruling élite in, 231-6; and strategic élite, 236-8; rural middle class in, 239-43; and skilled urban workers, 243-4

Elazar, General David, 287, 300
Erikson, Erik, 302
Esher, Lord, 297

Finer, Samuel E., 161
Fisher, Lord, 297
Foreign investment and aid, 275
Free Officer Corps, Egypt, 204-5, 206, 207, 225, 233-6, 238, 245, 247
Frederick the Great, 291 & n, 296
French, 12, 255; Syria and, 130, 131-2, 134, 135; General Staff, 297

Gamasi, General Abd-al-Ghani, 5-6, 7
Garrison State/Soldier, concept of, 162, 163
General Staff, 296-8
Germany (Prussia), 255, 256-7, 299; junker bureaucracy in, 78, 87, 90; General Staff, 296-7
Gibb, H.A.R., 74
Gibbon, Edward, 291
Gooch, Herbert, 253
Gooch, John, 291n, 297-8

al-Hafiz, General Amin, 131, 140, 145, 146, 147
al-Hafiz, Yassin, 148-9
Haig, Earl, 285, 287, 289, 298
Halpern, Manfred, 41-70, 97-112, 165, 182; Perlmutter's critiques of, 71-96, 113-228
Hama military academy, 135, 137, 139
Hamdun, Col Mustafa, 137, 139, 142
al-Hariri, General Ziad, 144, 145
Harsanyi, John, 85
Hart, Liddel, 301
Hatum, General Salim, 147
Hawrani, Akram, 136, 137, 139, 142, 143, 148
Haykal, Muhammad Hasanyan, 92, 221, 223
Heaphey, James, 88, 90, 233

Herzog, General Chaim, 302
Hinnawi, Colonel, 135, 137, 141
Hindenburg, Field-Marshal von, 285, 287, 297, 299
Hitler, Adolf, military coups against, 21-2
Homs military academy, 135, 137, 139
Horowitz, Irving Lewis, 125
Hourani, Albert, 151
Humanitarian socialism, 138
Huntington, S.P., 160n, 161, 162, 163, 164, 166-7, 168, 169, 248, 252, 254, 255, 272, 289
Hurewitz, Jacob C., 160n, 168-74, 188, 189
Husain, Kamal al-Din, 213
Hussein, King of Jordan, 172

Ibanez, General Carlos, 27
Ibrahim, Hasan, 204, 208
Indonesia, 30, 31, 33
Industrialization, 73, 74-6, 77-8, 86-7, 171
Intelligentsia, 42, 66n, 144, 151; as predominant force of NMC, 45-7, 82, 85
Iran, 49, 51-3, 59
Iraq, 33, 34, 82, 83, 84, 127, 138, 155, 158n, 171, 176, 187, 188, 197, 199, 262; military interventions in, 24, 125, 185, 186; and Qassem régime, 30, 33, 144, 146, 179-81, 182, 247
Iraq under Qassem (Dann), 160n, 179-81, 181
Isma'il, Khedive of Egypt, 74, 175
Israel, 3, 89, 131, 171, 172, 176, 285, 300, 302; see also Arab-Israeli wars
Issawi, Charles, 244

Jabar, Dr. 'Ali, 140
Jadid, Gen. Salah, 145, 147, 148
Janissaries, 10, 11, 173, 174
Janowitz, Morris M., 161, 162, 163-4
Japan, 78, 87, 90

Johnson, Prof. John J., 65n, 66n, 71, 72, 100, 119, 124-5, 126, 164, 165
Jordan, 49, 59, 147, 172, 176
al-Jundi, 'Abd Karim, 147

Keller, Suzanne, 243
Kemal, Mustafa (Atatürk), 30, 32, 53, 170-1, 172, 178, 179, 193
Khadduri, Prof. Majid, 178-9
Kitchener, Lord, 287, 298
Kleptocracy, 265, 275
Kuwait, 172

Landes, David, 78
Lang, Kurt, 2, 160
Lasswell, Harold, 161. 162, 163, 230
Latin America, 13, 18, 21, 25, 28, 65n, 256, 262, 265, 268, 269, 270, 274, 275; relationships between military and middle class in, 124-6
Law of Local Government (1960), 214
Lebanon, 131, 151, 154
Lederer, Emil, 118, 119
Legitimacy, 13-15, 23, 29, 32, 152, 167, 174, 175, 184-5, 257, 259, 272
Le Tourneau, Roger, 47
Liberation Rally, Egypt, 205-6, 208, 219n, 220, 224, 271
Libya, 30, 197
Linz, Juan, 16n
Lloyd George, David, 289
Ludendorff, General, 279, 299
Lukács, Georg, 67n

Mahmud II, Sultan, 56
al-Malki, Adnan, 139, 142
Marschak, Jakob, 118, 119
Middle class, 18, 20-1; birth of NMC in Middle East, 41-64; and bureaucracy in Egypt, 73-9; the military and, 122-6; in rural Egypt, 238, 239-43, 245, 246
Middle East Politics: The Military Dimension (Hurewitz), 168-72
Military coups, 1, 8, 24, 28, 33,

83, 125, 168, 172, 253, 262, 264; political explanation of, 19-23; middle-class, 20-1; in Middle East, 182-7, 190-2; in Egypt, 125, 186-7, 246-7; and in Syria, 125, 130, 131, 134, 135, 137, 143, 144, 185, 186, 191-2, 247; and in Iraq, 125, 185, 186, 247
Military establishment, 15, 270
Military executive, 268, 270-1
Military incompetence and failure, 283-303
Military interventionism, 2-3, 7, 8, 12, 13, 14-15, 18, 21, 22-3, 166-7, 168, 172, 181-2, 183-7, 190-1, 192
Military middle-class coup, 20-1
Military modernization, 165-7, 168-70, 171, 177
Military party, 270-1, 272, 273
Military professionalism, 2, 11, 27, 28, 31, 34, 162-3, 167, 168, 174, 254-5, 257, 258; *see also* Military incompetence
Military technology, 163-4
Mills, C. Wright, 232, 233
al-Misri, General Aziz 'Ali, 178, 182
Mitchell, Richard P., 187-8
Moltke, Field-Marshal von, 296-7, 299
Morocco, 55, 59
Mosca, Gaetano, 256
Moslems, in Syria, 132, 133, 140, 143
Muhammad 'Ali of Egypt, 56, 74-6, 77, 78-9, 87-9, 169, 170, 175
Muhi al-Din, Khaled, 204
Muhi al-Din, Zakariyah, 204, 224
Muslim Brotherhood, Egypt, 187-8, 205, 219

al-Nafuri, Amin, 139
Nagib, General, 26, 205-6, 244
Nahlawi, Colonel, 143, 144
Napoleon Bonaparte, Emperor, 285-6
Nasser, Gamal Abdel, 5, 6, 8, 14, 26, 30, 32, 33-4, 46, 47, 49, 53, 69-70n, 83-92 *passim,* 103, 118,

125, 136, 137, 141-2, 146, 150, 153, 170-1, 172, 178, 179, 181, 182, 186-7, 190, 192, 193, 196, 239, 246-7, 248, 276; political parties and, 203-7, 273, 263-4, 271; and National Union, 208-19; and Socialist Union, 219-27; and ruling elite, 231, 232, 233-4, 235, 236, 247

Nasser Academy, 3-4, 6

National Bloc, Syria, 132

National Party, Syria, 133

National Union, Egypt, 88, 142, 143, 220, 224; creation of, 208-9; and ideology, 209-18; and failure of, 218-19

Nationalism, 262

Neo-Destour Party, Tunisia, 64n

New Middle Class (NMC); Halpern's theories on, 41-70, 97-112, 165; intelligentsia as predominant force of, 45-7; conflicts within, 49-55; relationships to other classes, 55-60; prospects for, 60-4; Egypt and the myth of the, 71-96; the myth of the myth of the, 113-29; see also Middle class

Nieuwenhuijze, Professor C.A.O., 111n

Nkrumah, Kwame, 84

Nordlinger, Professor Eric, 122-4, 125

Nun, José, 125, 128

Nuri al-Sa'id, Pasha, 61

Officers, officer corps, 29)-6; in arbitrator army, 27; and in ruler army, 29, 31, 34; Egyptian, 83, 85, 175, 181, 190; Beeri's views on, 174-8, 181, 182; Iraqi, 180-1; class-consciousness of, 191, 193

Oligarchy, military, 15-16, 165, 261, 265-6, 268, 270-1, 273, 274, 275, 277

Ottoman Empire, 10, 11, 21, 25, 73, 75, 131-2, 134, 135, 155-6n, 169, 171, 172, 173-5, 177, 178; see also Turkey

Packenham, Robert, 41

Pakistan, 30-1

Palestine war (1949), 134, 135, 140, 191, 192

Parti Populaire Syrien (PPS), 133, 136, 137, 139, 141, 188

Patrimonialism, 10-11, 13, 173-5, 264-5

People's Party, Syria, 133

Peron, Juan, 25

Peru, 29, 32, 126, 268, 270, 275

Pinilla, Rojas, 31

Polarity of Boundary-Management, 107, 108, 109, 112n

Polarity of Direct Bargaining, 106, 107, 108, 109

Polarity of Emanation, 111-12n

Polarity of Transformation, 108-9

Political Bureau, Egypt, 222

Portugal, 20, 23, 30, 273

Practorian army, 23-35; arbitrator, 24, 25-8, 197, 199-200, 203; ruler, 24, 28-35, 197, 200-1

Praetorianism, 8-35, 166-8; in Egypt, 3-7 (see also Egypt); definitions, 9, 166-7, 173; historical, 9-12, 252; in advanced agricultural societies, 10-11; imperial-colonial legacies, 11-12; modern, 12-16, 268-9; types of, 15-16, 264-71; autocratic, 15, 261, 264-5, 268; oligarchic, 15-16, 261, 265-6, 268, 273, 274, 275; authoritarian, 15, 16, 260-71; social conditions contributing to, 16-19, 168; political explanations for military régimes, 19-23, 177-8; patrimonialism and, 173-5; structural evolution of régimes, 196-203; arbitrator régime type, 199-200, 203; and ruler régime type, 200-1; ideology of, 262-4; corporate, 261, 266-9, 270, 273-5; political support for, 270; auxiliary structures, 270-1; the future of, 276-9; see also Civil-military relations

Professional Soldier, concept of, 162-3
Progressive Modernizing Soldier model, 165-6, 177-8
Pronunciamiento, Spanish, 260
Pye, Lucian, 165

Qanut, 'Abd al Ghani, 142
Qassem, Brigadier 'Abd al-Karim, 24, 30, 125, 144, 146, 179-81, 182, 186, 187, 189, 190, 191, 247
al-Qudus, Ikhsan 'Abd, 219, 220
al-Quwwatli, Shukri, President of Syria, 211

al-Razaaz, Dr Mu'nif, 140
Red National Guard, Syria, 147
Revolutionary Command Council (RCC), 32, 186, 197, 200-1, 203, 270-1, 272; Egyptian, 26, 200, 204, 205, 206-7, 208, 219, 220, 233; Syrian, 145
Riad, Mahmud, 237
Rifa't, Kamal, 211 & n
Roberts, Michael, 292, 293-4
Roman Praetorian Guard, 9
Ruler praetorian army, 28-35, 197, 200-1
Rural middle class and landowner-ship in Egypt, 77, 78-9, 238, 239-43, 245, 246
Rustow, Dankwart A., 181, 230-1

Sa'adah, Antun, 133
al-Sabbagh, 178, 179
Sabri, 'Ali, 220, 222-4, 225, 227
Sadat, Anwar, President of Egypt, 3, 5, 6, 7, 153, 155, 204, 208-9, 214, 232, 236, 237, 276
al-Sa'di, 'Ali Salah, 146
Safran, Professor, 128
Said (1845-1863), of Egypt, 76
Salem, Gamal, 204, 208
Salem, Salah, 204
al-Sarraj, 'Abd al-Hamid, 139, 142, 143
Seeckt, General Hans von, 297
Sharon, General Ariel, 287, 302

Shawaaf army mutiny, Iraq (1959), 187
Shils, Edward, 164-5
Shishakly, Adib, 32, 34, 125, 135-7, 140, 186, 188-9, 201, 205n, 247
Social classes/system, 16-19, 275-6; *see also* New Middle Class
Society of Free Officers, Egypt, 21, 26
Spain, 13-14, 20, 256
Speier, Hans, 161
Stouffer, Samuel, 161, 162
Suez Canal, 5, 221, 237
Suharto, General, 30
Sukarno, President, 30, 31, 33, 84
Sulaiman, Sidqi, 224
Suleiman the Magnificent, Sultan, 11, 174
Sultanism, 11, 173, 178, 179, 181
Sulzberger, C.L., 178
Sunnis, in Syria, 132, 133, 140, 143, 149
Swaidani, Ahmed, 147
Syria, 82, 83, 84, 88, 126, 127, 130-59, 197, 262, 263; arbitrator régime in, 199, 200; ruler army régime in, 201; military coups in, 125, 130, 131, 134, 135, 137, 143, 144, 185, 186, 186, 191-2, 247; background of army domin-ation in politics, 131-5; religious communities in, 133; Shishakly era, 135-7, 188-9, 201; Ba'th Par-ty and the Army (1954-58), 137-41; Ba'th, Army and the U.A.R. (1958-61), 141-3, 180, 209, 210, 211-12, 214, 217-19; years of as-cendancy and fratricide (1961-69), 143-51; prospects of Ba'th, 151-4; and prospects of the Army, 154-5; National Union in, 212, 214, 217-19

Tawfiq of Egypt, 79
Taylor, A.J.P., 301
Thompson, William, 19, 20
Trades unions, 55-6, 244
Tunisia, 56, 64n

Turkey, 21, 23, 25, 26, 30, 32, 171; *see also* Ottoman Empire
Tyranny, 261, 264-5, 268, 270, 274, 275, 277

U.A.R. (1958-61), 139, 141-3, 144, 146, 150, 180, 182, 189; National Union and, 209-19; *see also* Egypt; Syria
Ubayad, Hamed, 148
Underdeveloped countries, role of military in, 164-7, 168
United National Front, Iraq, 125, 247
United States, 98, 126, 162-3, 257
Urban workers, 17-18, 238, 243-4
USSR, 20, 139

Veteran Free Officers, Egypt, 86, 89, 234; *see also* Free Officers Corps

Watkins, F.M., 9, 258
Weber, Max, 11, 13n, 173
Wilson, Sir Henry, 300
World Coup Zone, 278

Yemen, 126, 127, 171, 172
Young, Professor T. Cuyler, 65n, 71
Young Turks, 177

Zahar al-Din, General 'Abd al-Krim, 144, 145
al-Za'im, Colonel Husni, 134, 135, 137, 138
Zeldin, Theodore, 260
Zu'ayn, Yousuf, 147, 148
Zurayq, Constantin, 151